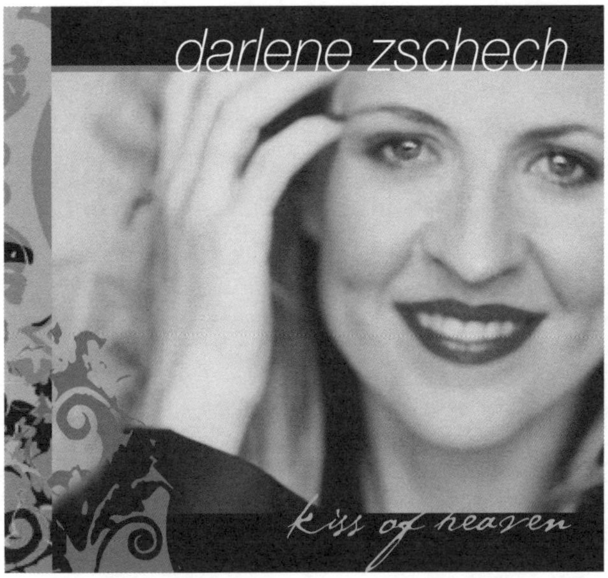

titles in alphabetical order *page*

INOTOF

Pray

Words and Music by
DARLENE ZSCHECH

Joyfully ♩ = 104

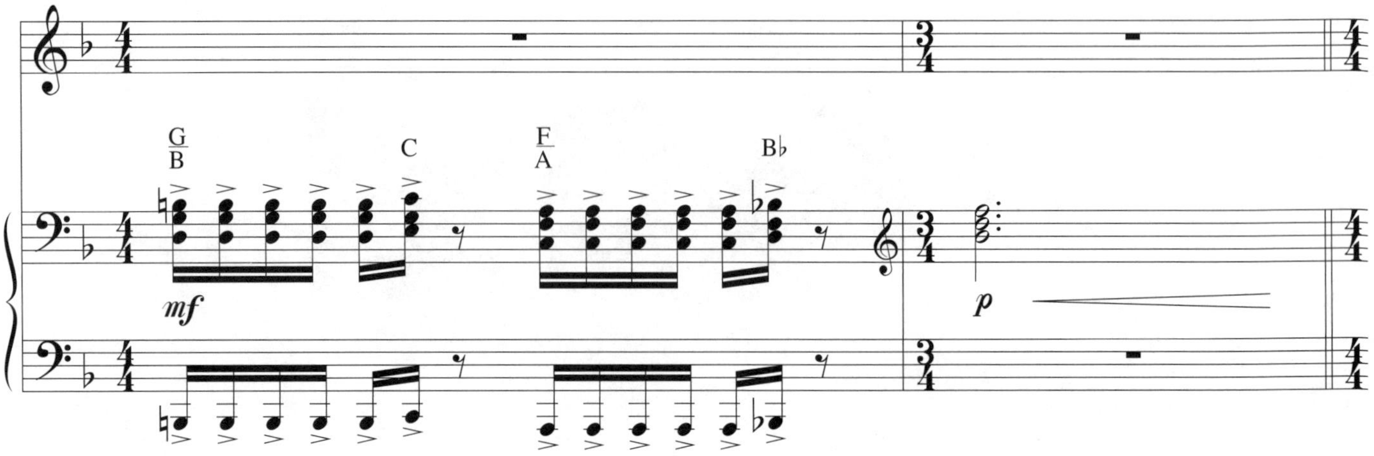

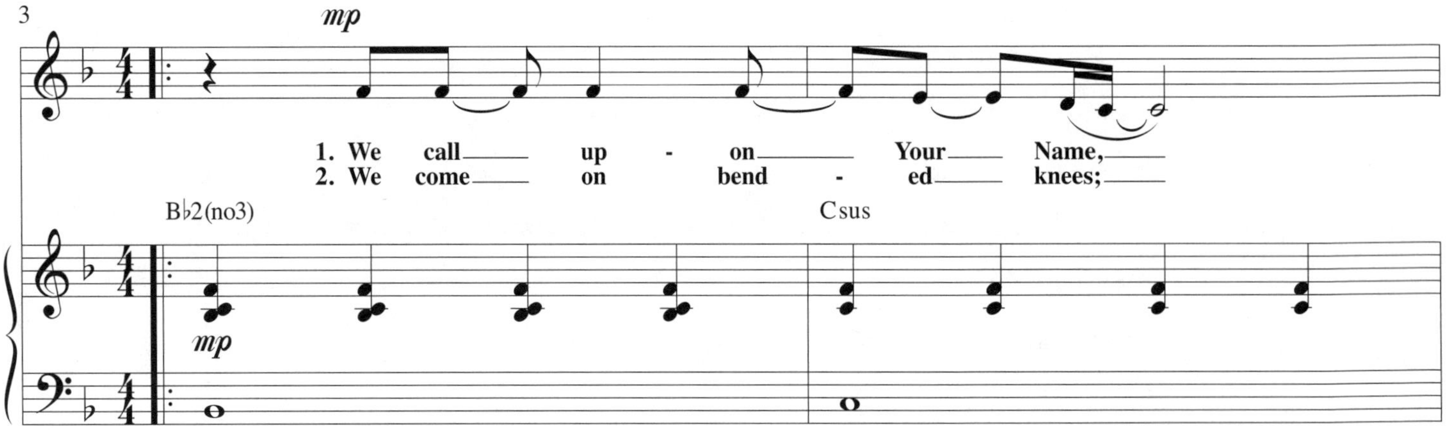

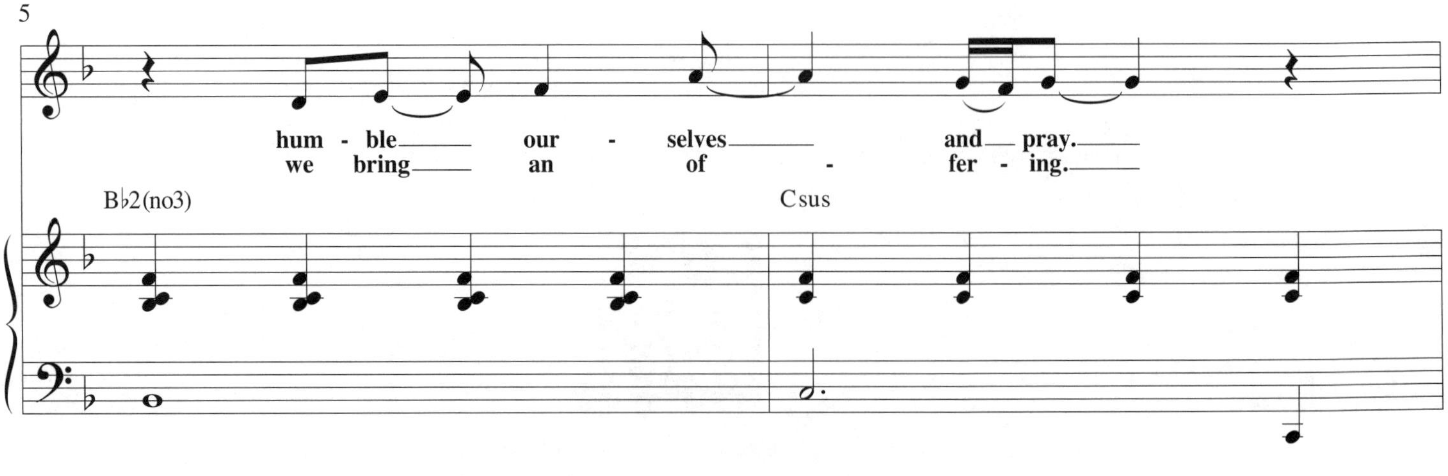

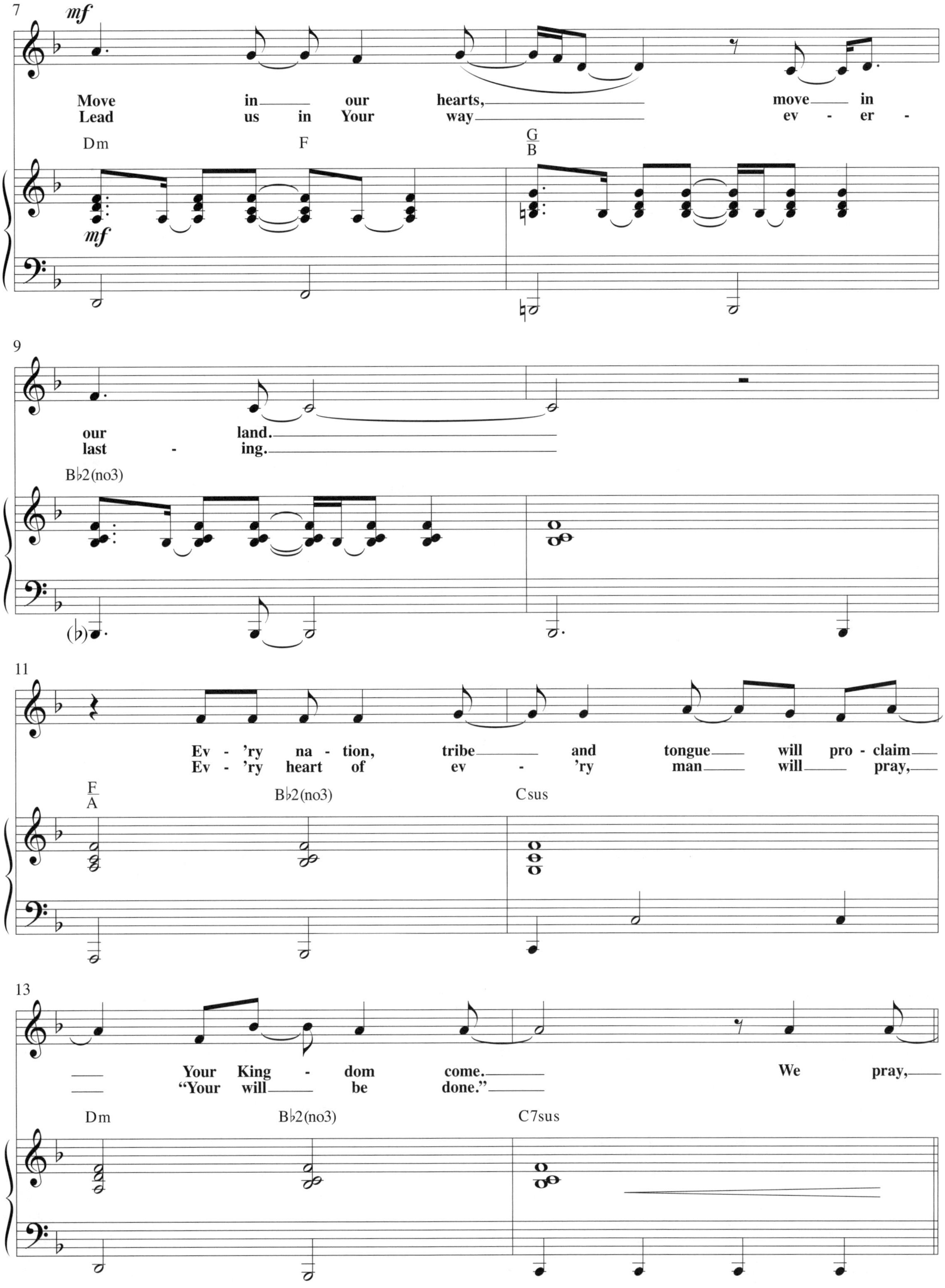
7
mf
Move in our hearts, move in
Lead us in Your way ev - er -
Dm
F
G/B
mf
9
our land.
last - ing.
B♭2(no3)
11
Ev - 'ry na - tion, tribe and tongue will pro - claim
Ev - 'ry heart of ev - 'ry man will pray,
F/A
B♭2(no3)
Csus
13
Your King - dom come. We pray,
"Your will be done."
Dm
B♭2(no3)
C7sus

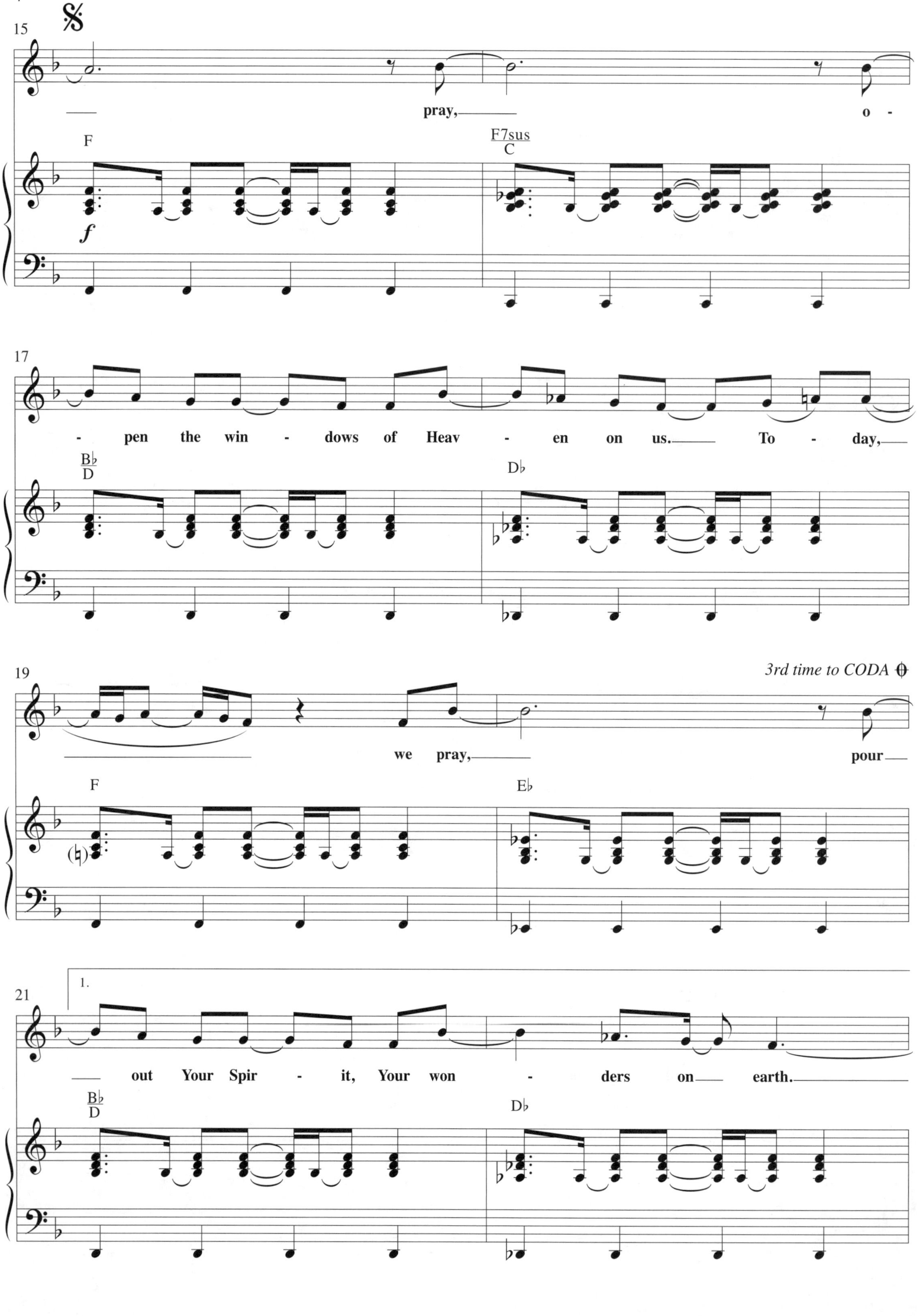
15
pray, o -
F
F7sus
C
f
17
- pen the win - dows of Heav - en on us. To - day,
B♭
D
D♭
19
3rd time to CODA
we pray, pour
F
E♭
21
1.
out Your Spir - it, Your won - ders on earth.
B♭
D
D♭

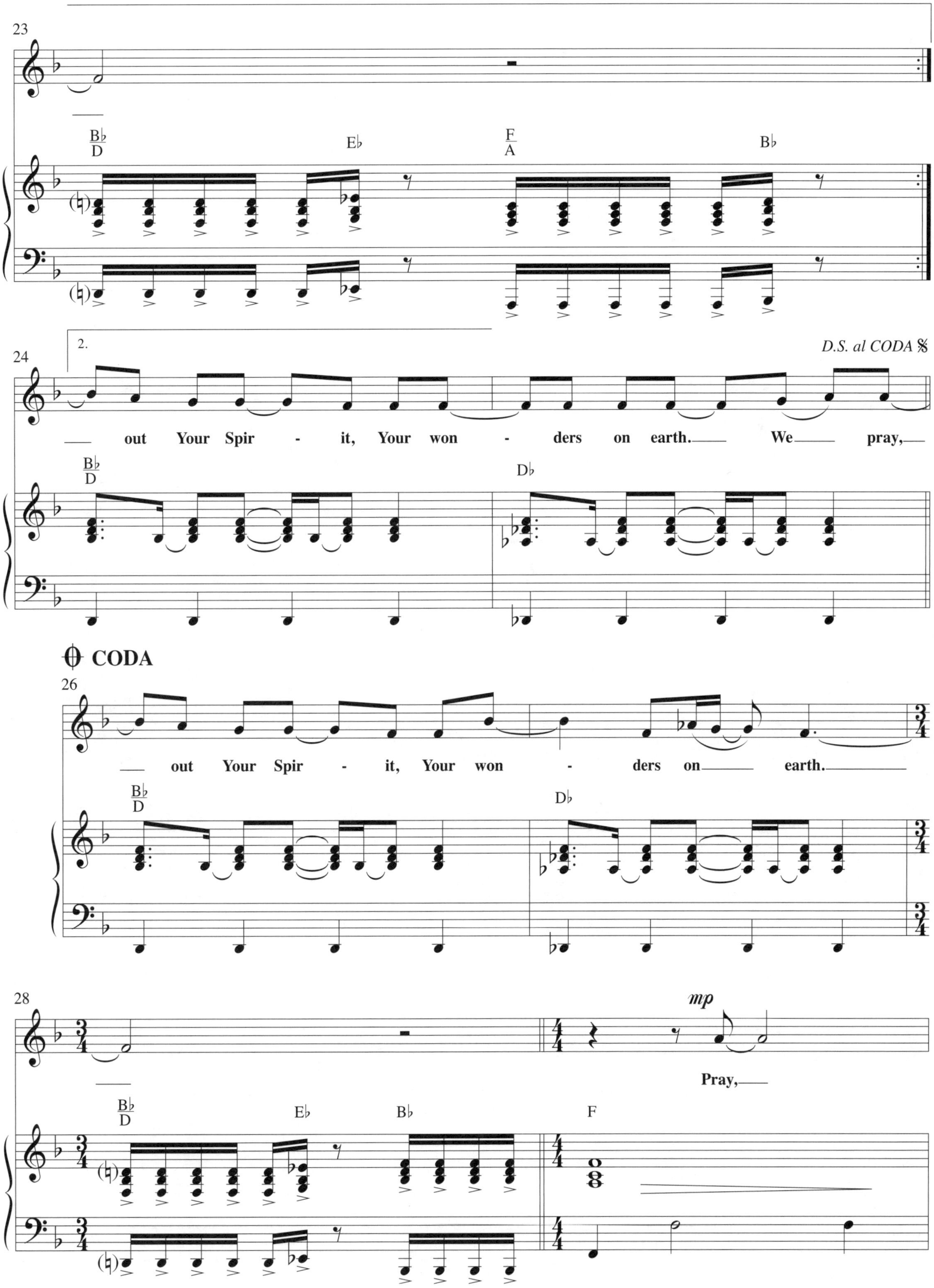
23
B♭/D
E♭
F/A
B♭
24
2.
D.S. al CODA 𝄋
out Your Spir - it, Your won - ders on earth. We pray,
B♭/D
D♭
CODA
26
out Your Spir - it, Your won - ders on earth.
B♭/D
D♭
28
mp
Pray,
B♭/D
E♭
B♭
F

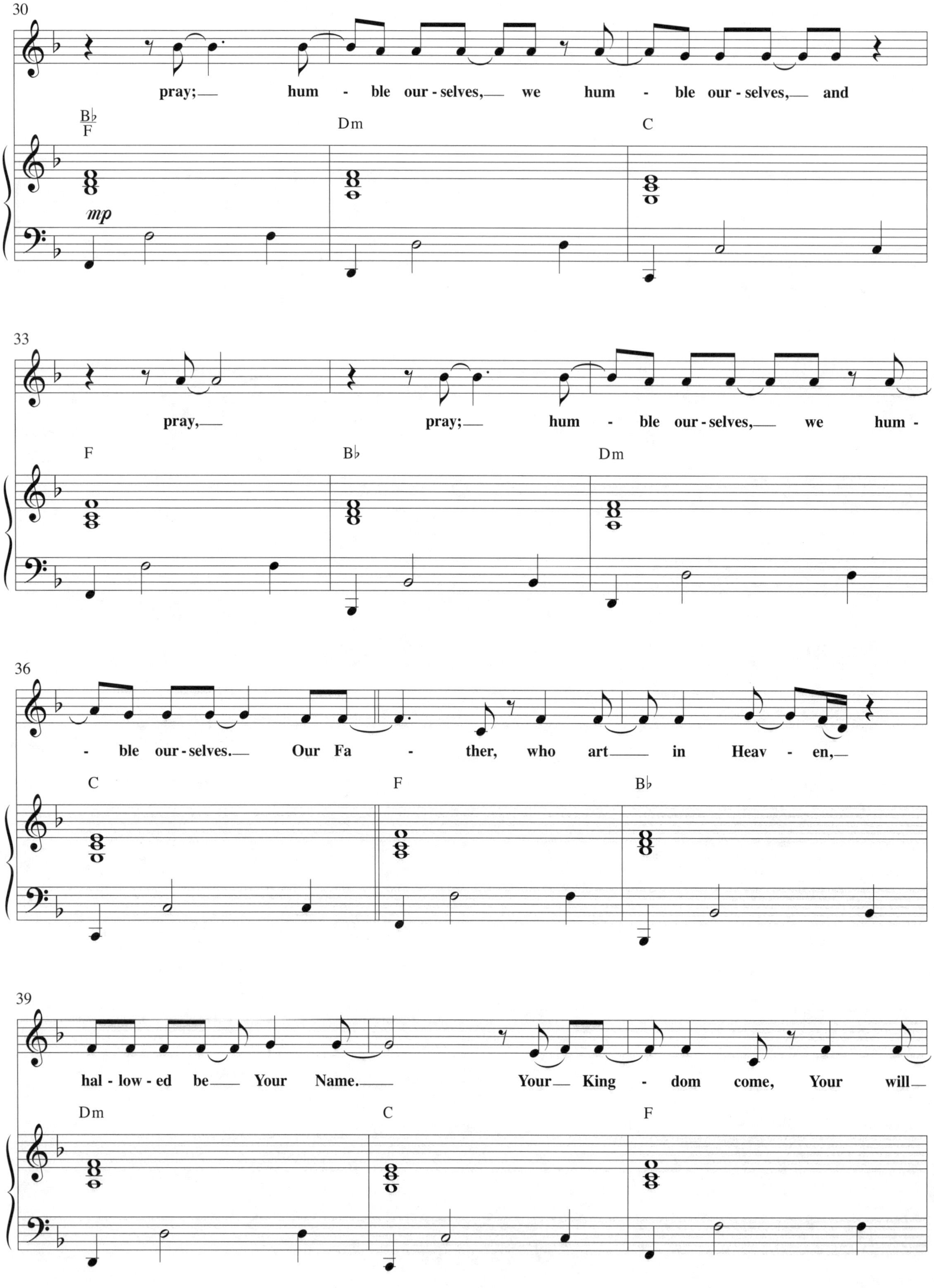
30
pray; hum - ble our - selves, we hum - ble our - selves, and
B♭/F
Dm
C
mp
33
pray, pray; hum - ble our - selves, we hum -
F
B♭
Dm
36
- ble our - selves. Our Fa - ther, who art in Heav - en,
C
F
B♭
39
hal - low - ed be Your Name. Your King - dom come, Your will
Dm
C
F

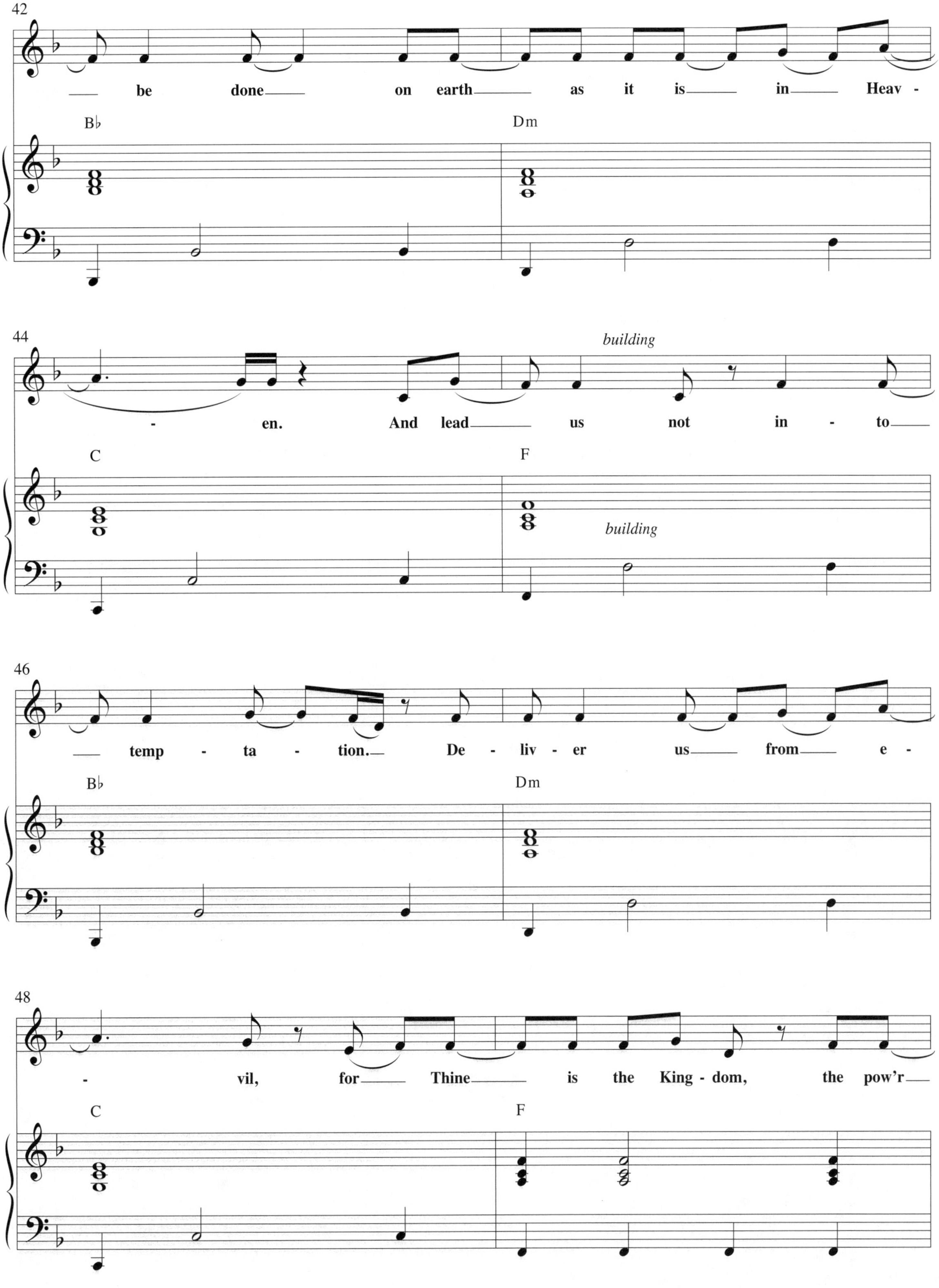
42
be done on earth as it is in Heav -
B♭
Dm
44
building
- en. And lead us not in - to
C
F
building
46
temp - ta - tion. De - liv - er us from e -
B♭
Dm
48
- vil, for Thine is the King - dom, the pow'r
C
F

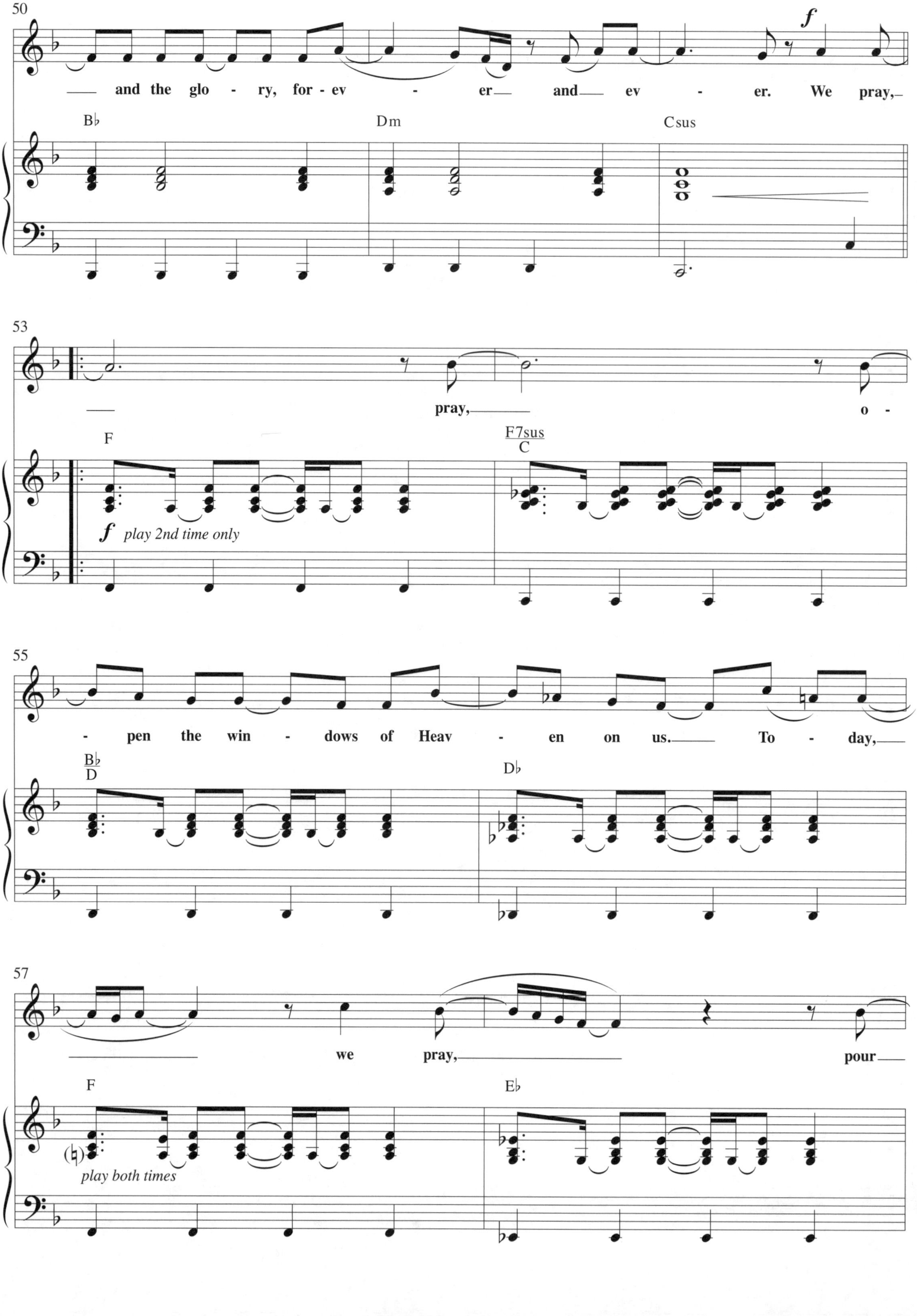
50
f
and the glo - ry, for - ev - er and ev - er. We pray,
B♭
Dm
Csus
53
pray, o -
F
F7sus
C
f play 2nd time only
55
- pen the win - dows of Heav - en on us. To - day,
B♭
D
D♭
57
we pray, pour
F
E♭
(♮)
play both times

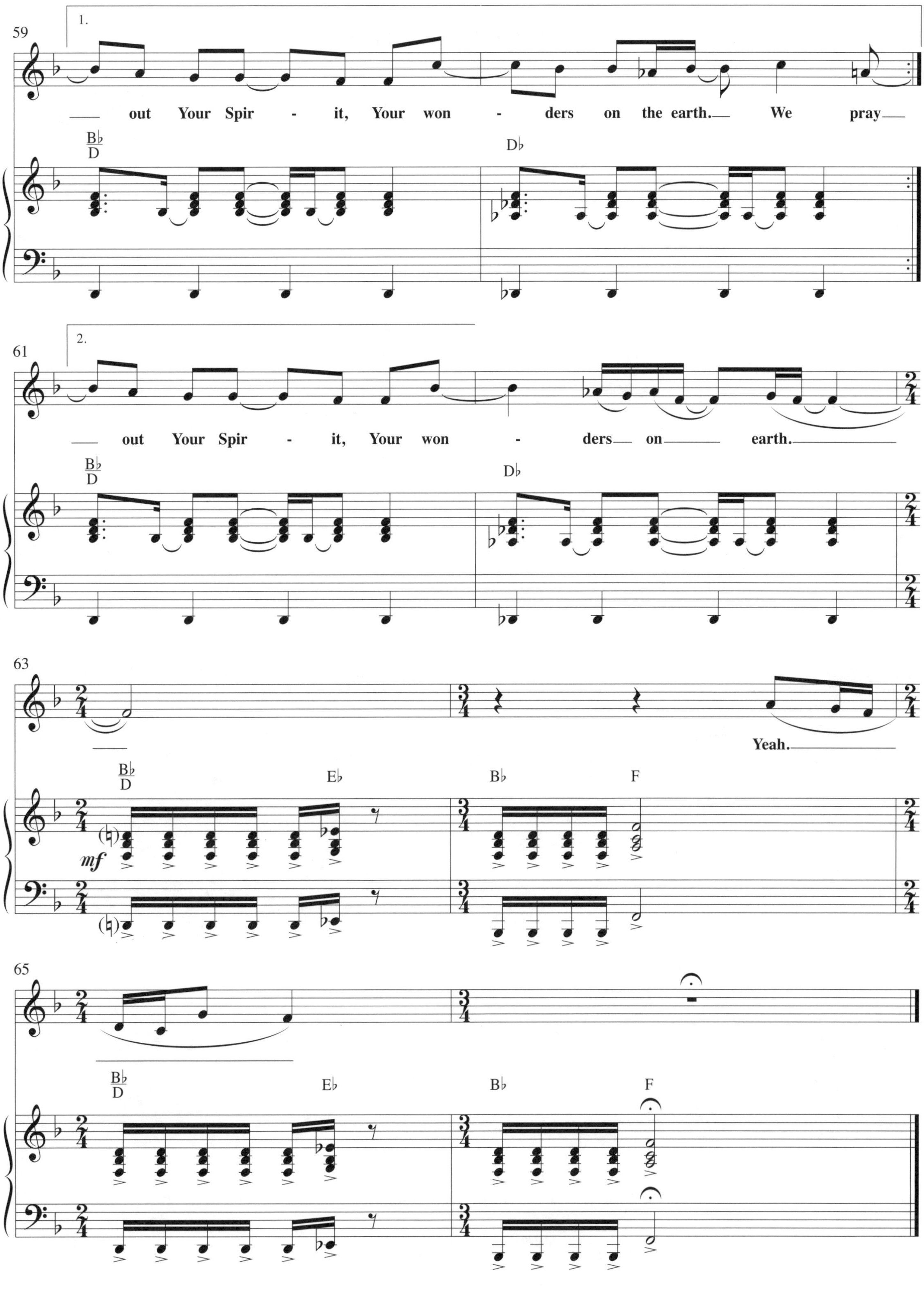
59
1.
out Your Spir - it, Your won - ders on the earth. We pray
B♭/D
D♭
61
2.
out Your Spir - it, Your won - ders on earth.
B♭/D
D♭
63
Yeah.
B♭/D
E♭
B♭
F
mf
65
B♭/D
E♭
B♭
F

Heaven On Earth

Words and Music by
DAVID HOLMES and
DARLENE ZSCHECH

Moderately ♩ = 76

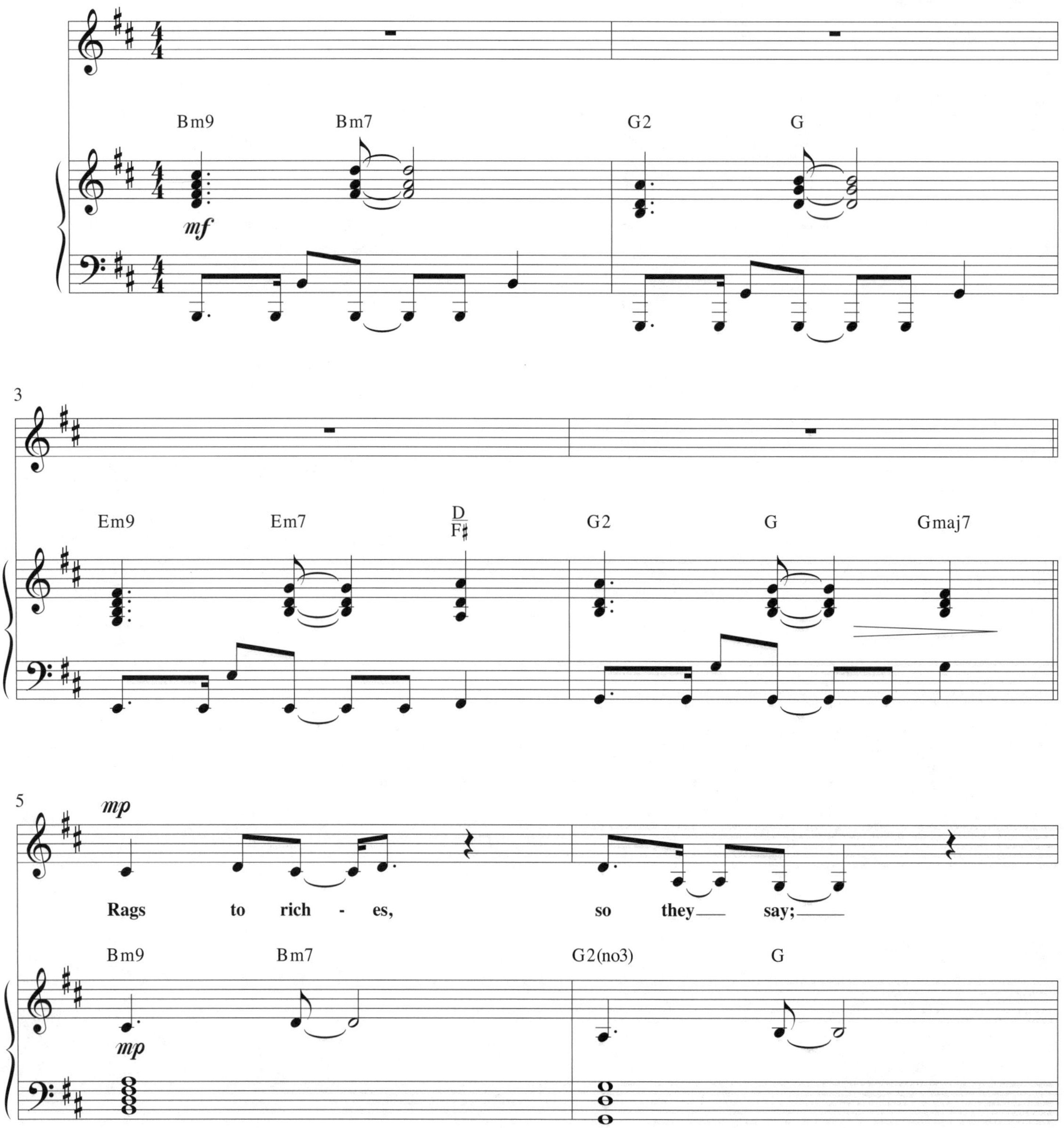

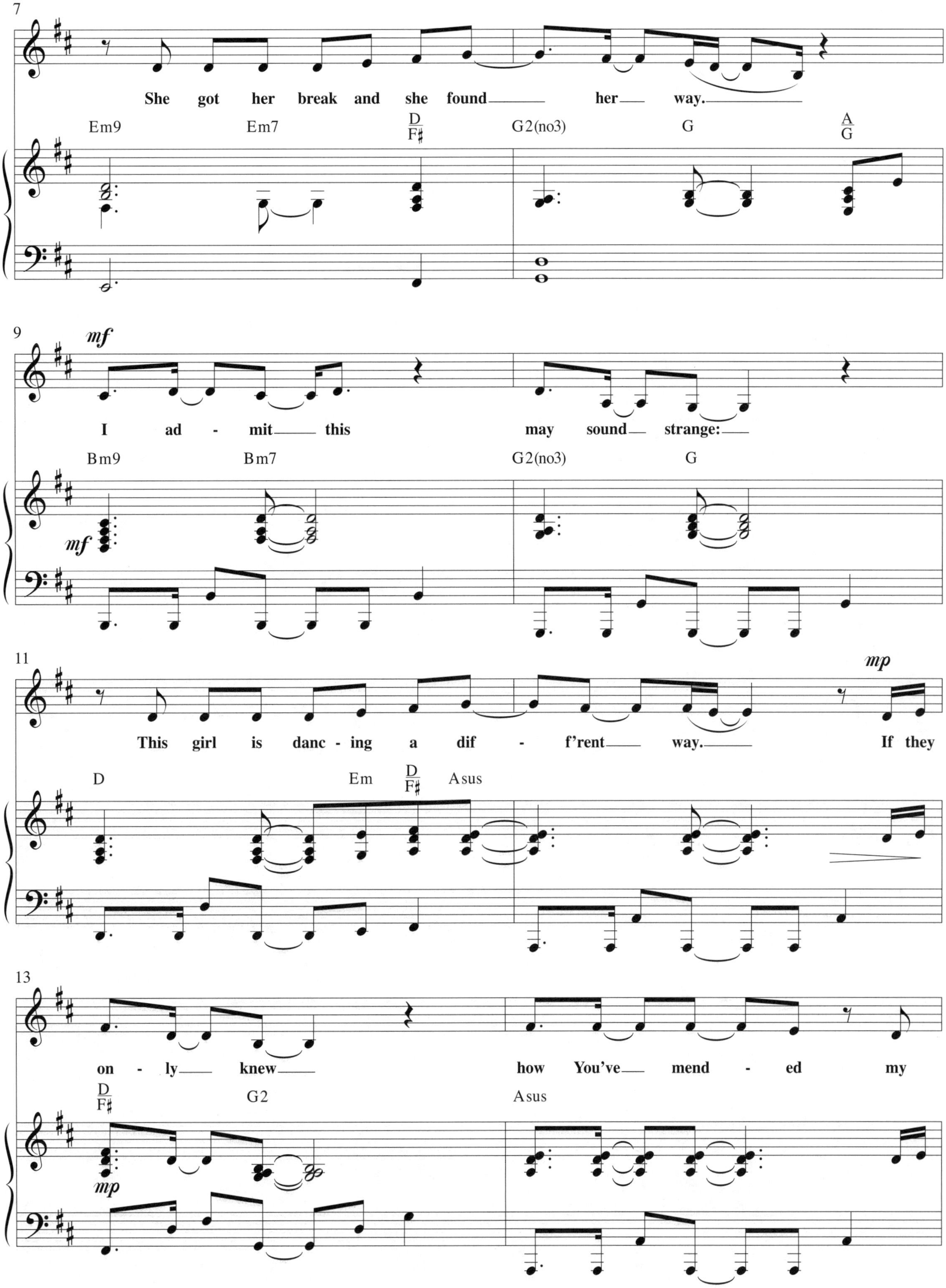
7
She got her break and she found her way.
Em9 Em7 D/F♯ G2(no3) G A/G
9
mf
I ad - mit this may sound strange:
Bm9 Bm7 G2(no3) G
mf
11
mp
This girl is danc - ing a dif - f'rent way. If they
D Em D/F♯ Asus
13
on - ly knew how You've mend - ed my
D/F♯ G2 Asus
mp

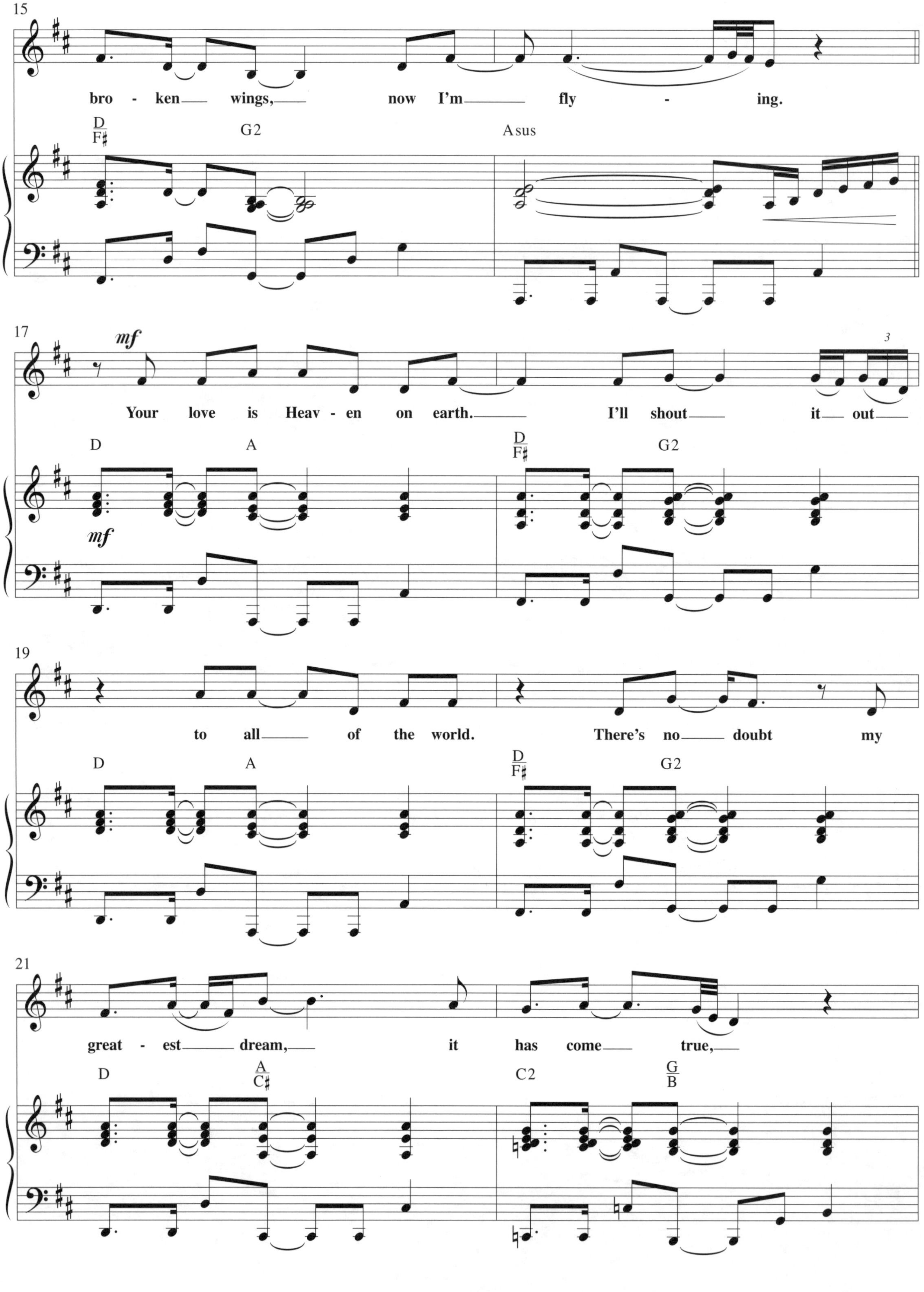
15
broken wings, now I'm fly - ing.
D/F♯ G2 Asus
17
mf
Your love is Heav - en on earth. I'll shout it out
D A D/F♯ G2
19
to all of the world. There's no doubt my
D A D/F♯ G2
21
great - est dream, it has come true,
D A/C♯ C2 G/B

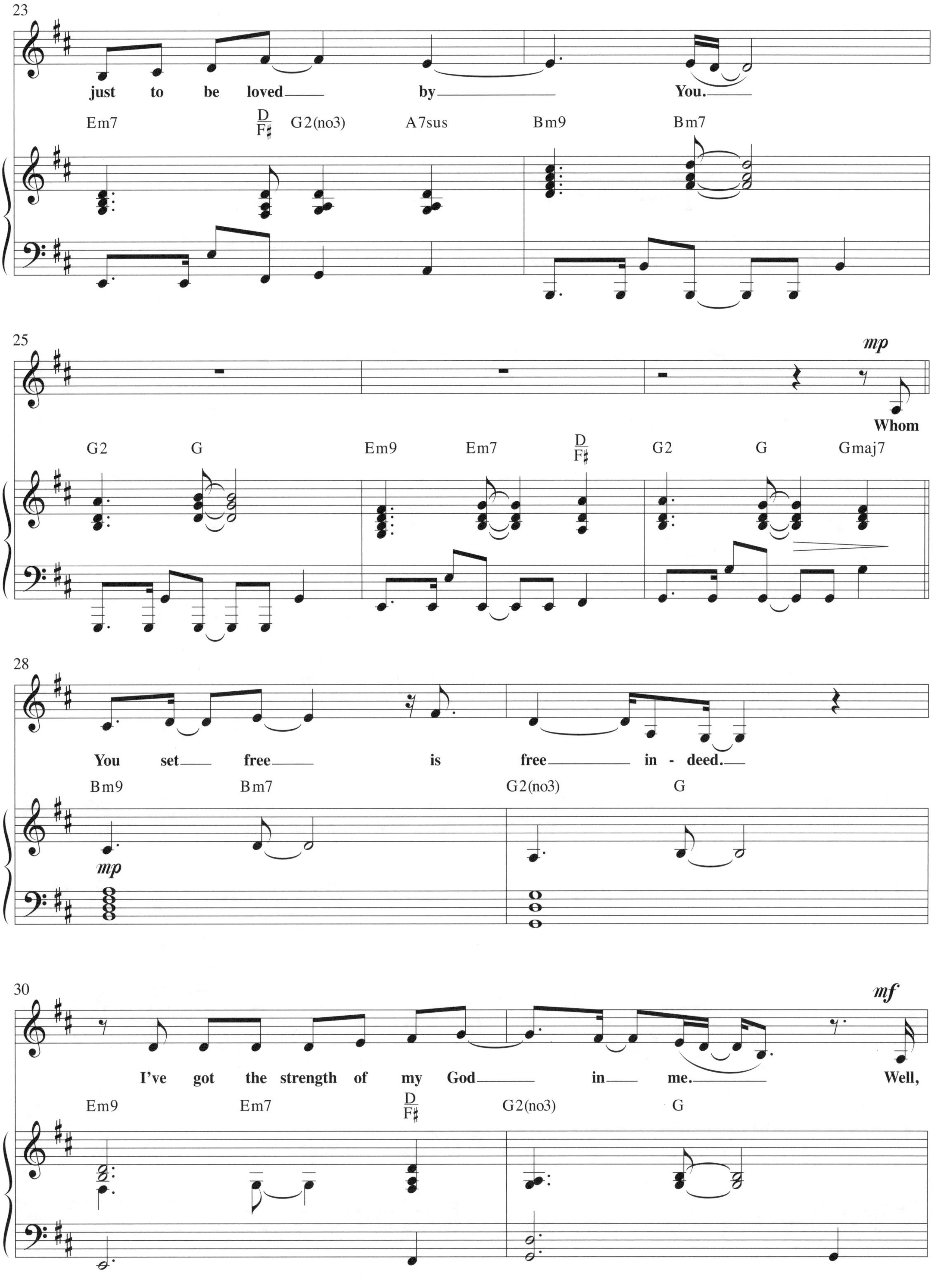
23
just to be loved by You.
Em7 D/F♯ G2(no3) A7sus Bm9 Bm7
25
mp
Whom
G2 G Em9 Em7 D/F♯ G2 G Gmaj7
28
You set free is free in - deed.
Bm9 Bm7 G2(no3) G
mp
30
mf
I've got the strength of my God in me. Well,
Em9 Em7 D/F♯ G2(no3) G

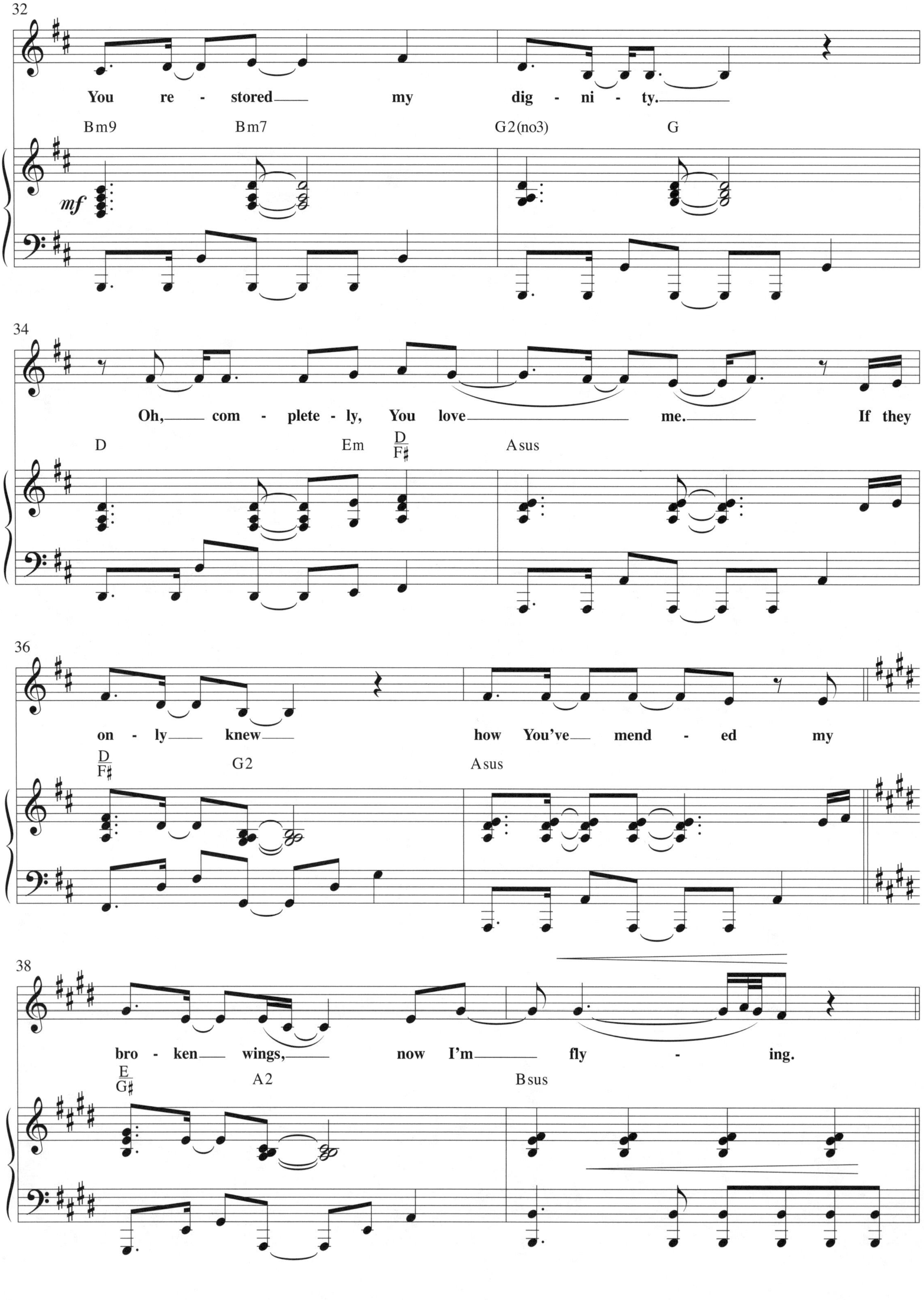
32
You re - stored my dig - ni - ty.
Bm9 Bm7 G2(no3) G
mf
34
Oh, com - plete - ly, You love me. If they
D Em D/F♯ Asus
36
on - ly knew how You've mend - ed my
D/F♯ G2 Asus
38
bro - ken wings, now I'm fly - ing.
E/G♯ A2 Bsus

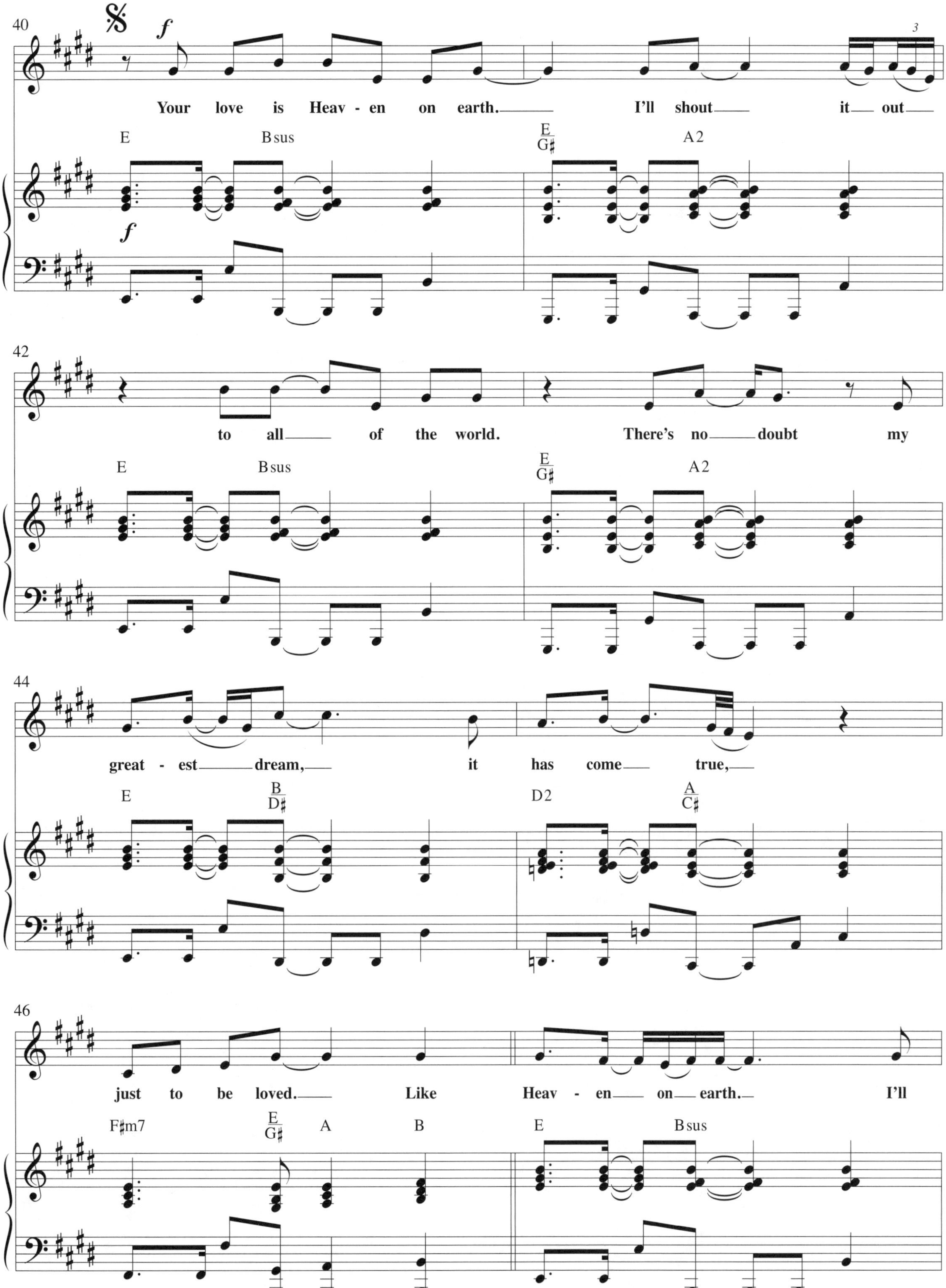
Your love is Heav - en on earth. I'll shout it out
E Bsus E/G♯ A2
to all of the world. There's no doubt my
E Bsus E/G♯ A2
great - est dream, it has come true,
E B/D♯ D2 A/C♯
just to be loved. Like Heav - en on earth. I'll
F♯m7 E/G♯ A B E Bsus

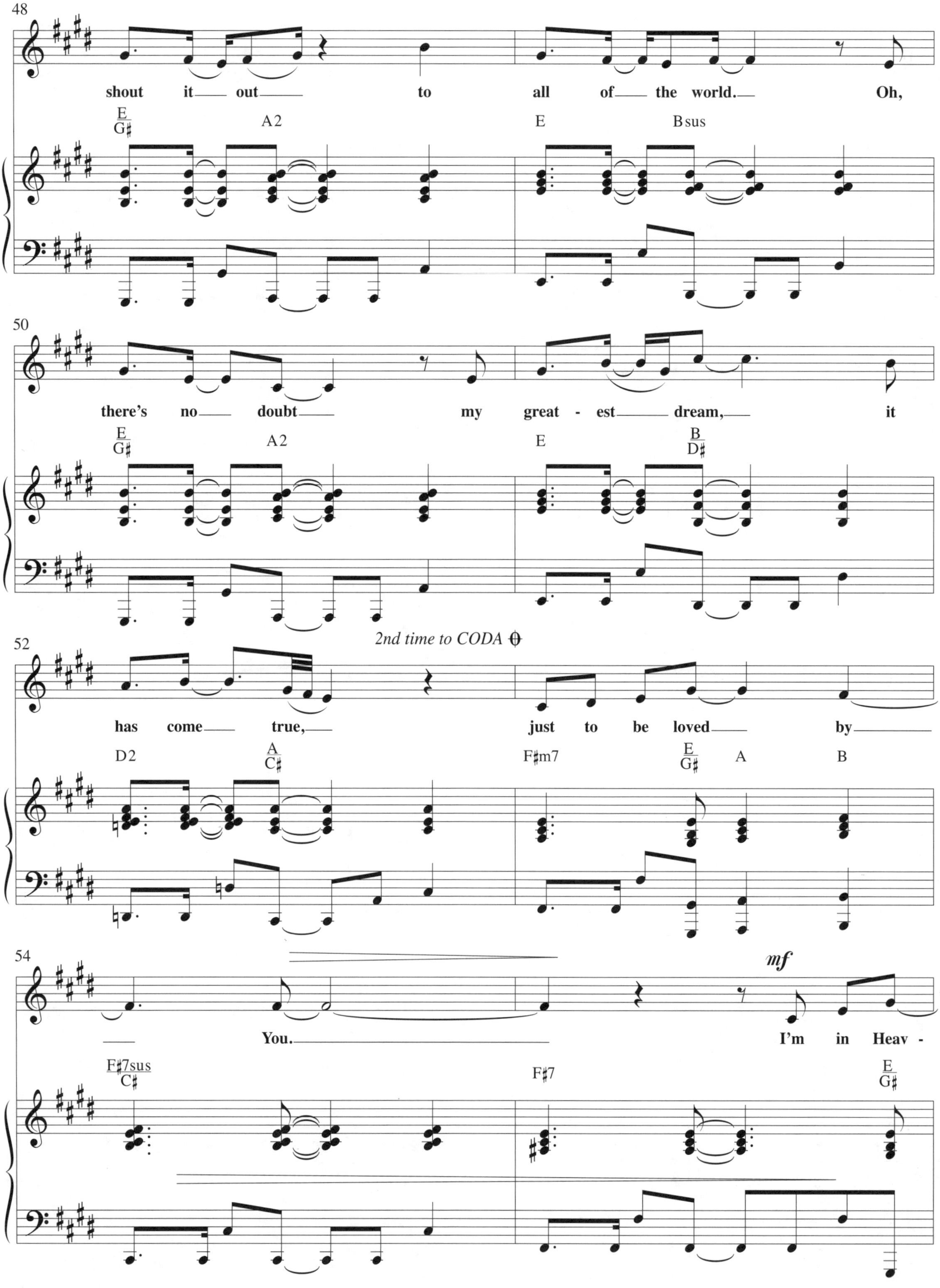
48
shout it out to all of the world. Oh,
E/G♯ A2 E Bsus
50
there's no doubt my great - est dream, it
E/G♯ A2 E B/D♯
2nd time to CODA
52
has come true, just to be loved by
D2 A/C♯ F♯m7 E/G♯ A B
54
mf
You. I'm in Heav -
F♯7sus/C♯ F♯7 E/G♯

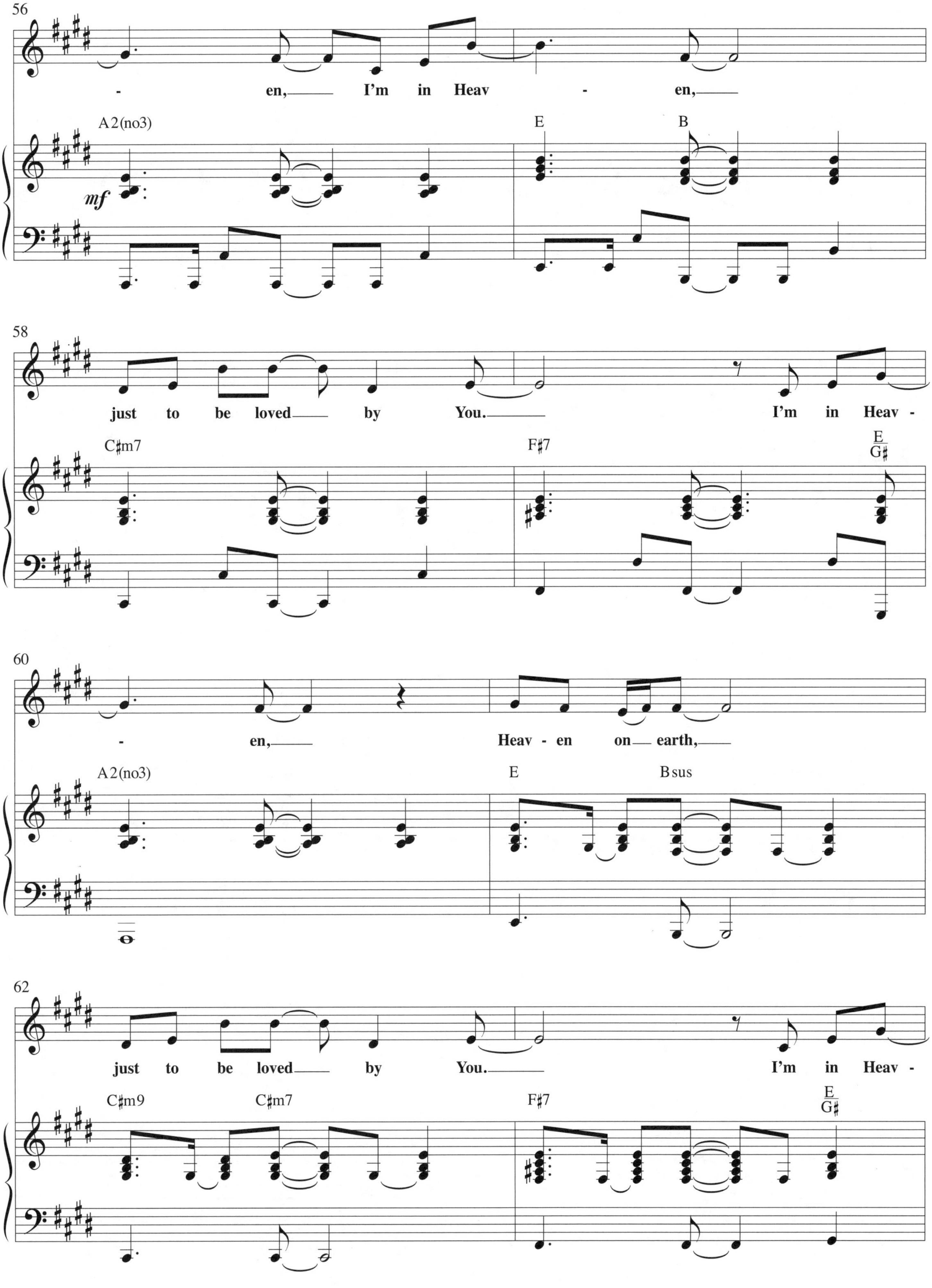
56
- en, I'm in Heav - en,
A2(no3)
mf
E
B
58
just to be loved by You. I'm in Heav -
C♯m7
F♯7
E/G♯
60
- en, Heav - en on earth,
A2(no3)
E
Bsus
62
just to be loved by You. I'm in Heav -
C♯m9
C♯m7
F♯7
E/G♯

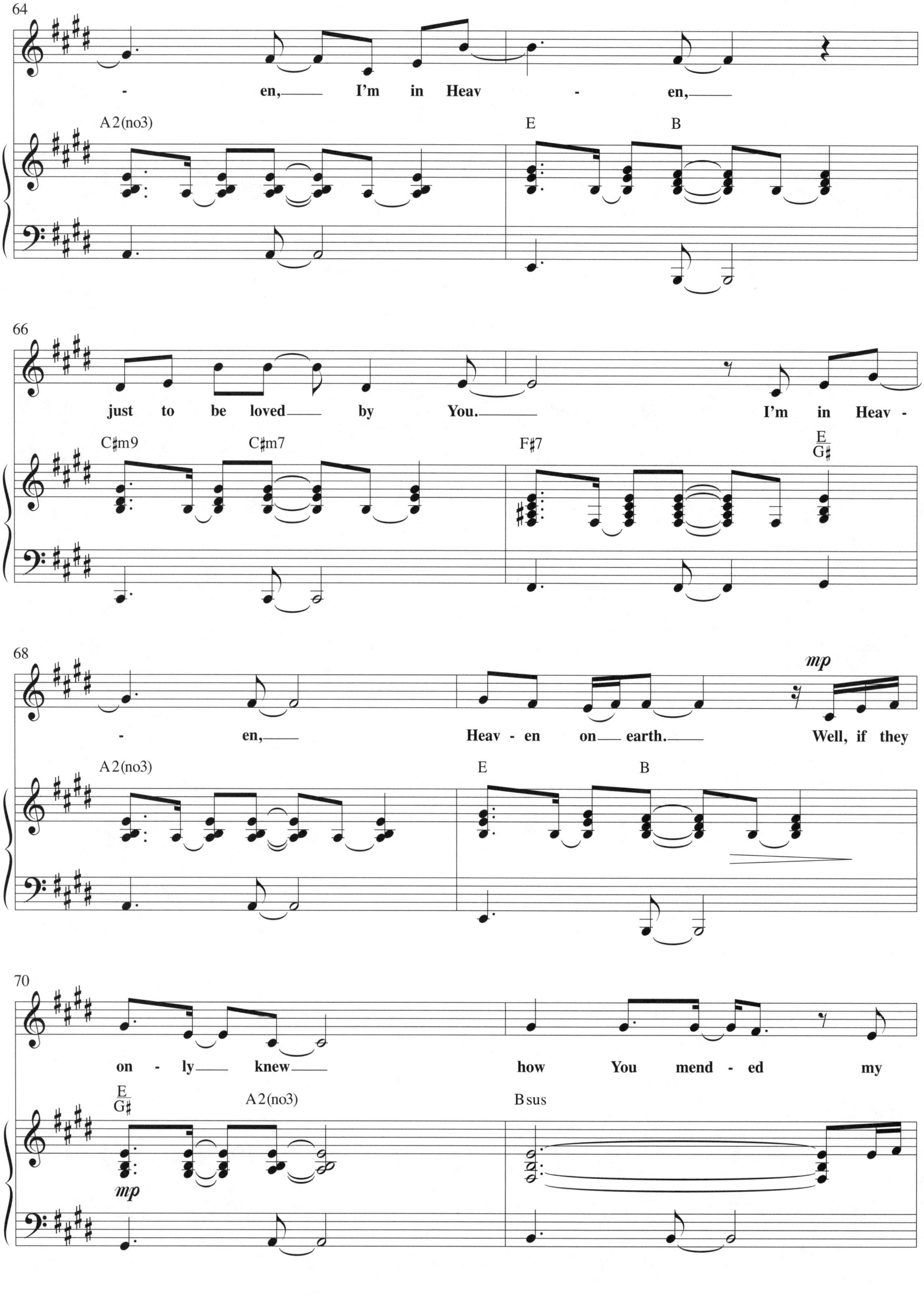
64
- en, I'm in Heav - en,
A2(no3)
E
B
66
just to be loved by You. I'm in Heav -
C♯m9
C♯m7
F♯7
E/G♯
68
- en, Heav - en on earth. Well, if they
mp
A2(no3)
E
B
70
on - ly knew how You mend - ed my
E/G♯
A2(no3)
Bsus
mp

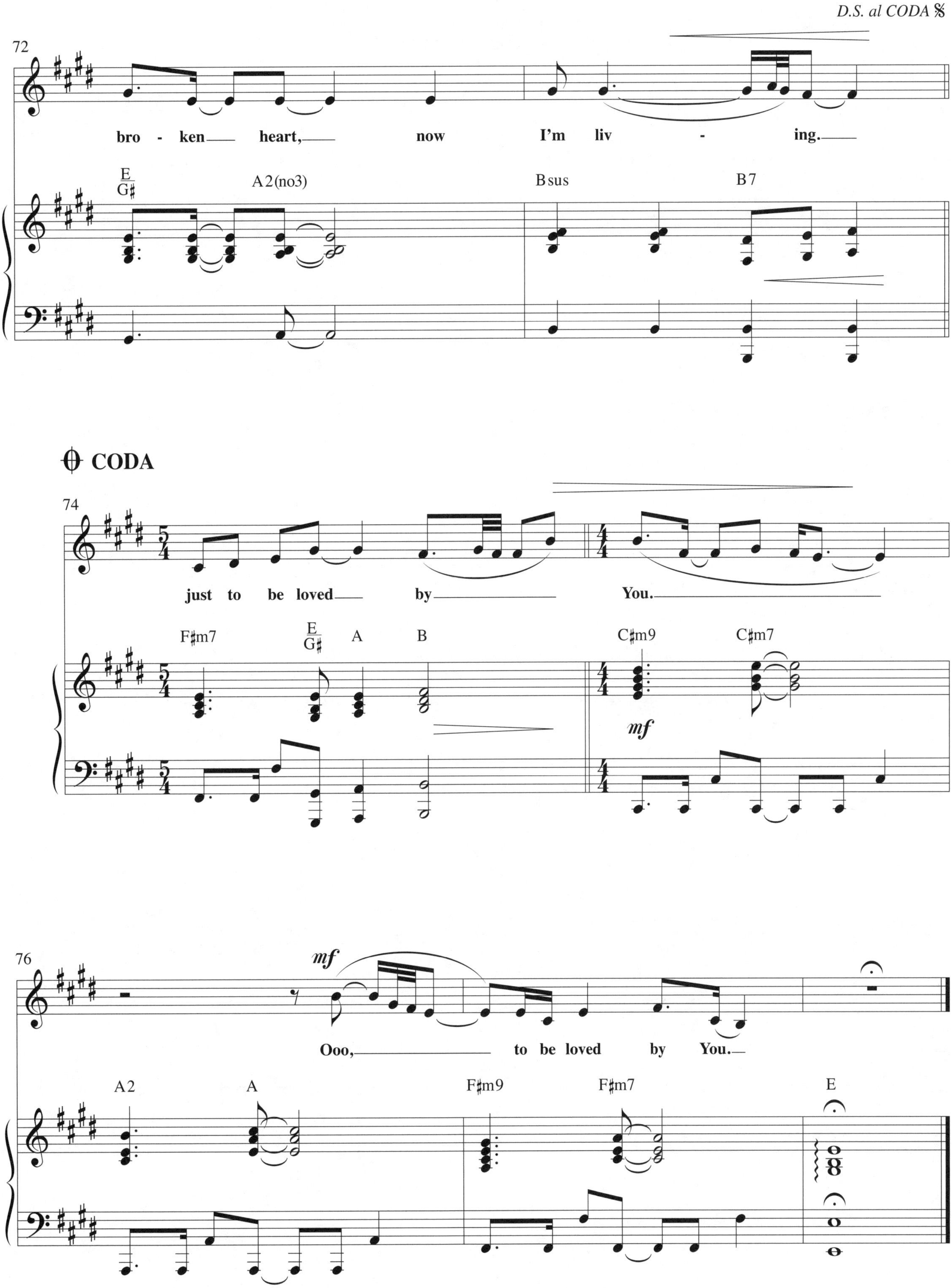
D.S. al CODA
72
bro - ken heart, now I'm liv - ing.
E/G♯ A2(no3) Bsus B7
CODA
74
just to be loved by You.
F♯m7 E/G♯ A B C♯m9 C♯m7
mf
76
mf
Ooo, to be loved by You.
A2 A F♯m9 F♯m7 E

Faithful

Words and Music by
DARLENE ZSCHECH
and DAVID HOLMES

Easy rhythm ♩ = 116

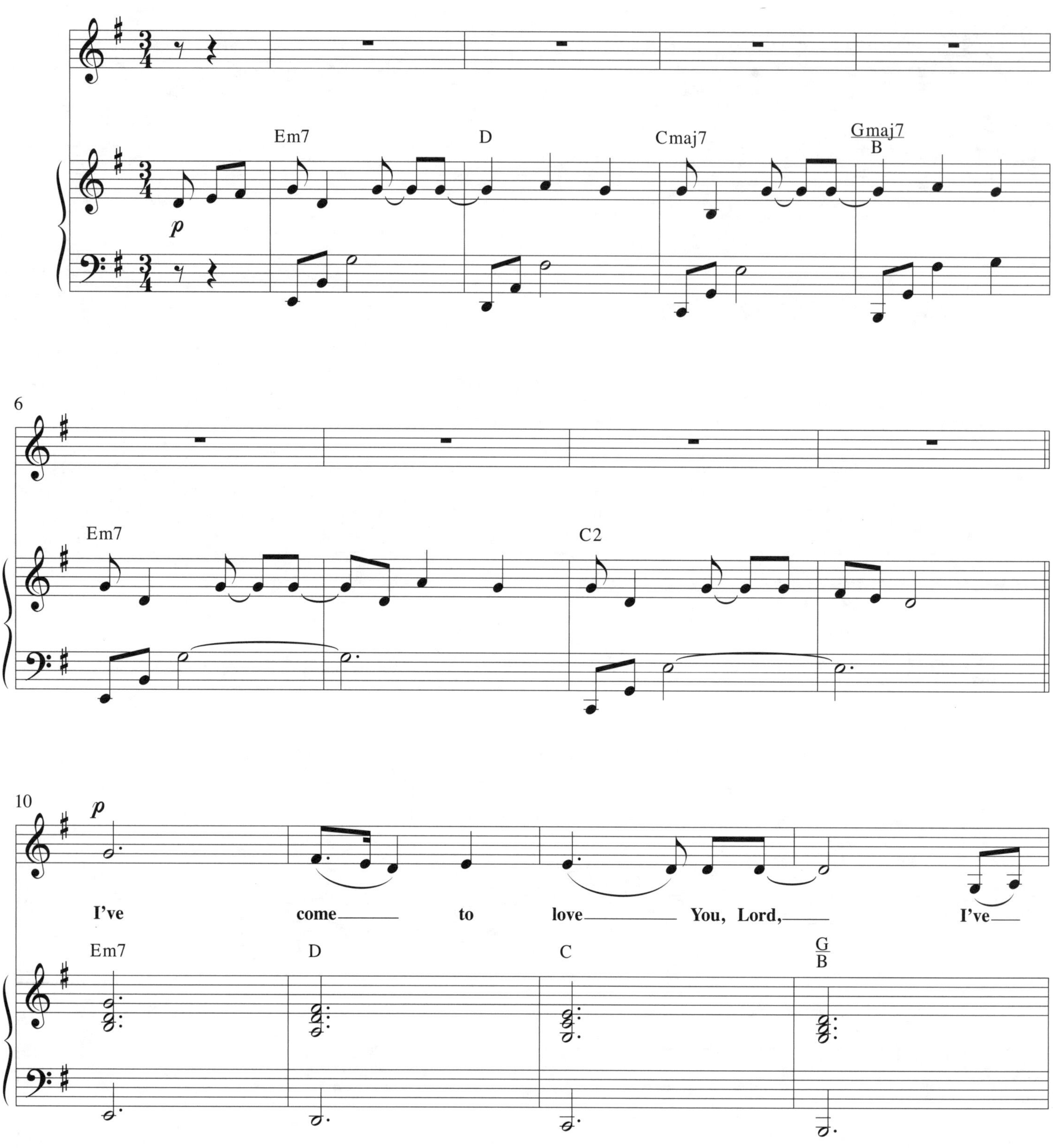

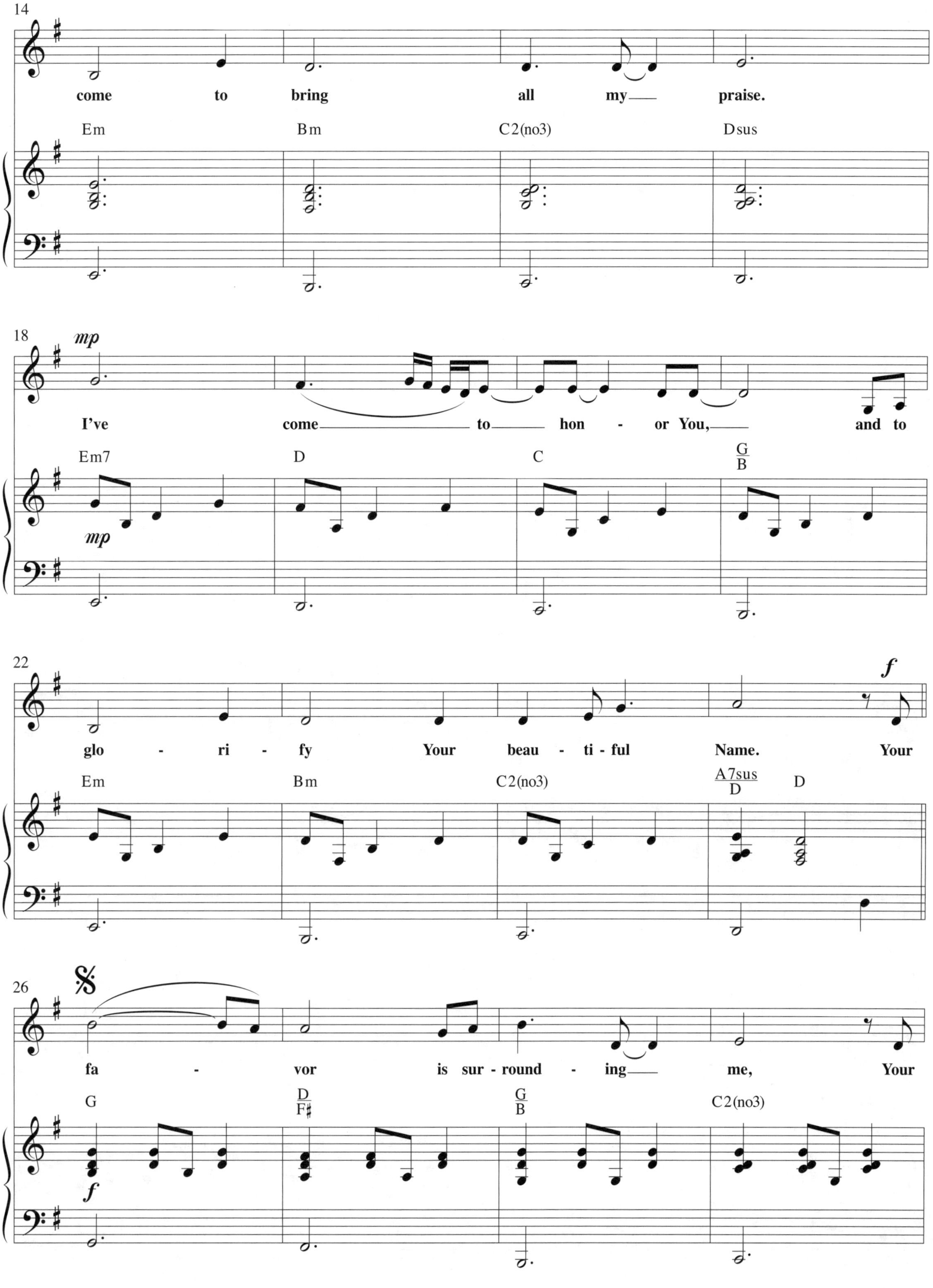
14
come to bring all my praise.
Em Bm C2(no3) Dsus
18
mp
I've come to hon - or You, and to
Em7 D C G/B
mp
22
f
glo - ri - fy Your beau - ti - ful Name. Your
Em Bm C2(no3) A7sus/D D
26
fa - vor is sur - round - ing me, Your
G D/F♯ G/B C2(no3)
f

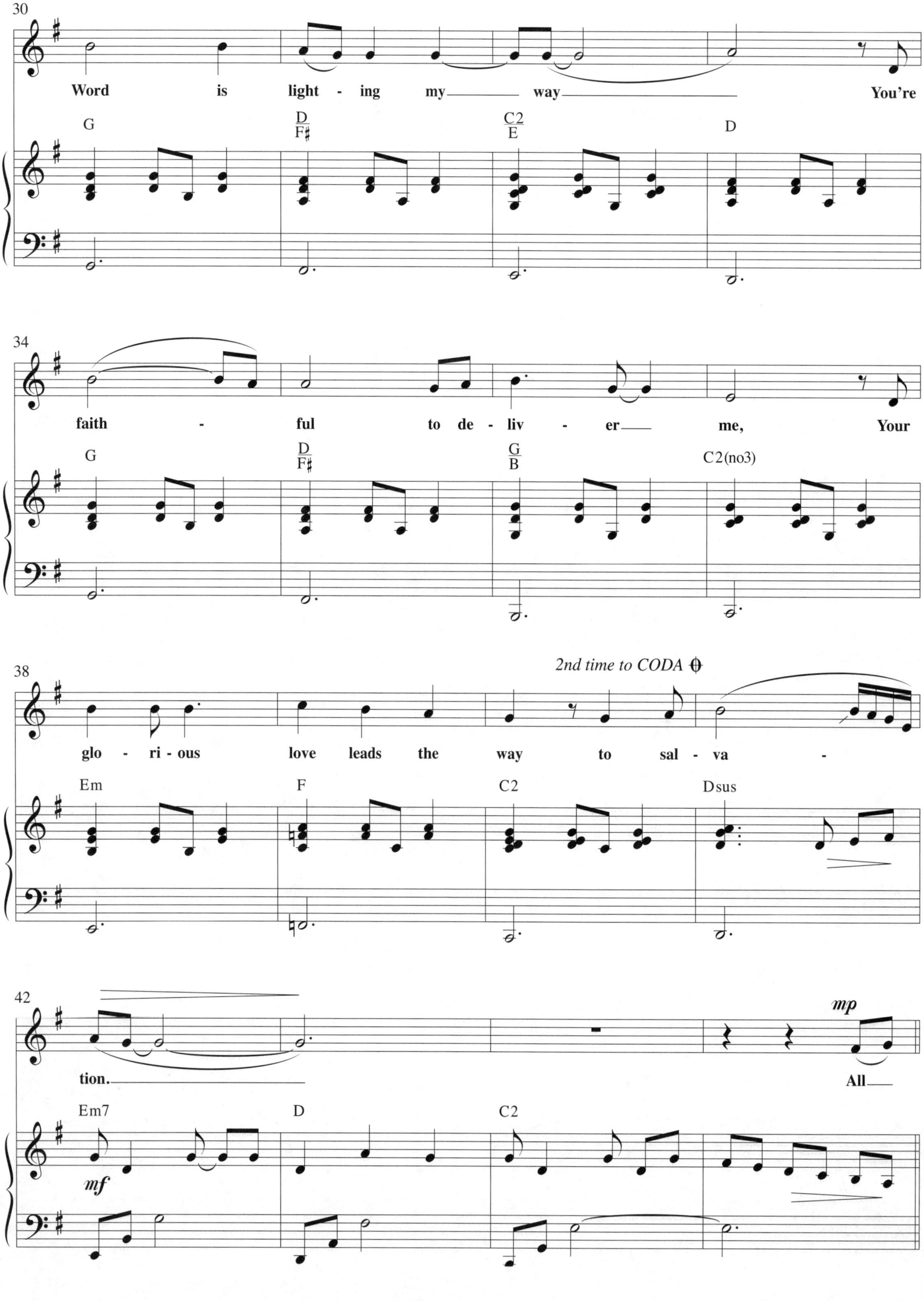
30
Word is light - ing my way You're
G
D F♯
C2 E
D
34
faith - ful to de - liv - er me, Your
G
D F♯
G B
C2(no3)
38
2nd time to CODA
glo - ri - ous love leads the way to sal - va -
Em
F
C2
Dsus
42
mp
tion. All
Em7
D
C2
mf

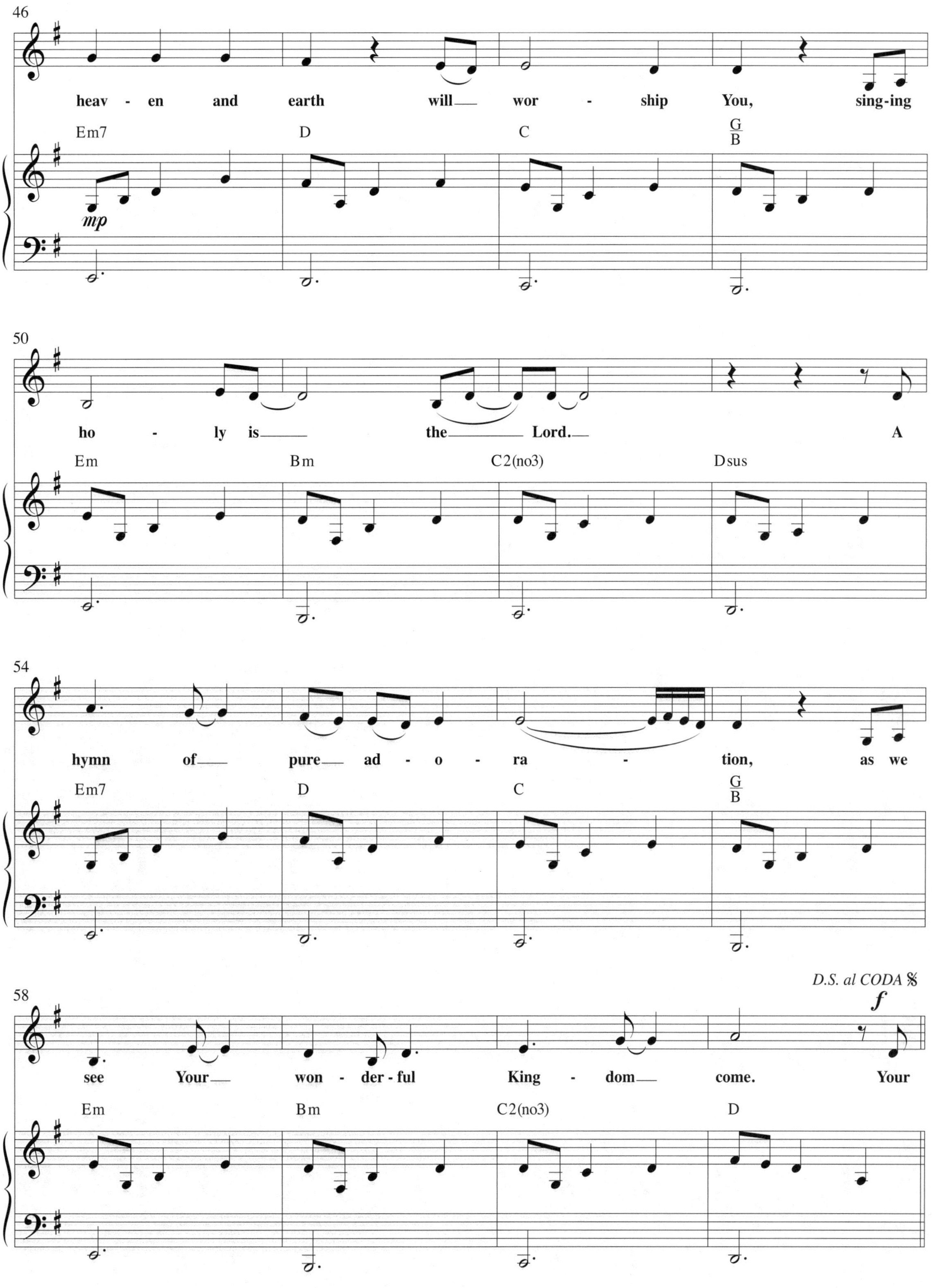
46
heav - en and earth will wor - ship You, sing-ing
Em7 D C G/B
mp
50
ho - ly is the Lord. A
Em Bm C2(no3) Dsus
54
hymn of pure ad - o - ra - tion, as we
Em7 D C G/B
D.S. al CODA 𝄋
f
58
see Your won - der - ful King - dom come. Your
Em Bm C2(no3) D

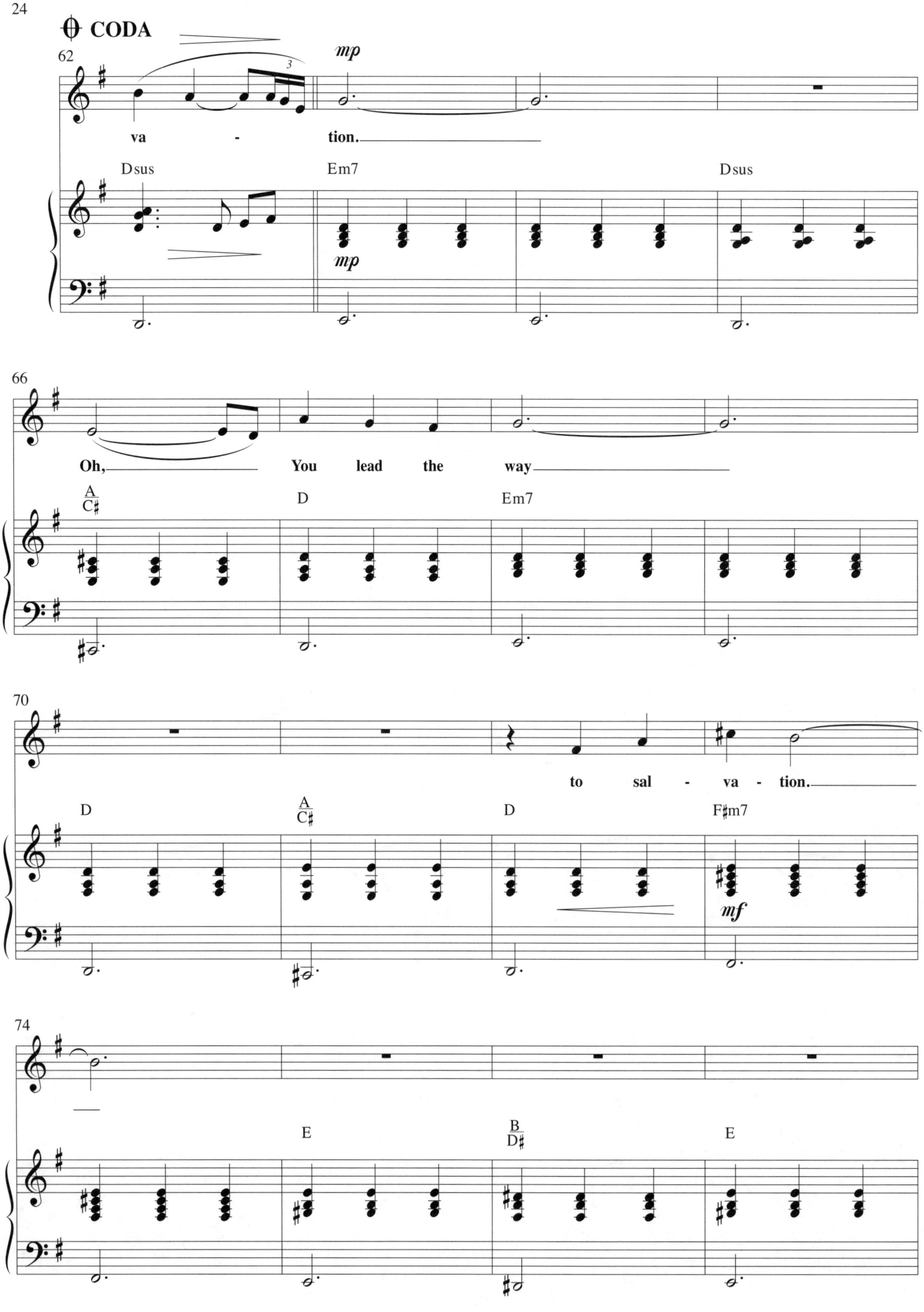
CODA
62
mp
va - tion.
Dsus
Em7
Dsus
mp
66
Oh, You lead the way
A/C♯
D
Em7
70
to sal - va - tion.
D
A/C♯
D
F♯m7
mf
74
E
B/D♯
E

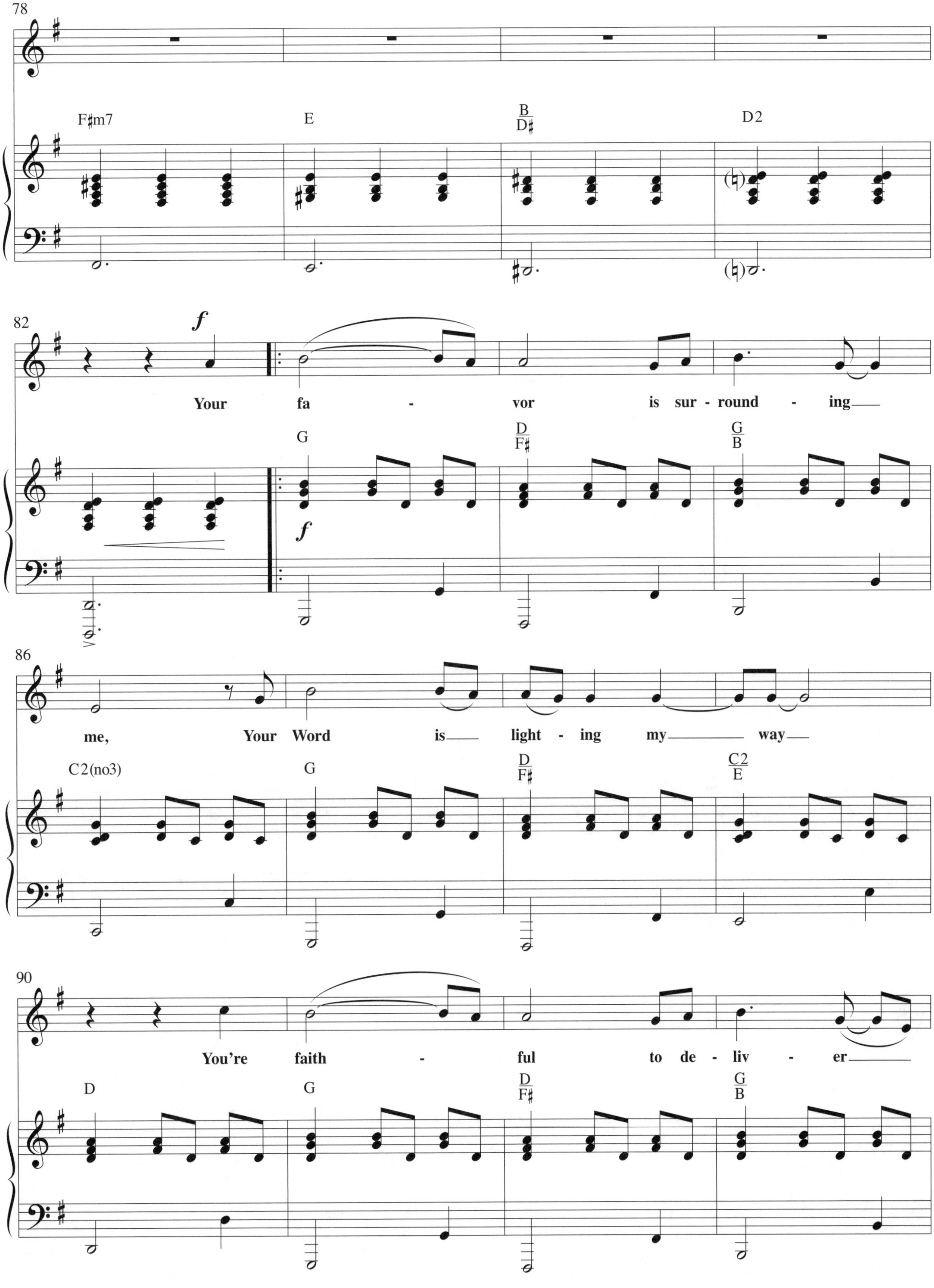
78
F♯m7
E
B/D♯
D2
82
f
Your fa - vor is sur - round - ing
G
D/F♯
G/B
f
86
me, Your Word is light - ing my way
C2(no3)
G
D/F♯
C2/E
90
You're faith - ful to de - liv - er
D
G
D/F♯
G/B

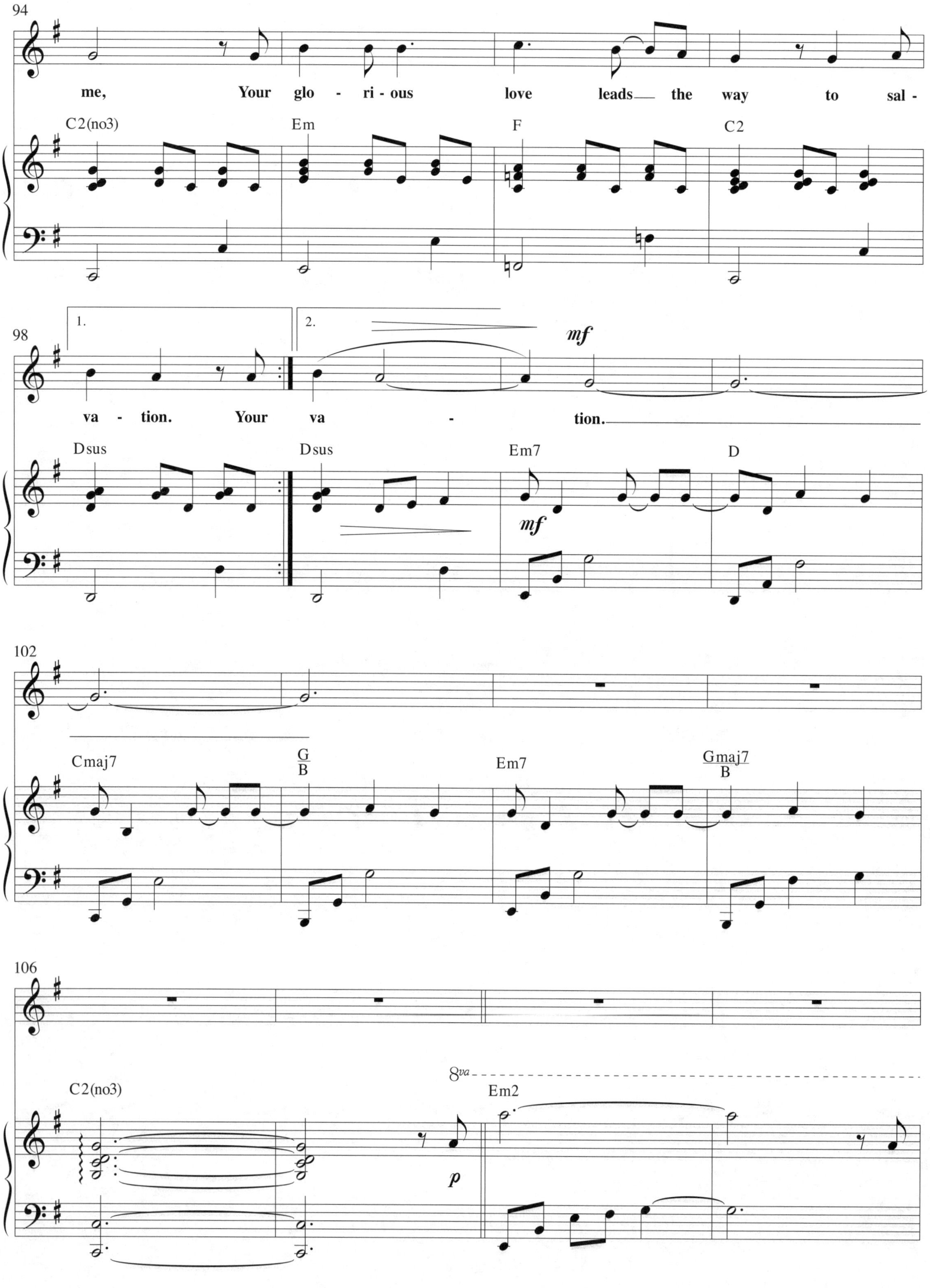
94
me, Your glo - ri - ous love leads the way to sal -
C2(no3) Em F C2
98
1. 2.
va - tion. Your va - tion.
mf
Dsus Dsus Em7 D
mf
102
Cmaj7 G/B Em7 Gmaj7/B
106
C2(no3) Em2
8va
p

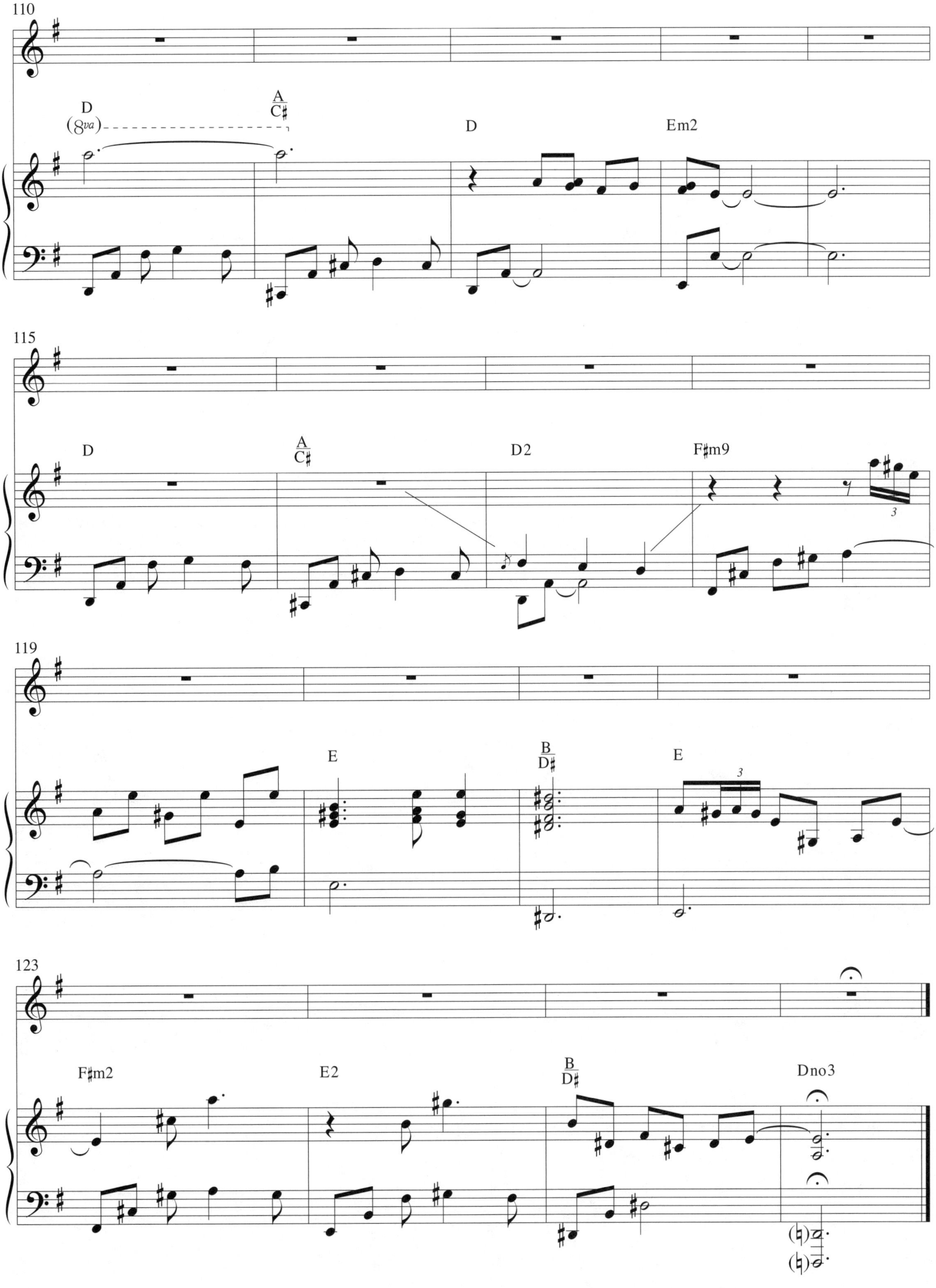
110
D
(8va)
A
C♯
D
Em2
115
D
A
C♯
D2
F♯m9
119
E
B
D♯
E
123
F♯m2
E2
B
D♯
Dno3

Beautiful Savior

TRADITIONAL - Public Domain
Author unknown - translated 1677 by Joseph A. Seiss

With wonder and awe ♩ = 72

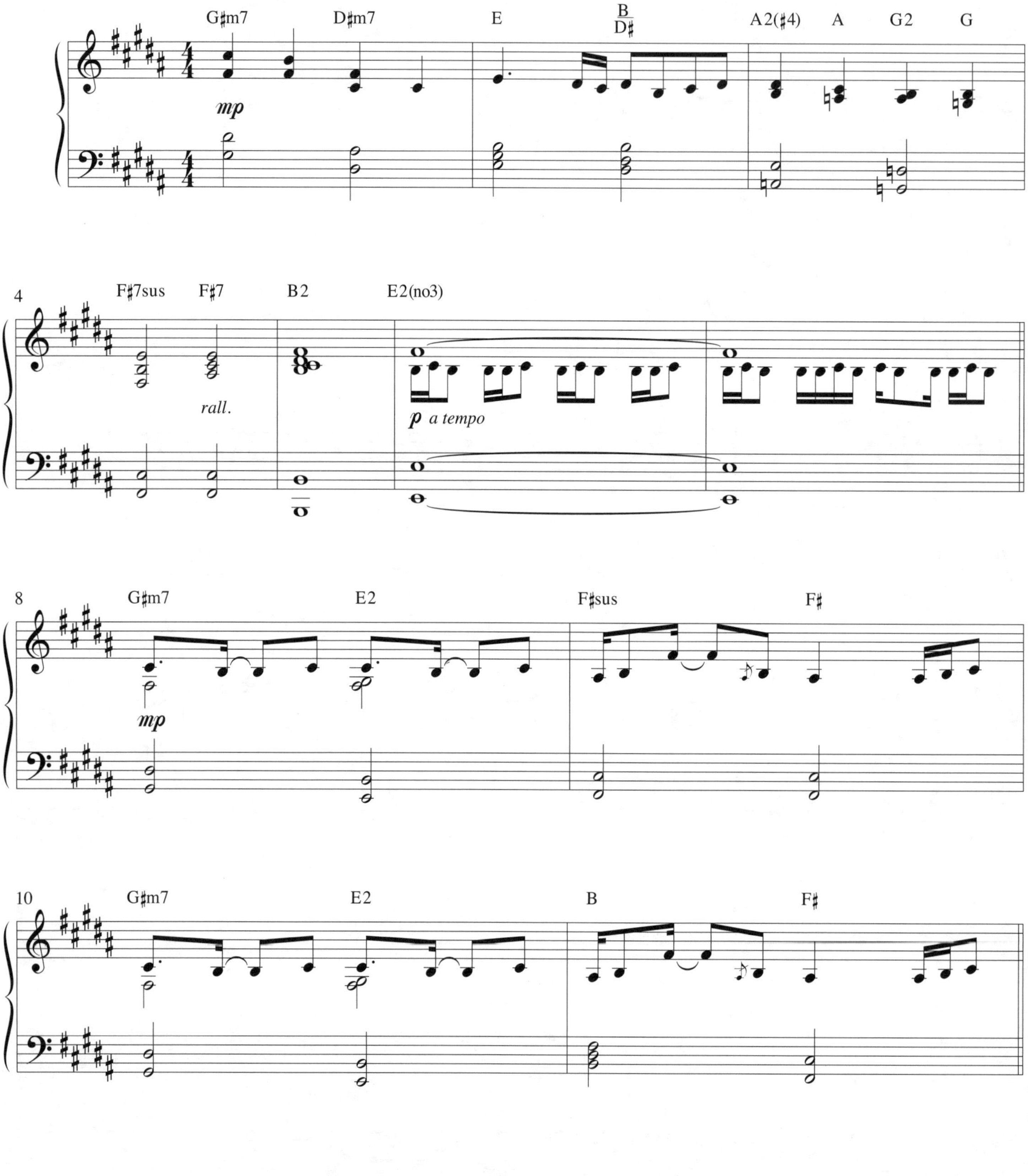

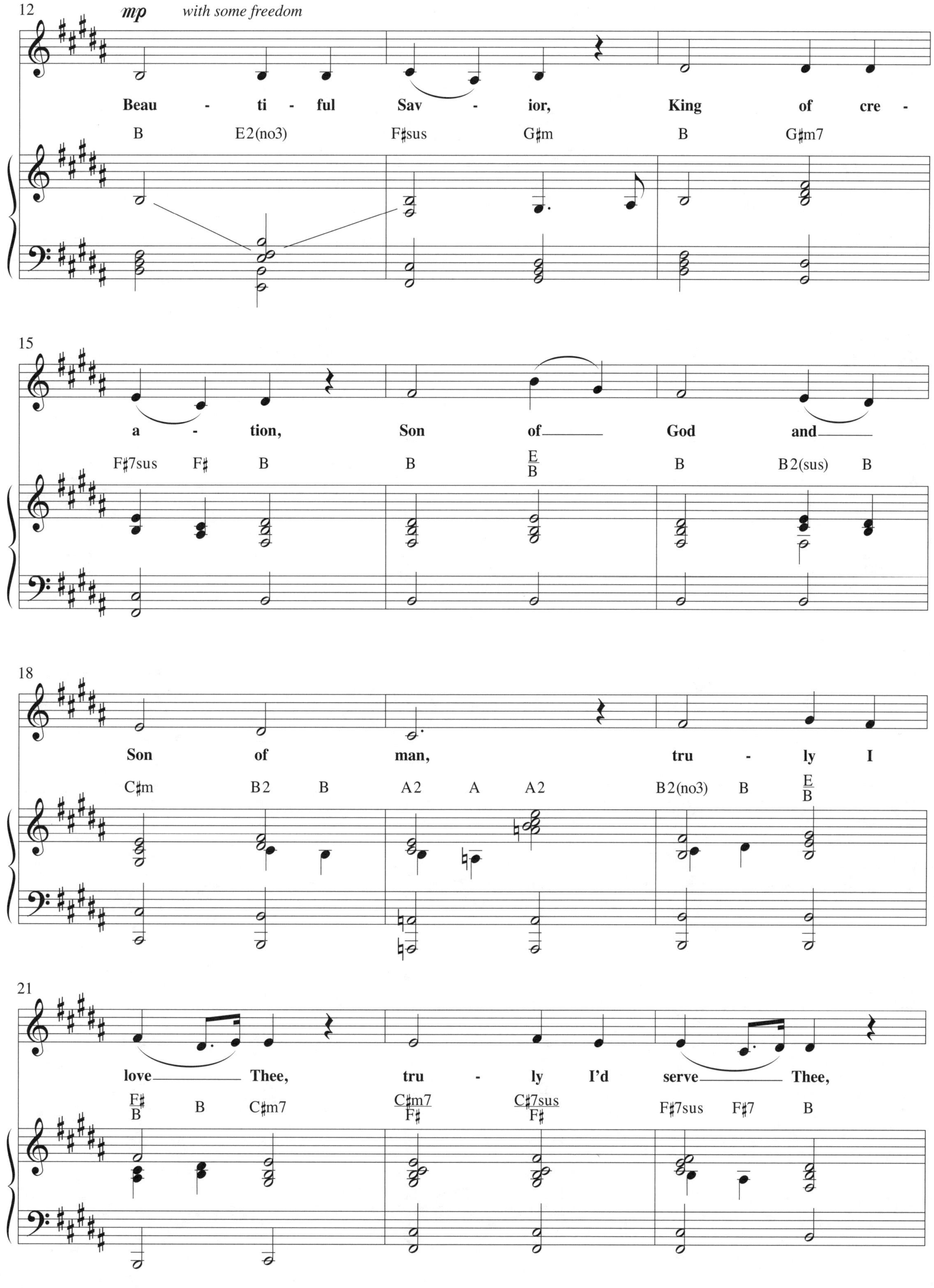
12
mp with some freedom
Beau - ti - ful Sav - ior, King of cre -
B E2(no3) F♯sus G♯m B G♯m7
15
a - tion, Son of God and
F♯7sus F♯ B B E/B B B2(sus) B
18
Son of man, tru - ly I
C♯m B2 B A2 A A2 B2(no3) B E/B
21
love Thee, tru - ly I'd serve Thee,
F♯/B B C♯m7 C♯m7/F♯ C♯7sus/F♯ F♯7sus F♯7 B

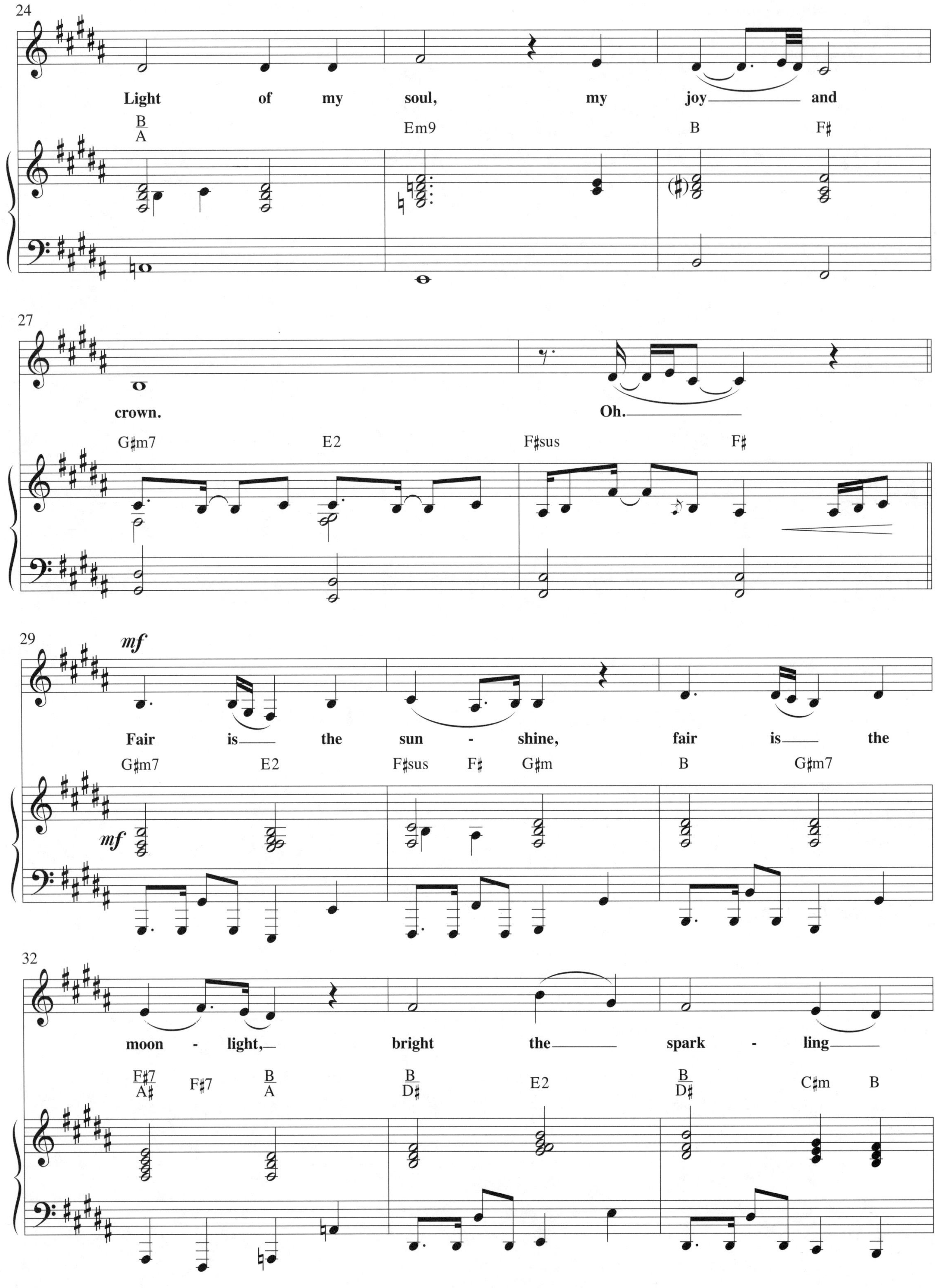
24
Light of my soul, my joy and
B/A Em9 B F♯
27
crown. Oh.
G♯m7 E2 F♯sus F♯
29
mf
Fair is the sun - shine, fair is the
G♯m7 E2 F♯sus F♯ G♯m B G♯m7
mf
32
moon - light, bright the spark - ling
F♯7/A♯ F♯7 B/A B/D♯ E2 B/D♯ C♯m B

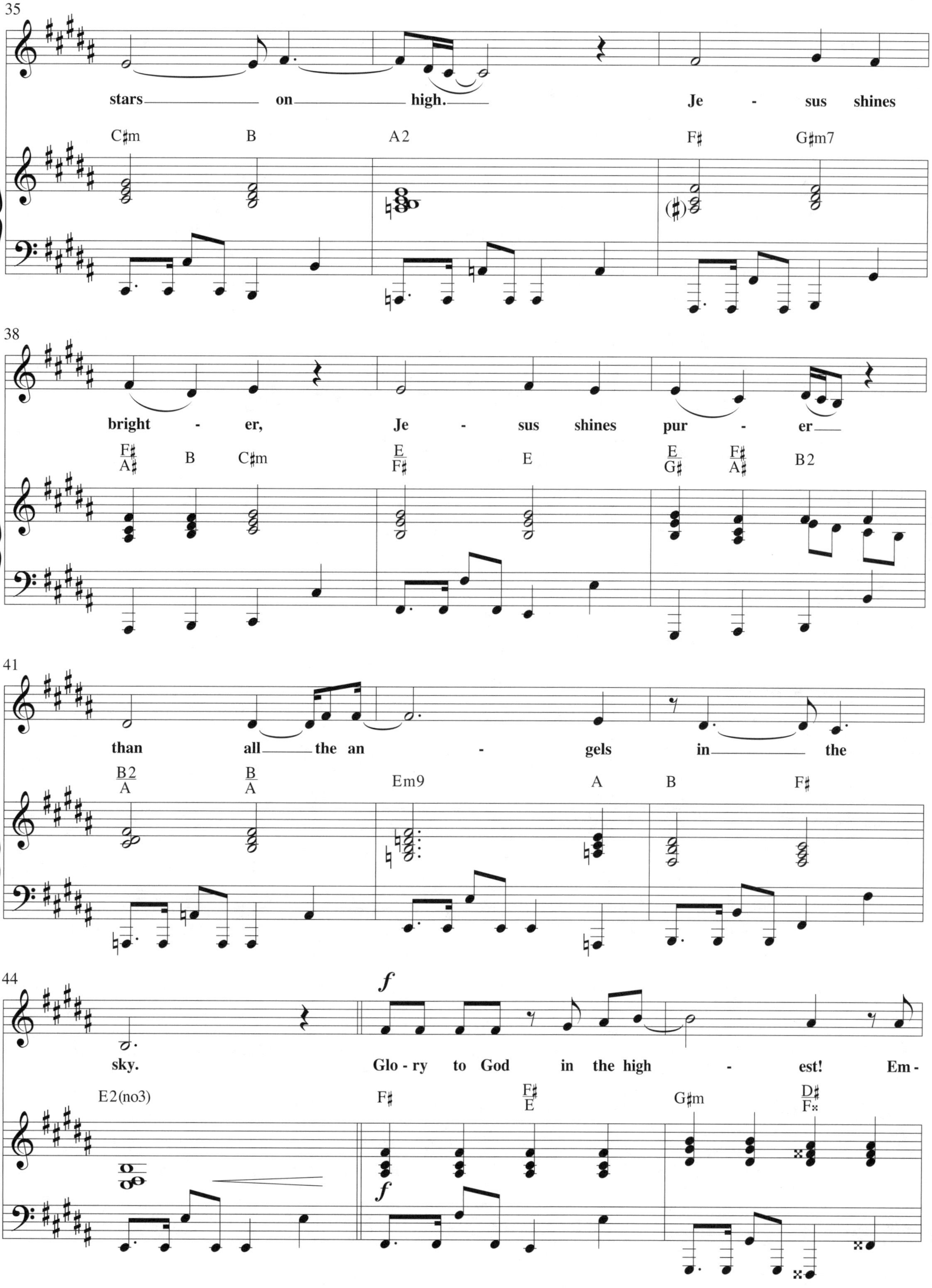
35
stars on high. Je - sus shines
C♯m B A2 F♯ G♯m7
38
bright - er, Je - sus shines pur - er
F♯/A♯ B C♯m E/F♯ E E/G♯ F♯/A♯ B2
41
than all the an - gels in the
B2/A B/A Em9 A B F♯
44
sky. Glo - ry to God in the high - est! Em -
E2(no3) F♯ F♯/E G♯m D♯/F𝄪
f
f

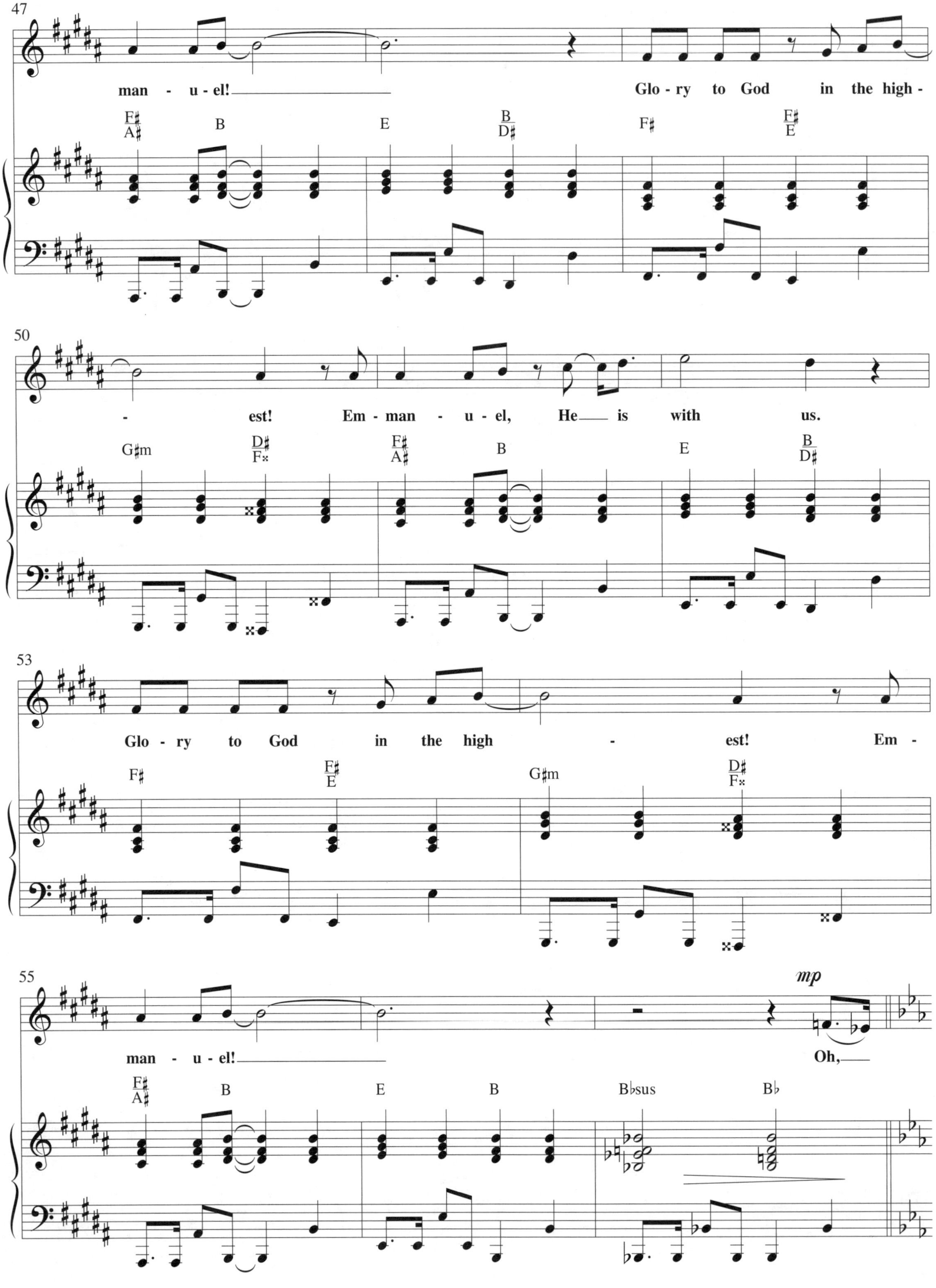
47
man - u - el!
Glo - ry to God in the high -
F♯/A♯ B E B/D♯ F♯ F♯/E
50
- est! Em - man - u - el, He is with us.
G♯m D♯/F𝄪 F♯/A♯ B E B/D♯
53
Glo - ry to God in the high - est! Em -
F♯ F♯/E G♯m D♯/F𝄪
55
mp
man - u - el! Oh,
F♯/A♯ B E B B♭sus B♭

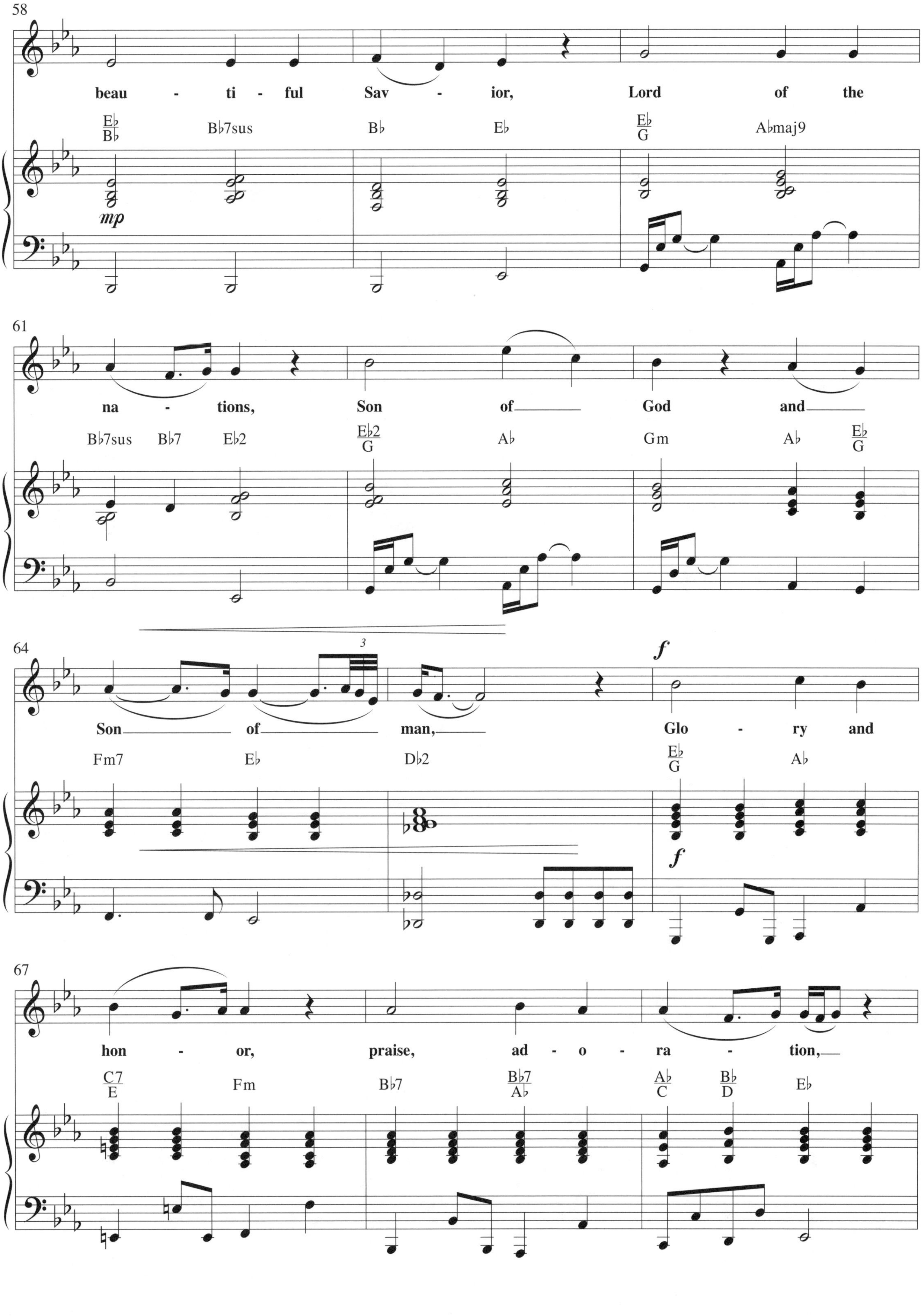
58
beau - ti - ful Sav - ior, Lord of the
Eb/Bb Bb7sus Bb Eb Eb/G Abmaj9
mp
61
na - tions, Son of God and
Bb7sus Bb7 Eb2 Eb2/G Ab Gm Ab Eb/G
64
Son of man,
Fm7 Eb Db2 Eb/G Ab
f
Glo - ry and
67
hon - or, praise, ad - o - ra - tion,
C7/E Fm Bb7 Bb7/Ab Ab/C Bb/D Eb

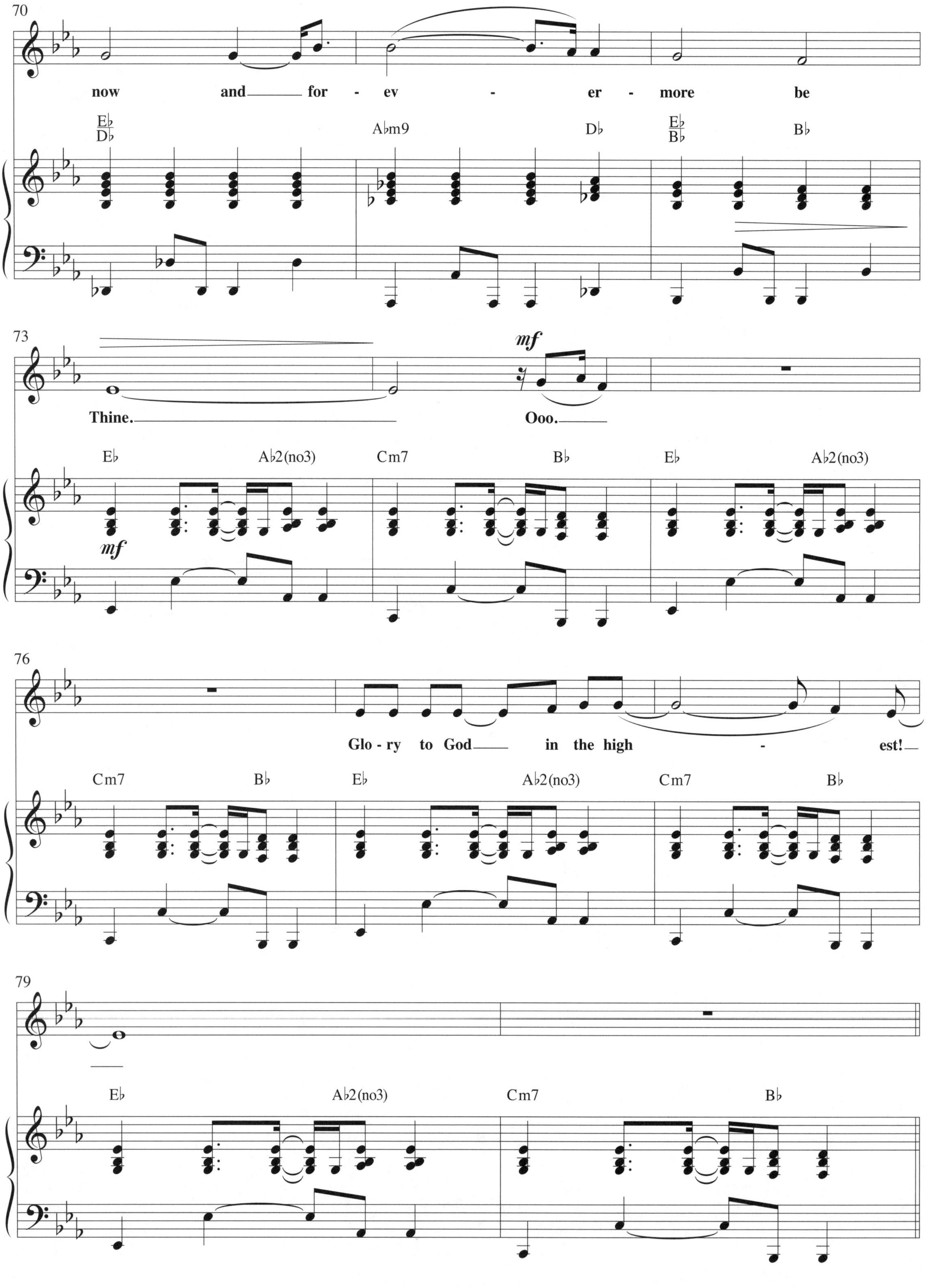
70
now and for - ev - er - more be
E♭/D♭
A♭m9
D♭
E♭/B♭
B♭
73
mf
Thine.
Ooo.
E♭
A♭2(no3)
Cm7
B♭
E♭
A♭2(no3)
mf
76
Glo - ry to God in the high - est!
Cm7
B♭
E♭
A♭2(no3)
Cm7
B♭
79
E♭
A♭2(no3)
Cm7
B♭

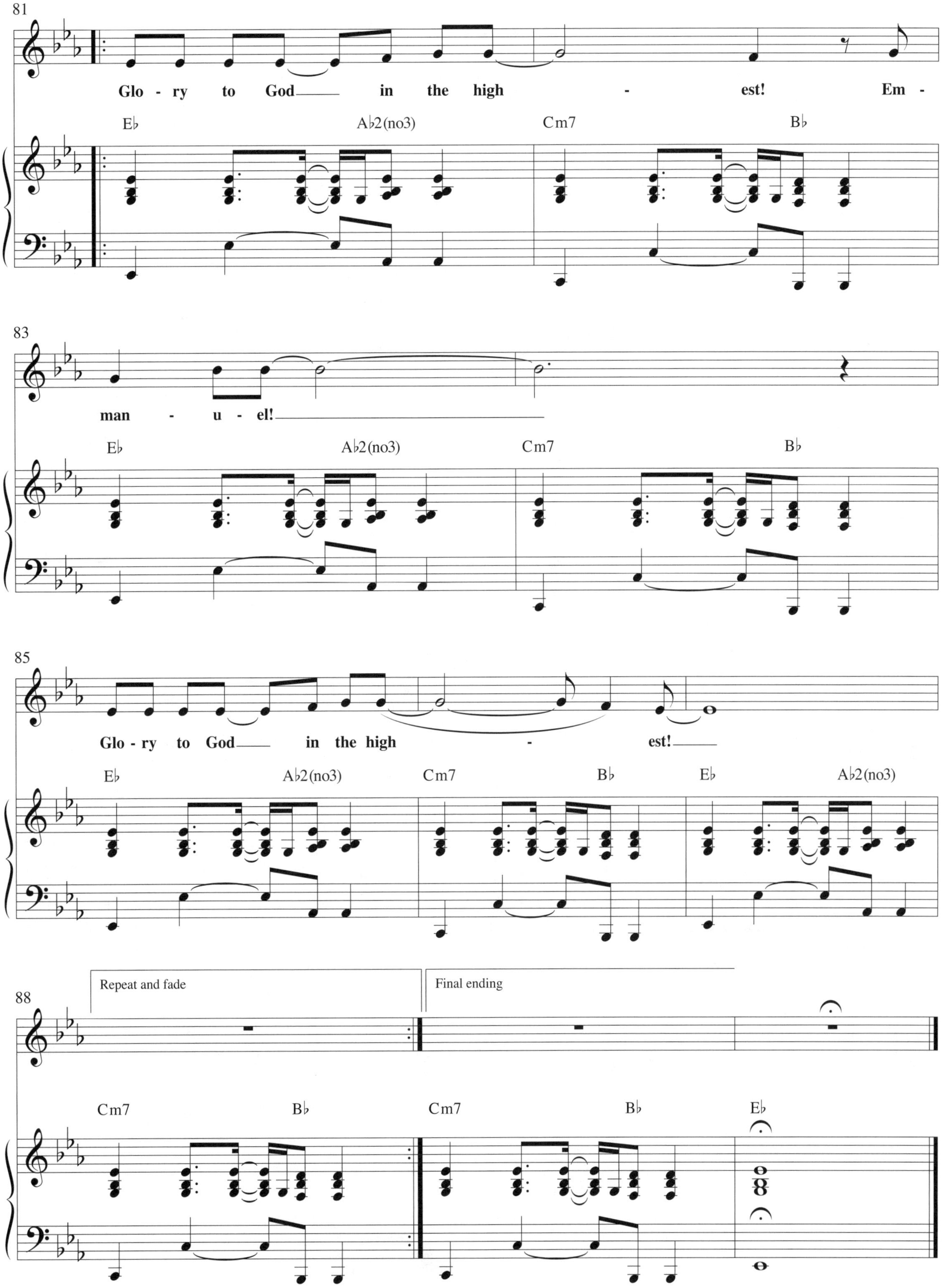
81
Glo - ry to God in the high - est! Em -
E♭ A♭2(no3) Cm7 B♭
83
man - u - el!
E♭ A♭2(no3) Cm7 B♭
85
Glo - ry to God in the high - est!
E♭ A♭2(no3) Cm7 B♭ E♭ A♭2(no3)
88
Repeat and fade
Final ending
Cm7 B♭ Cm7 B♭ E♭

Everything About You

Words and Music by
DARLENE ZSCHECH
and DAVID HOLMES

Slow four ♩ = 64

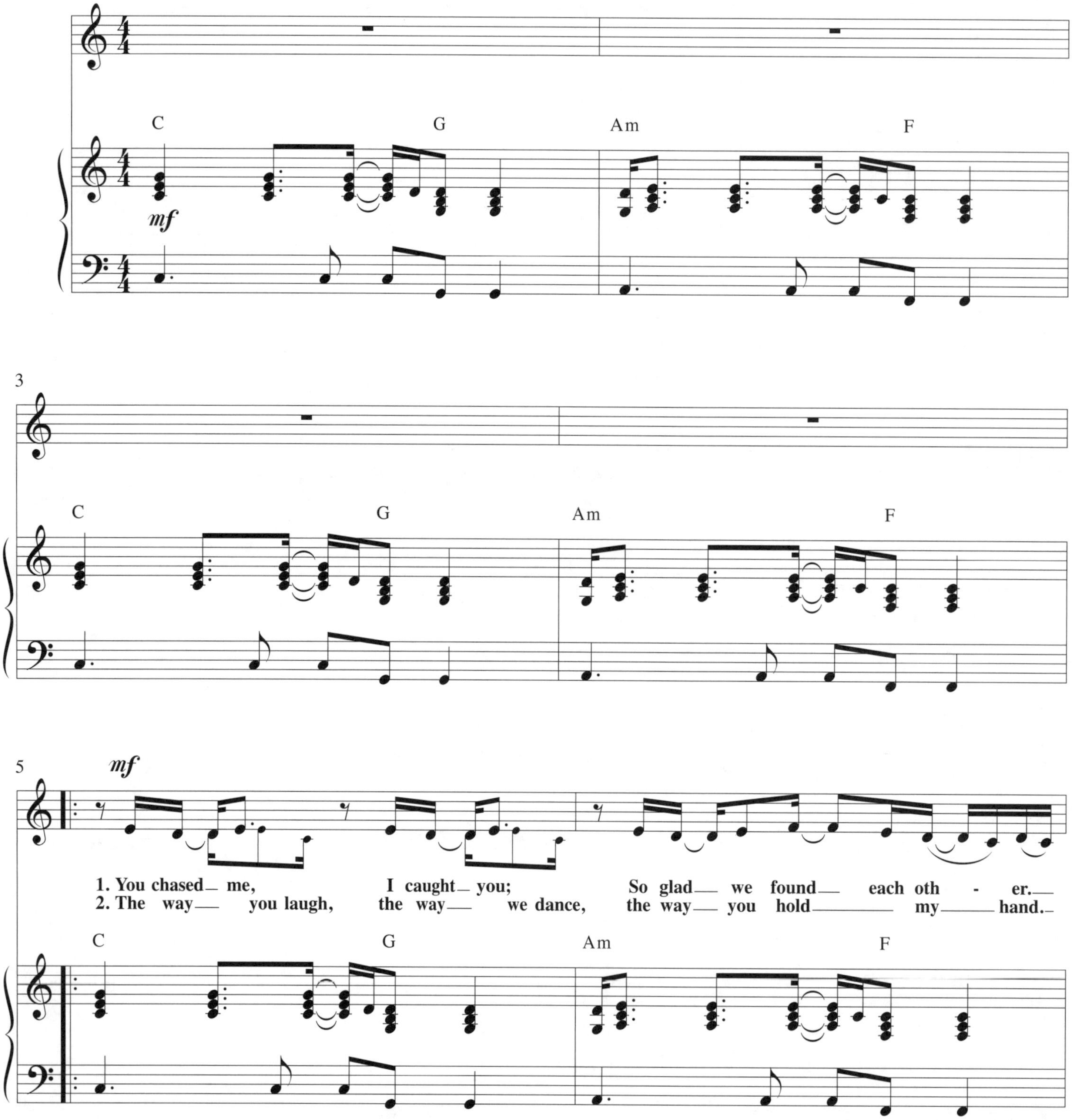

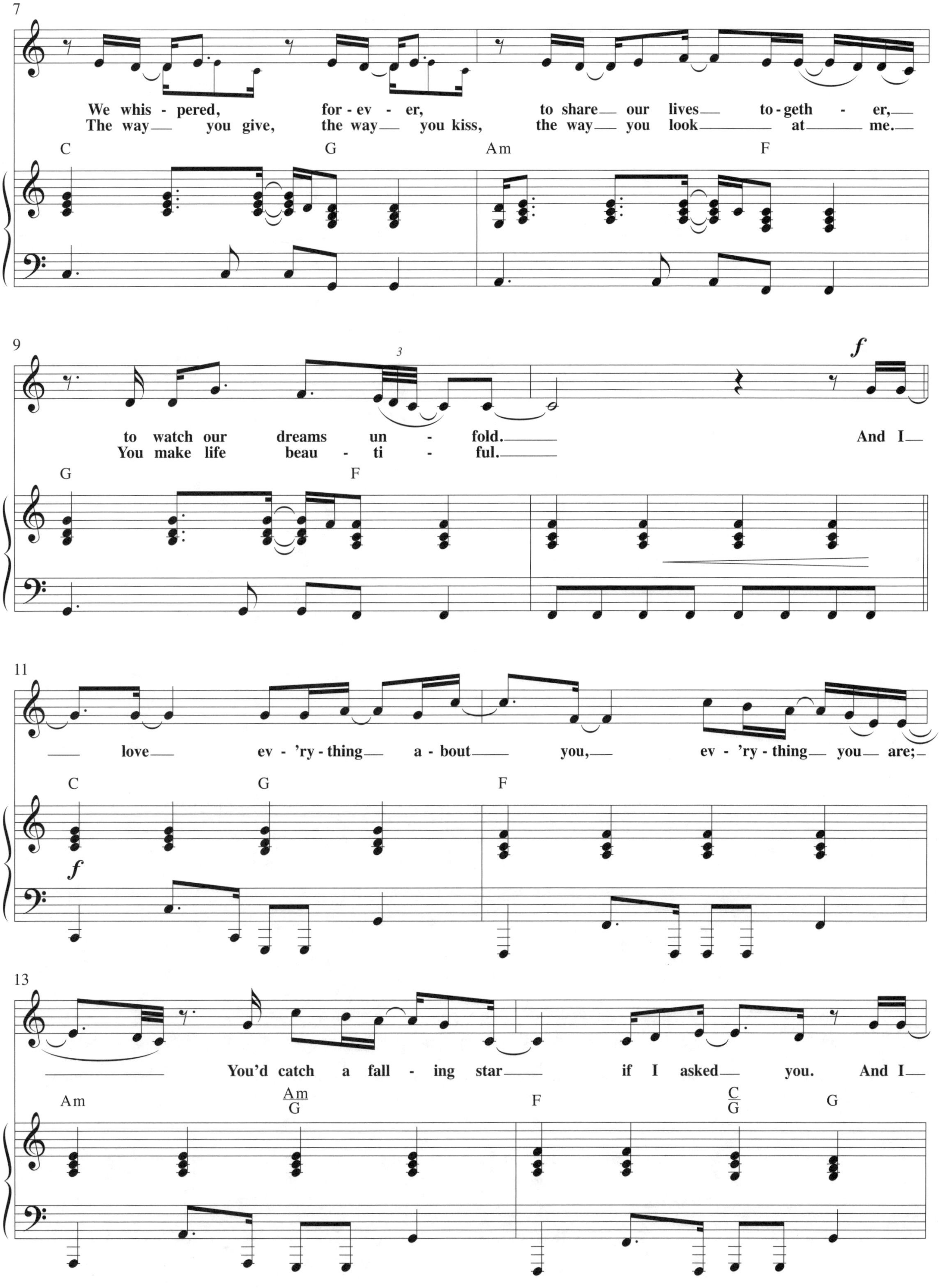
7
We whis - pered, for - ev - er, to share our lives to - geth - er,
The way you give, the way you kiss, the way you look at me.
C G Am F
9
to watch our dreams un - fold.
You make life beau - ti - ful.
And I
G F
f
3
11
love ev - 'ry - thing a - bout you, ev - 'ry - thing you are;
C G F
f
13
You'd catch a fall - ing star if I asked you. And I
Am Am/G F C/G G

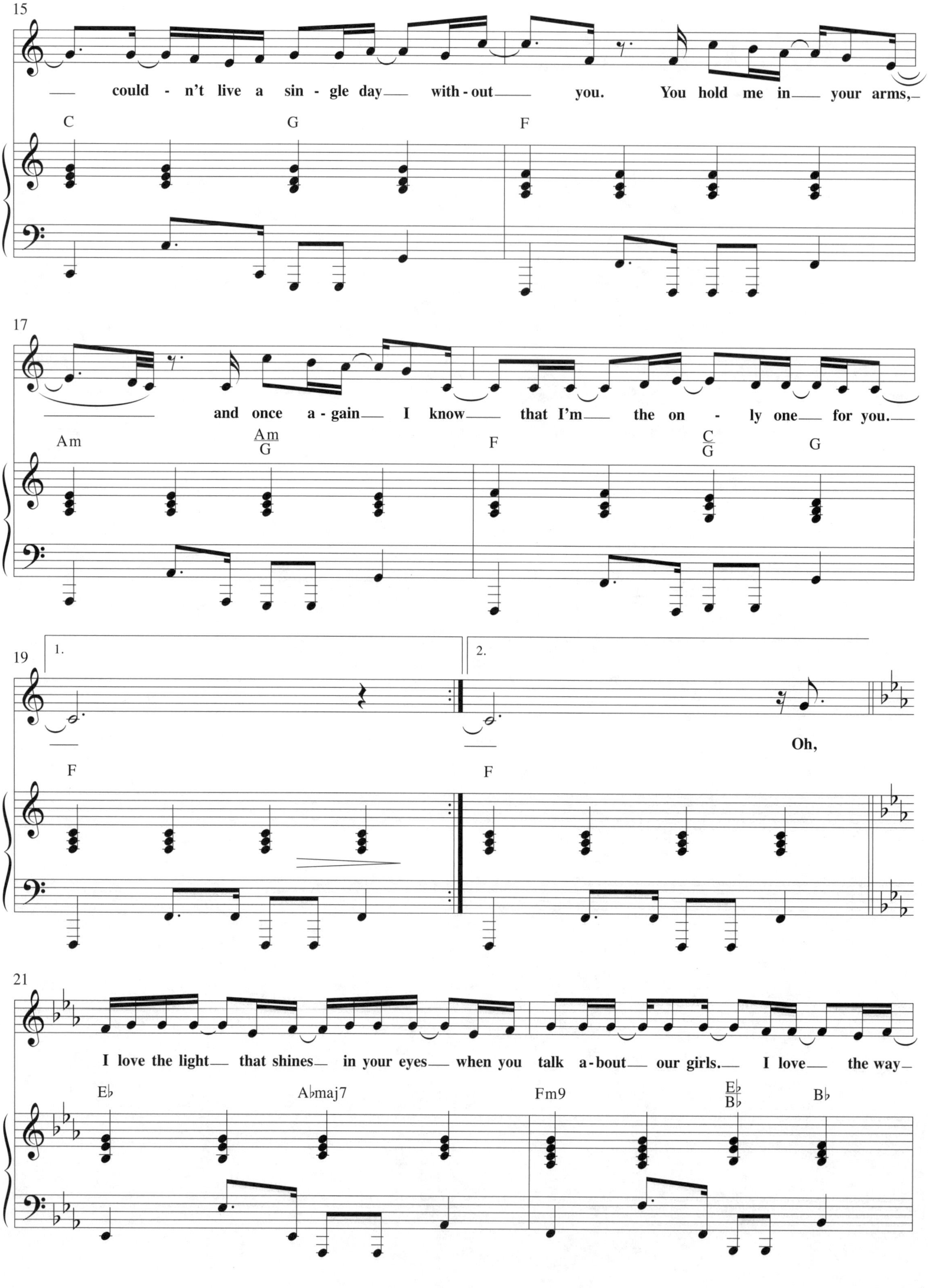
15
could - n't live a sin - gle day with - out you. You hold me in your arms,
C
G
F
17
and once a - gain I know that I'm the on - ly one for you.
Am
Am/G
F
C/G
G
19
1.
2.
Oh,
F
F
21
I love the light that shines in your eyes when you talk a - bout our girls. I love the way
E♭
A♭maj7
Fm9
E♭/B♭
B♭

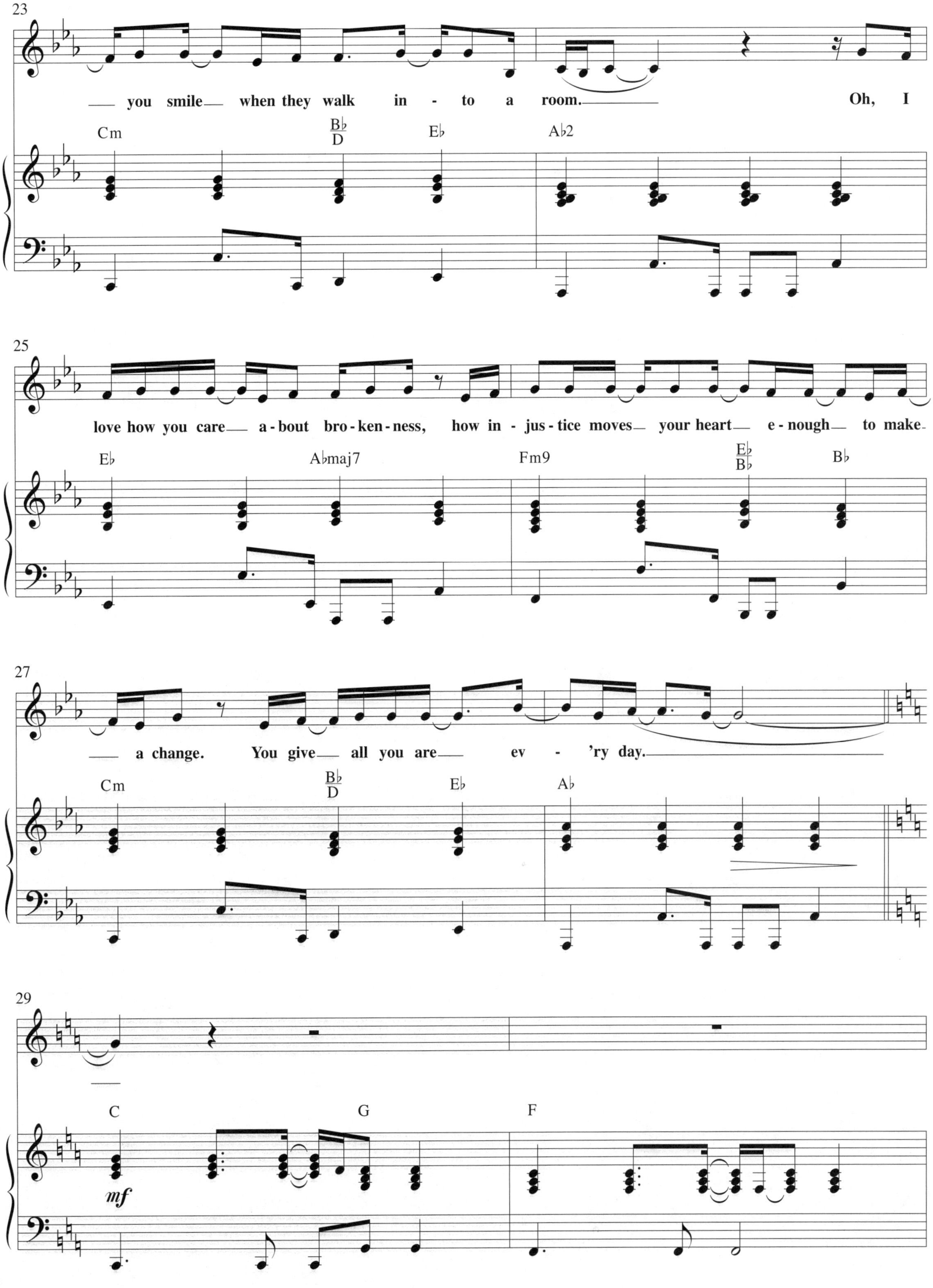
23
you smile when they walk in - to a room. Oh, I
Cm
B♭/D
E♭
A♭2
25
love how you care a - bout bro - ken - ness, how in - jus - tice moves your heart e - nough to make
E♭
A♭maj7
Fm9
E♭/B♭
B♭
27
a change. You give all you are ev - 'ry day.
Cm
B♭/D
E♭
A♭
29
C
G
F
mf

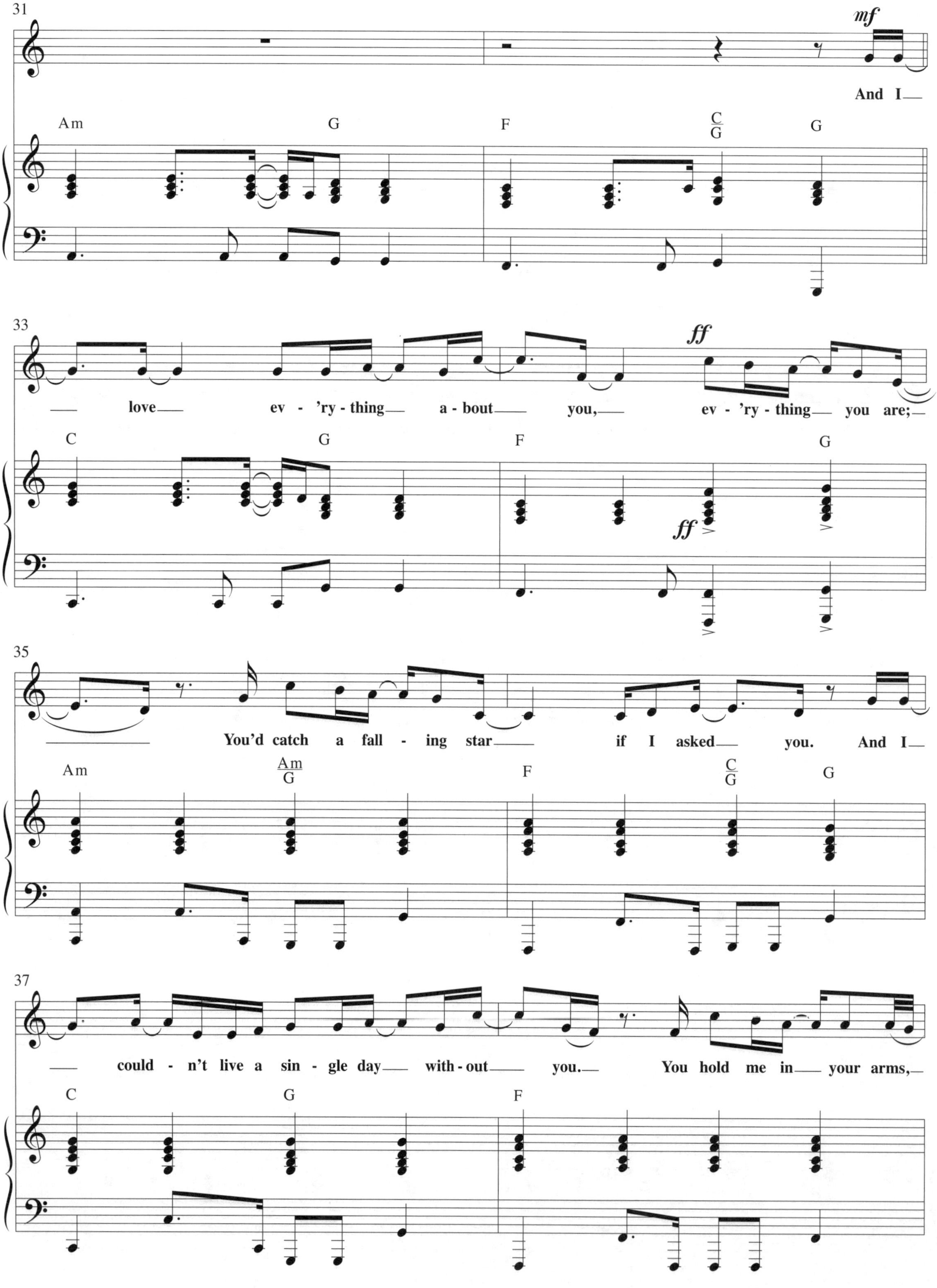
31
mf
And I
Am G F C/G G
33
ff
love ev - 'ry - thing a - bout you, ev - 'ry - thing you are;
C G F G
ff
35
You'd catch a fall - ing star if I asked you. And I
Am Am/G F C/G G
37
could - n't live a sin - gle day with - out you. You hold me in your arms,
C G F

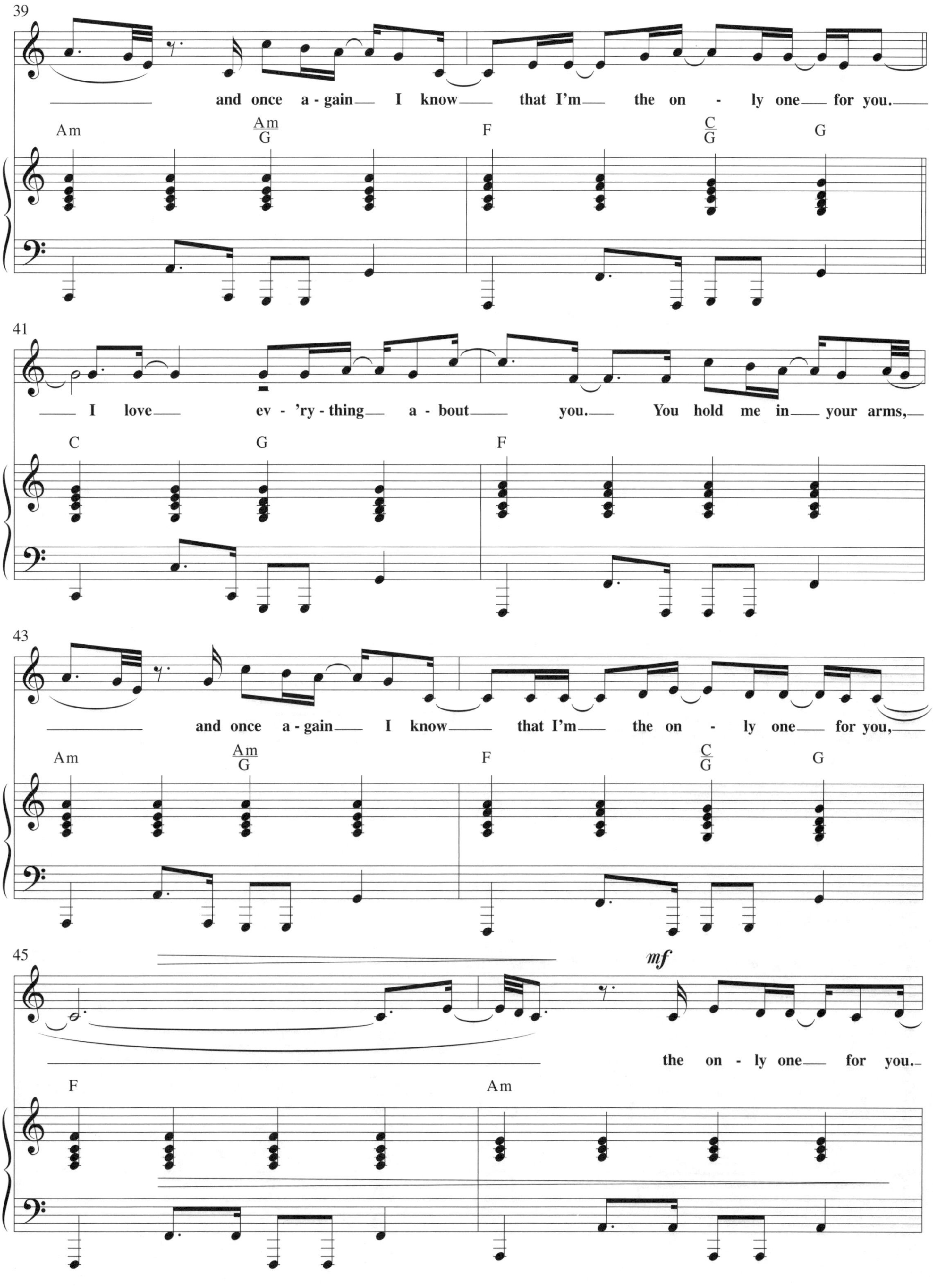
39
and once a-gain I know that I'm the on - ly one for you.
Am
Am/G
F
C/G
G
41
I love ev-'ry-thing a-bout you. You hold me in your arms,
C
G
F
43
and once a-gain I know that I'm the on - ly one for you,
Am
Am/G
F
C/G
G
45
mf
the on-ly one for you.
F
Am

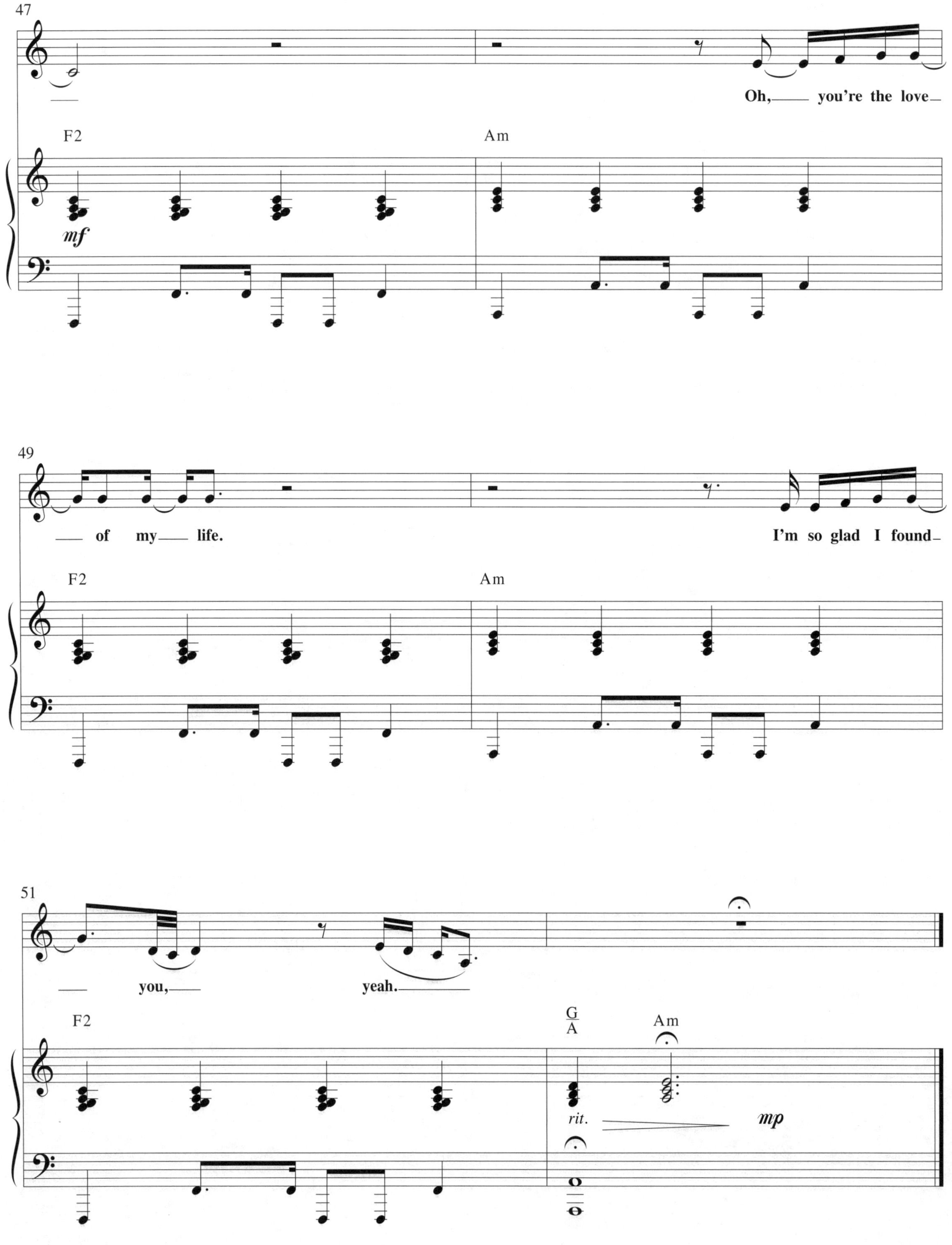
47
Oh, you're the love
F2
Am
mf
49
of my life.
I'm so glad I found
F2
Am
51
you, yeah.
F2
G
A
Am
rit.
mp

Promise

Words and Music by
DARLENE ZSCHECH
and DAVID HOLMES

Moderate rock beat ♩ = 80

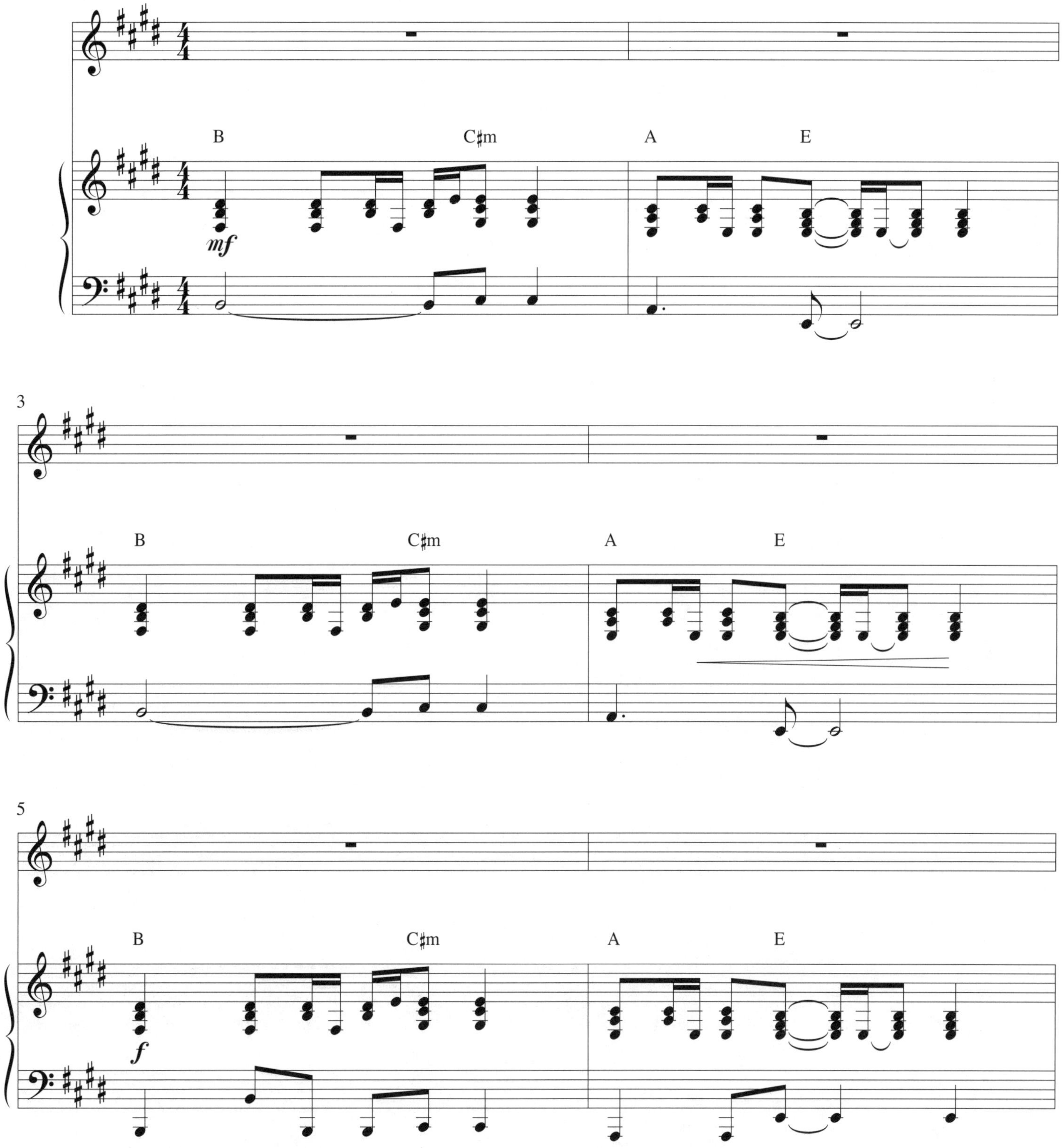

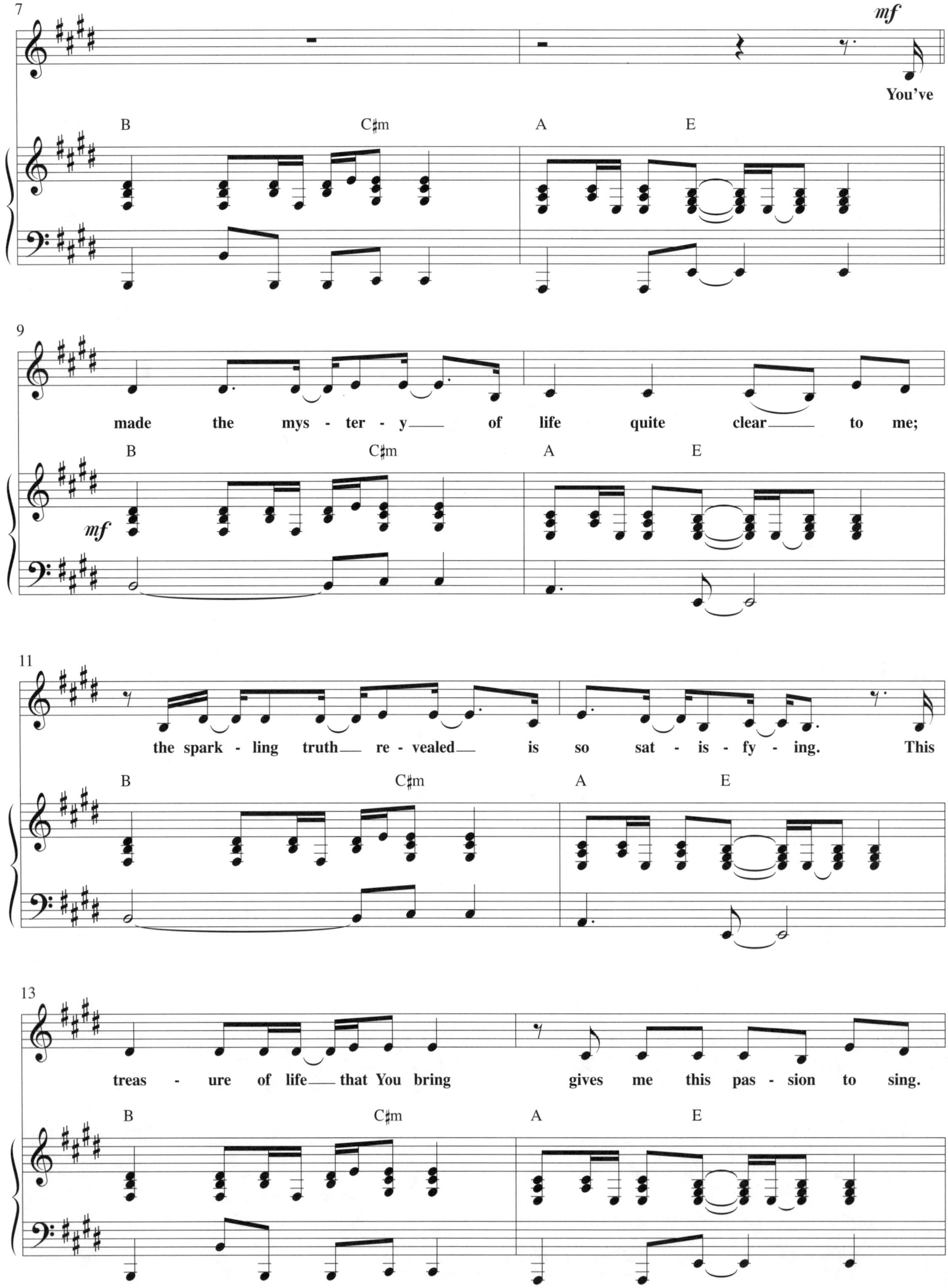
7
mf
You've
B C♯m A E
9
made the mys - ter - y of life quite clear to me;
B C♯m A E
mf
11
the spark - ling truth re - vealed is so sat - is - fy - ing. This
B C♯m A E
13
treas - ure of life that You bring gives me this pas - sion to sing.
B C♯m A E

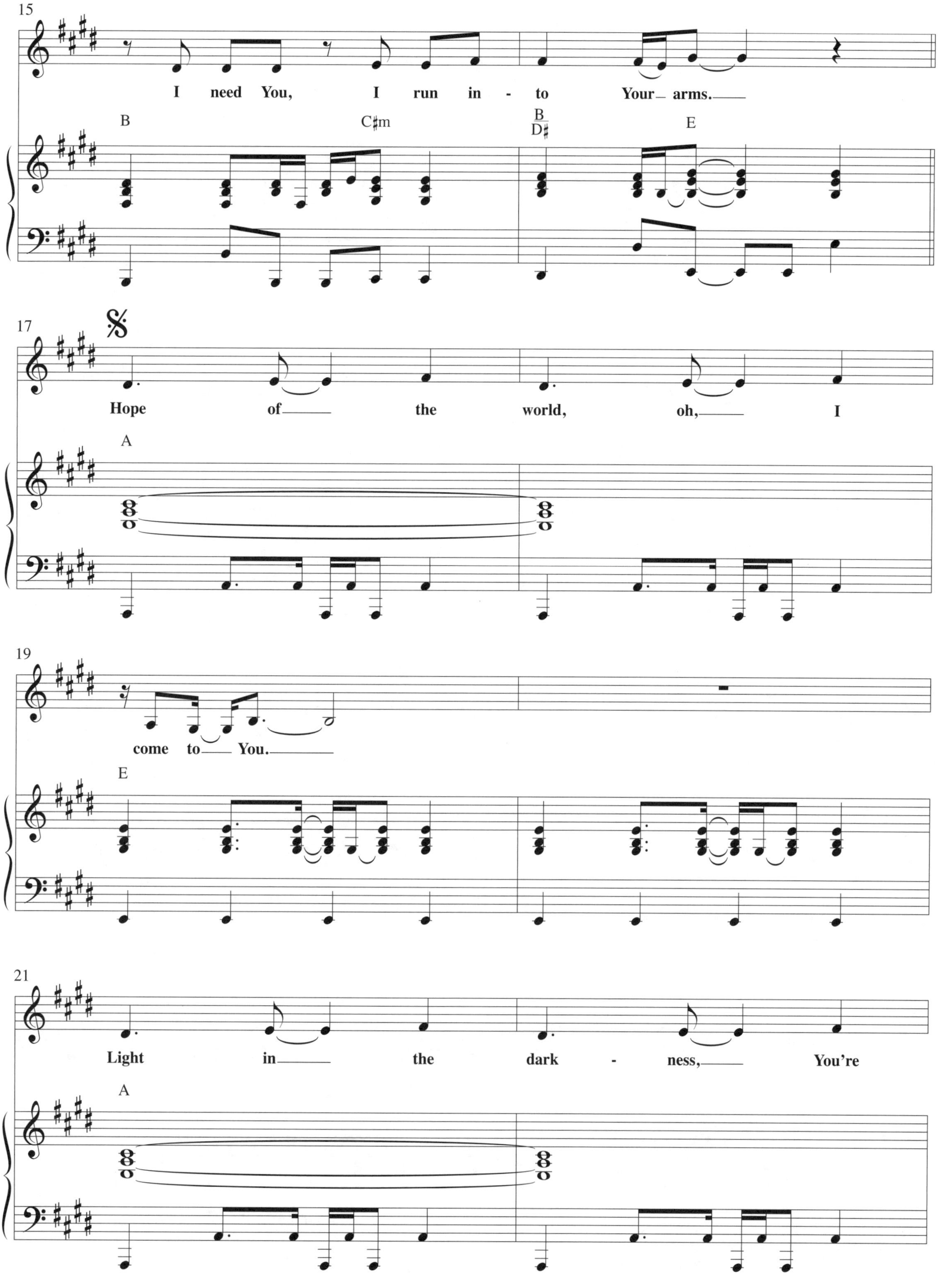
15
I need You, I run in - to Your arms.
B C♯m B/D♯ E
17
Hope of the world, oh, I
A
19
come to You.
E
21
Light in the dark - ness, You're
A

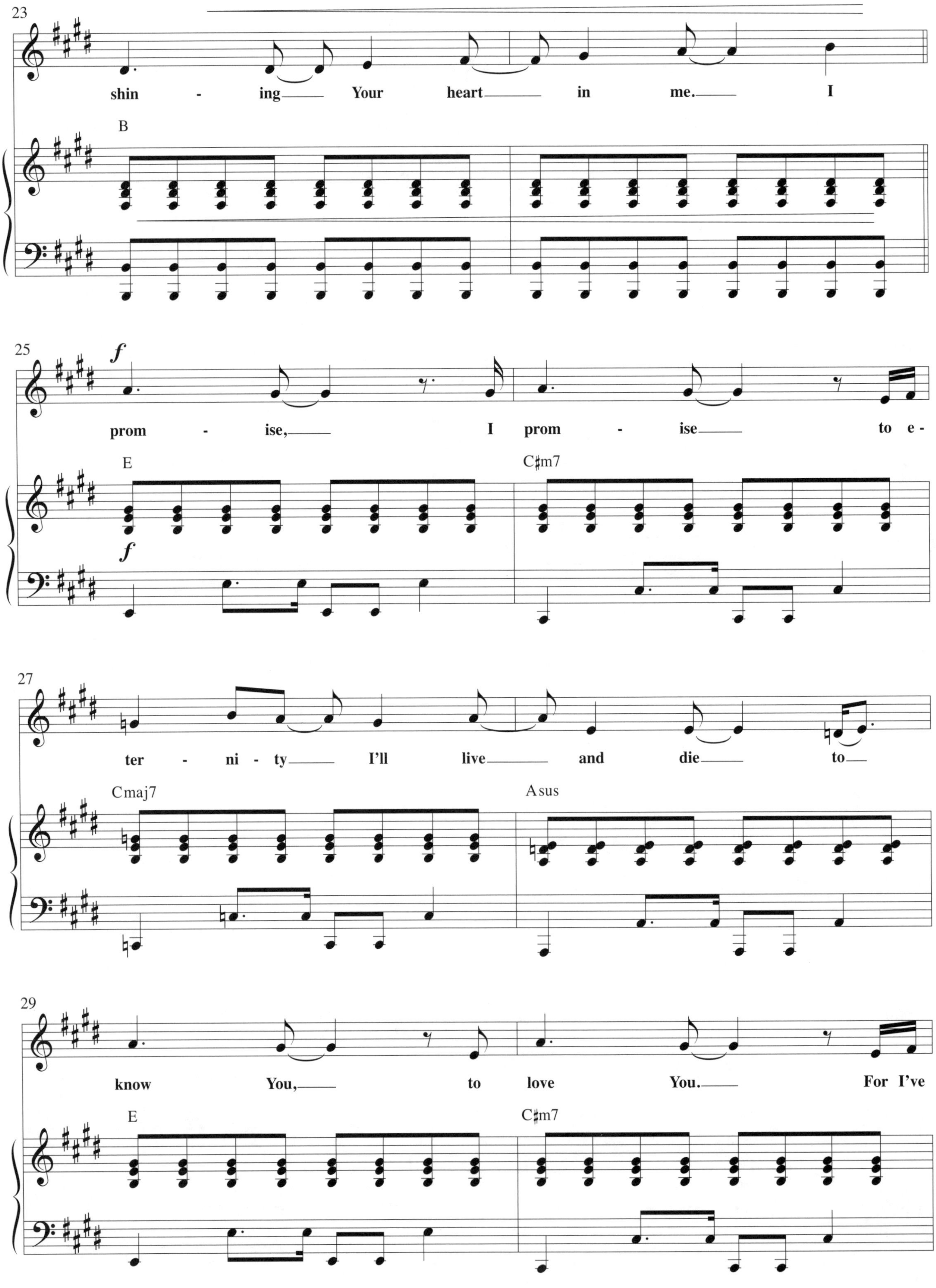
23
shin - ing Your heart in me. I
B
25
f
prom - ise, I prom - ise to e -
E
C♯m7
f
27
ter - ni - ty I'll live and die to
Cmaj7
Asus
29
know You, to love You. For I've
E
C♯m7

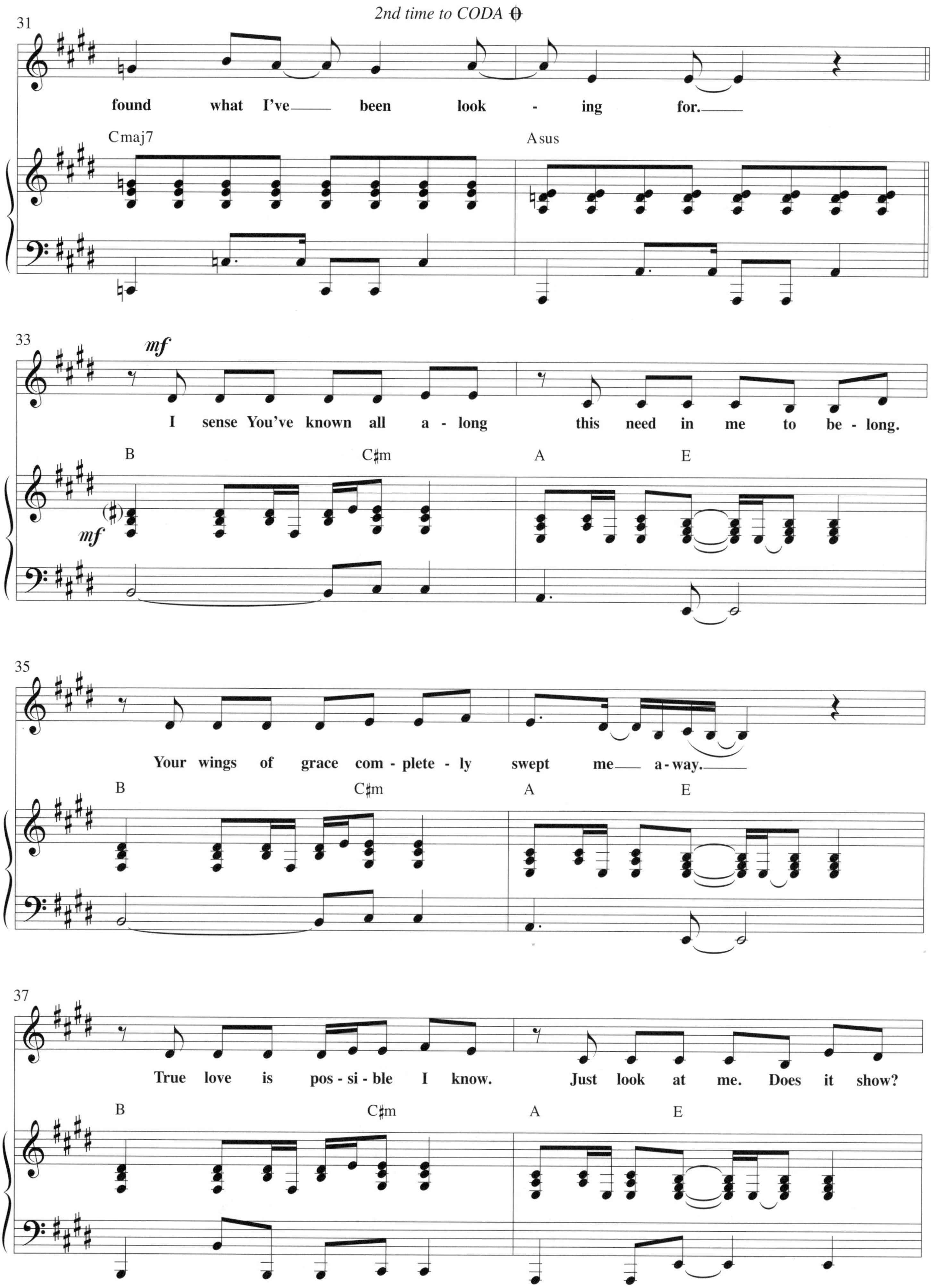
2nd time to CODA
31
found what I've been look - ing for.
Cmaj7
Asus
33
mf
I sense You've known all a - long this need in me to be - long.
B
C♯m
A
E
mf
35
Your wings of grace com - plete - ly swept me a - way.
B
C♯m
A
E
37
True love is pos - si - ble I know. Just look at me. Does it show?
B
C♯m
A
E

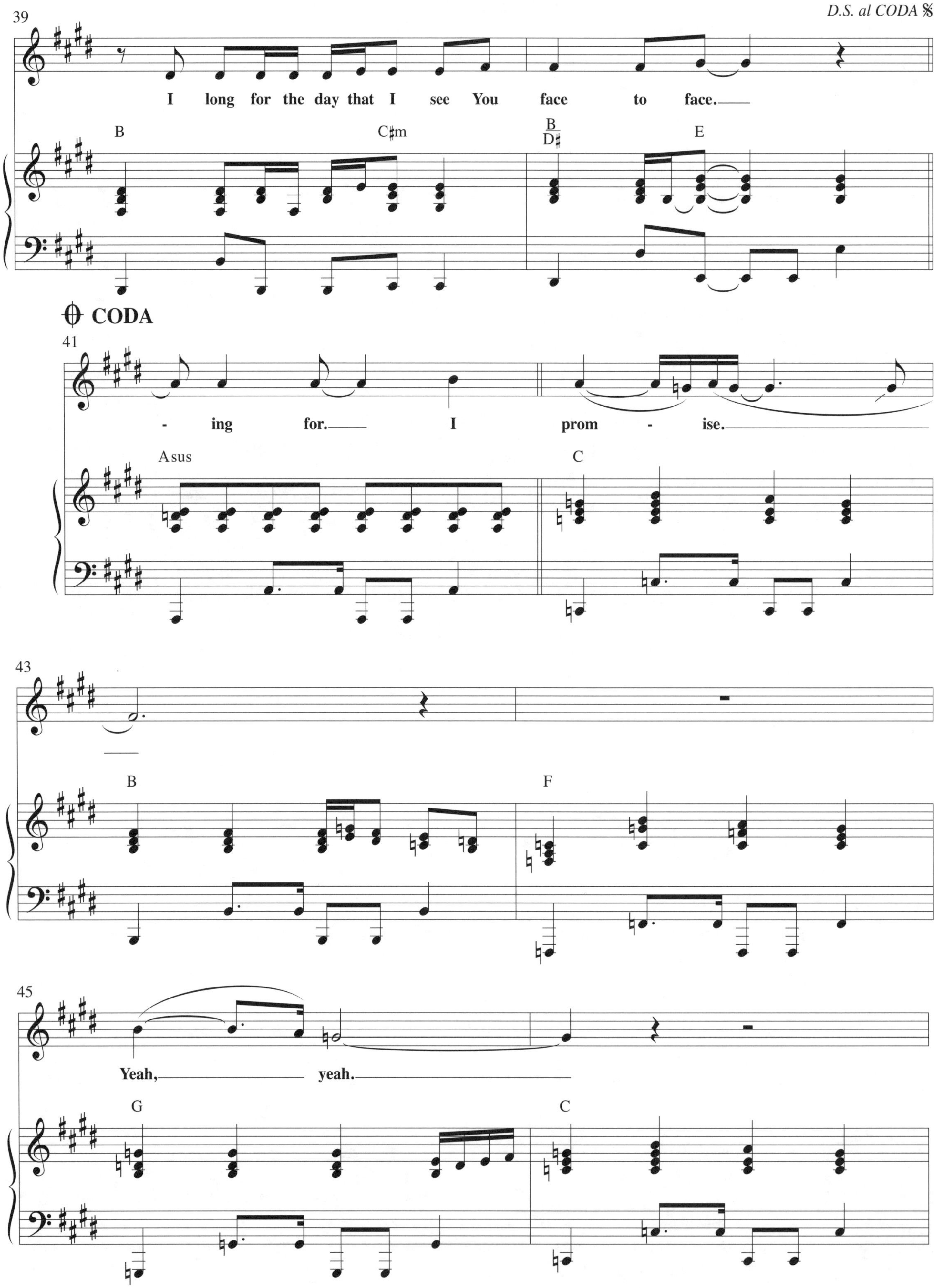
D.S. al CODA 𝄋
39
I long for the day that I see You face to face.
B
C♯m
B/D♯
E
CODA
41
-ing for. I prom - ise.
Asus
C
43
B
F
45
Yeah, yeah.
G
C

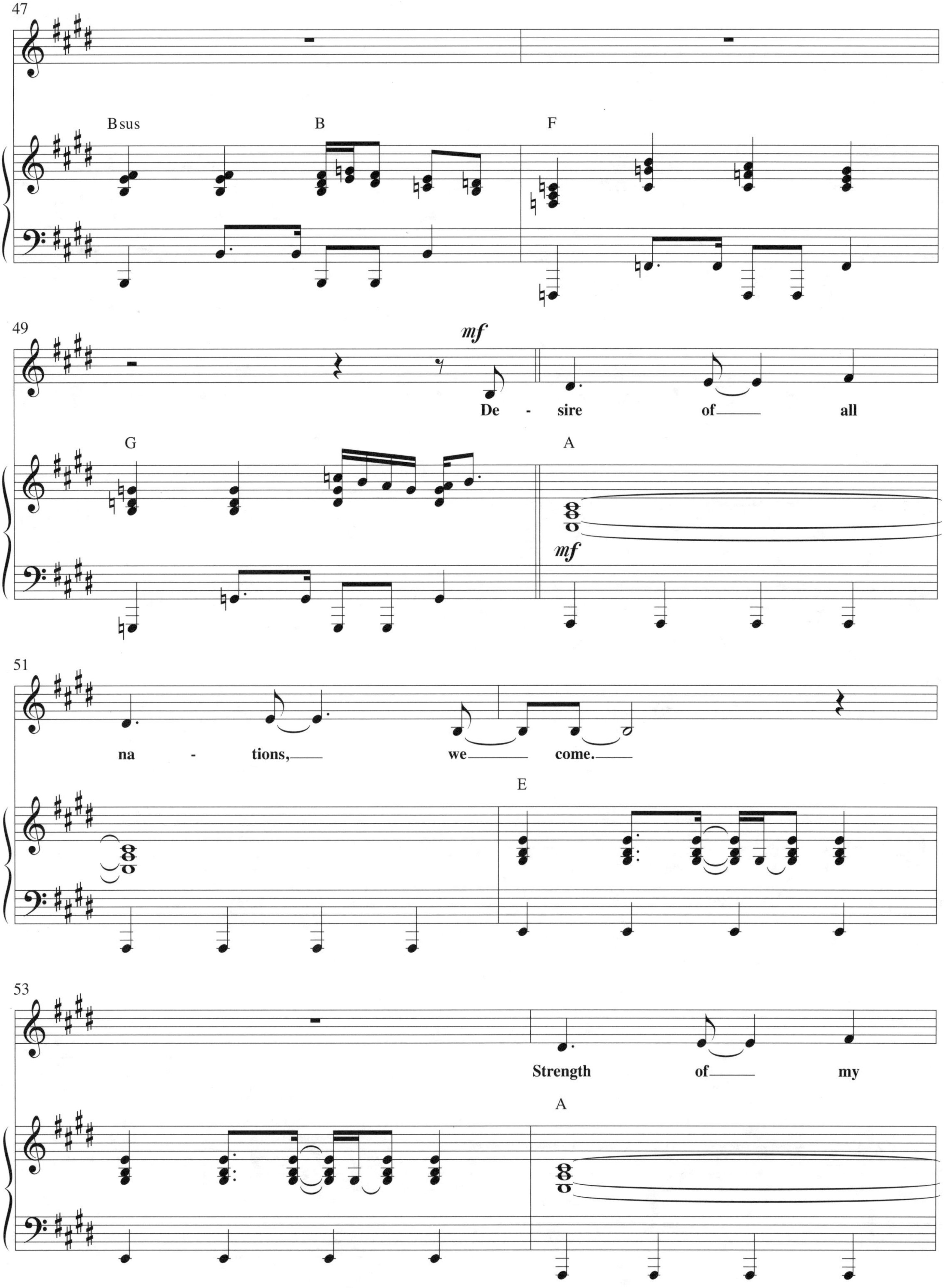
47
Bsus
B
F
49
mf
De - sire of all
G
A
mf
51
na - tions, we come.
E
53
Strength of my
A

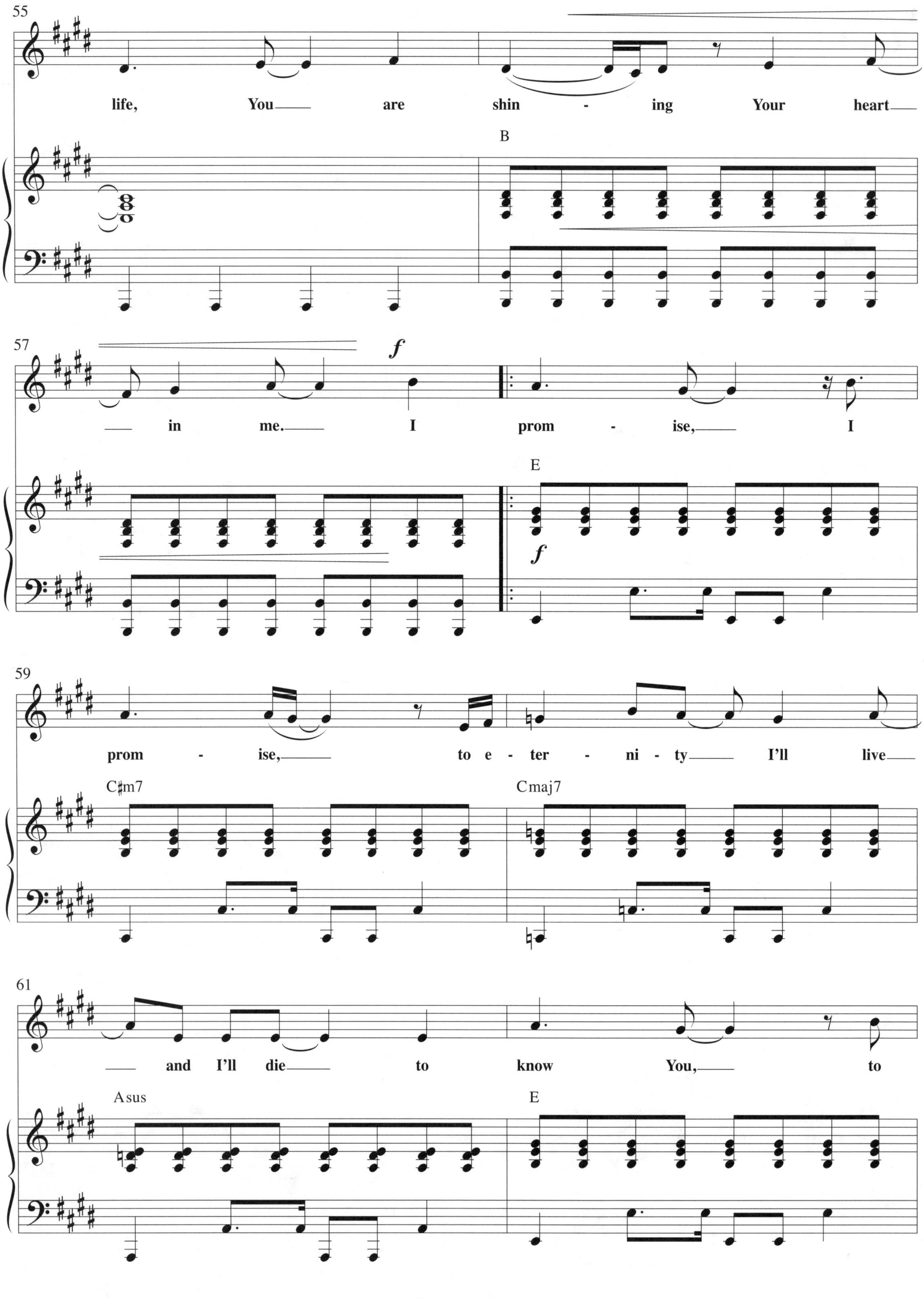
55
life, You are shin - ing Your heart
B
57
f
in me. I prom - ise, I
E
f
59
prom - ise, to e - ter - ni - ty I'll live
C♯m7
Cmaj7
61
and I'll die to know You, to
Asus
E

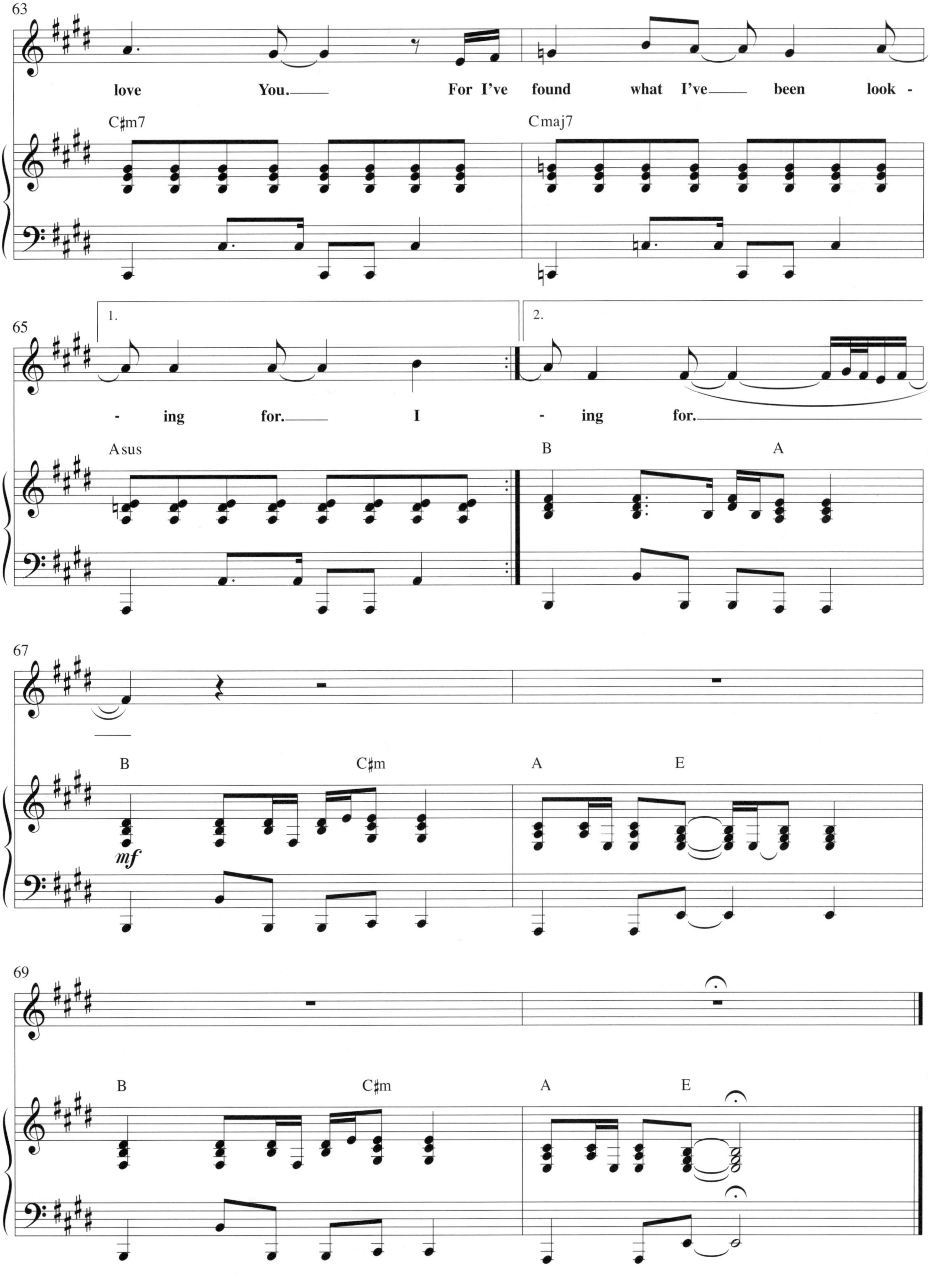
63
love You. For I've found what I've been look -
C♯m7
Cmaj7
65
1.
2.
- ing for. I - ing for.
Asus
B
A
67
B
C♯m
A
E
mf
69
B
C♯m
A
E

Irresistible

Words and Music by
DARLENE ZSCHECH

Steady four ♩ = 76

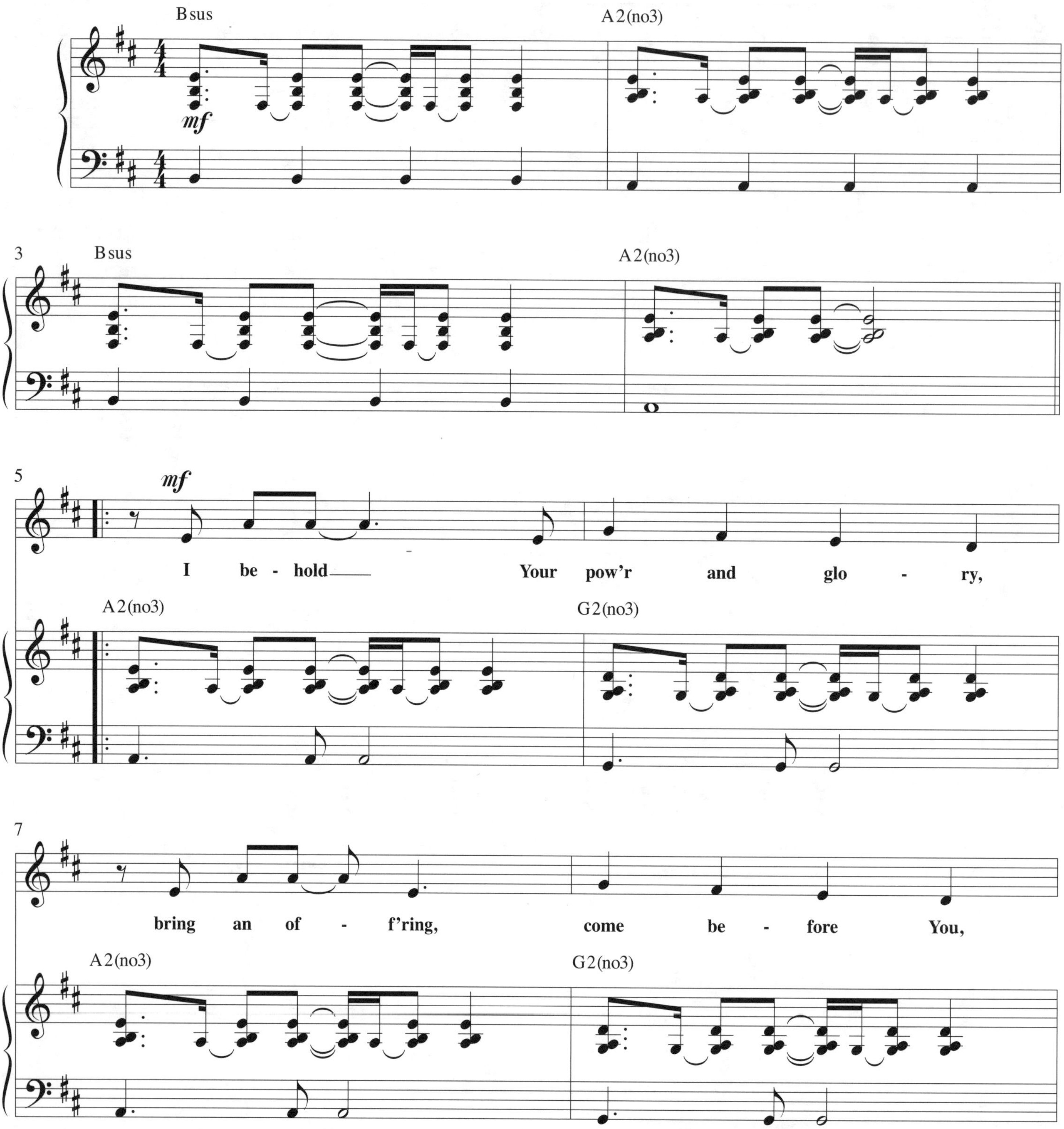

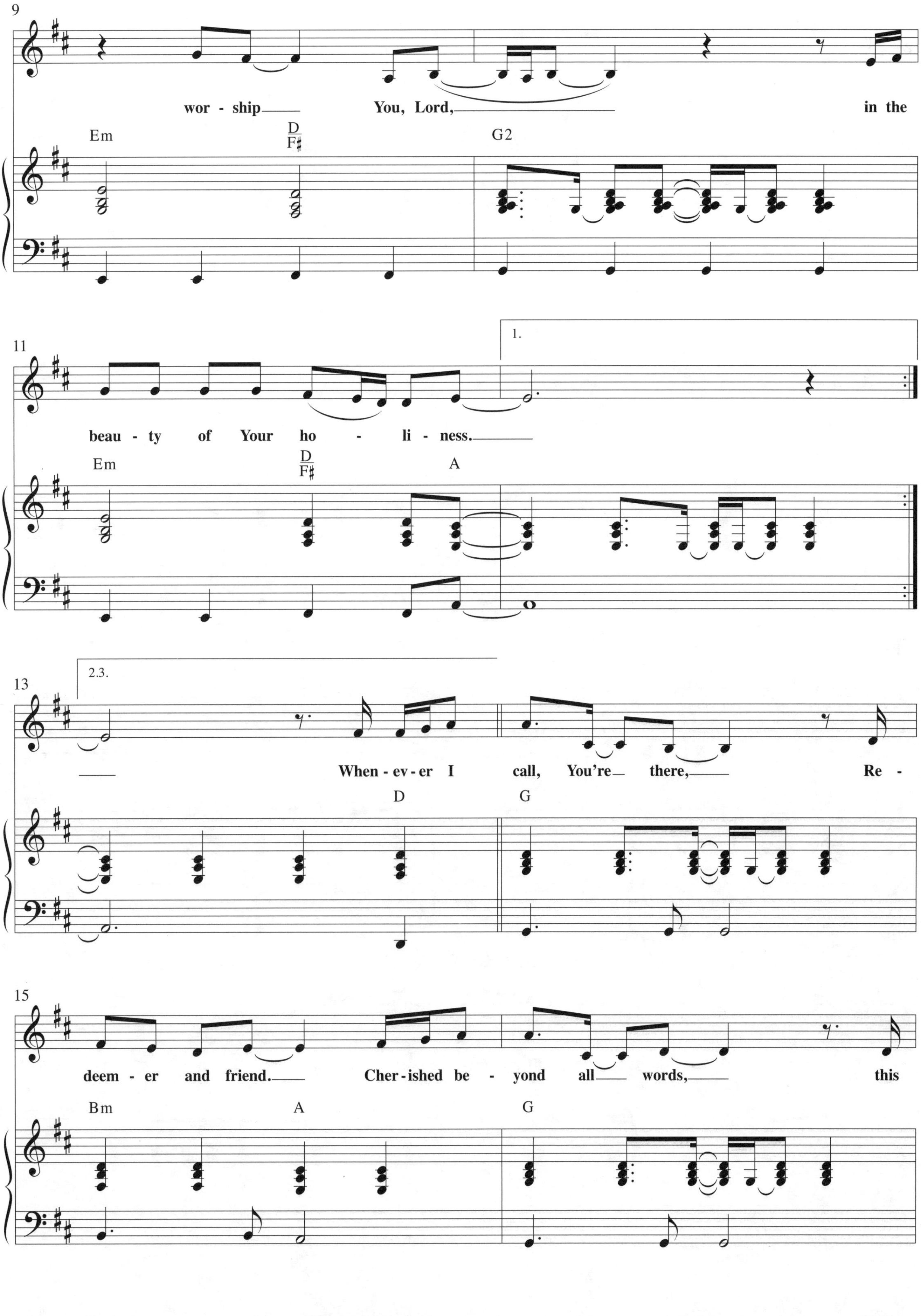
9
wor - ship You, Lord, in the
Em D/F♯ G2
11
1.
beau - ty of Your ho - li - ness.
Em D/F♯ A
13
2.3.
When - ev - er I call, You're there, Re -
D G
15
deem - er and friend. Cher - ished be - yond all words, this
Bm A G

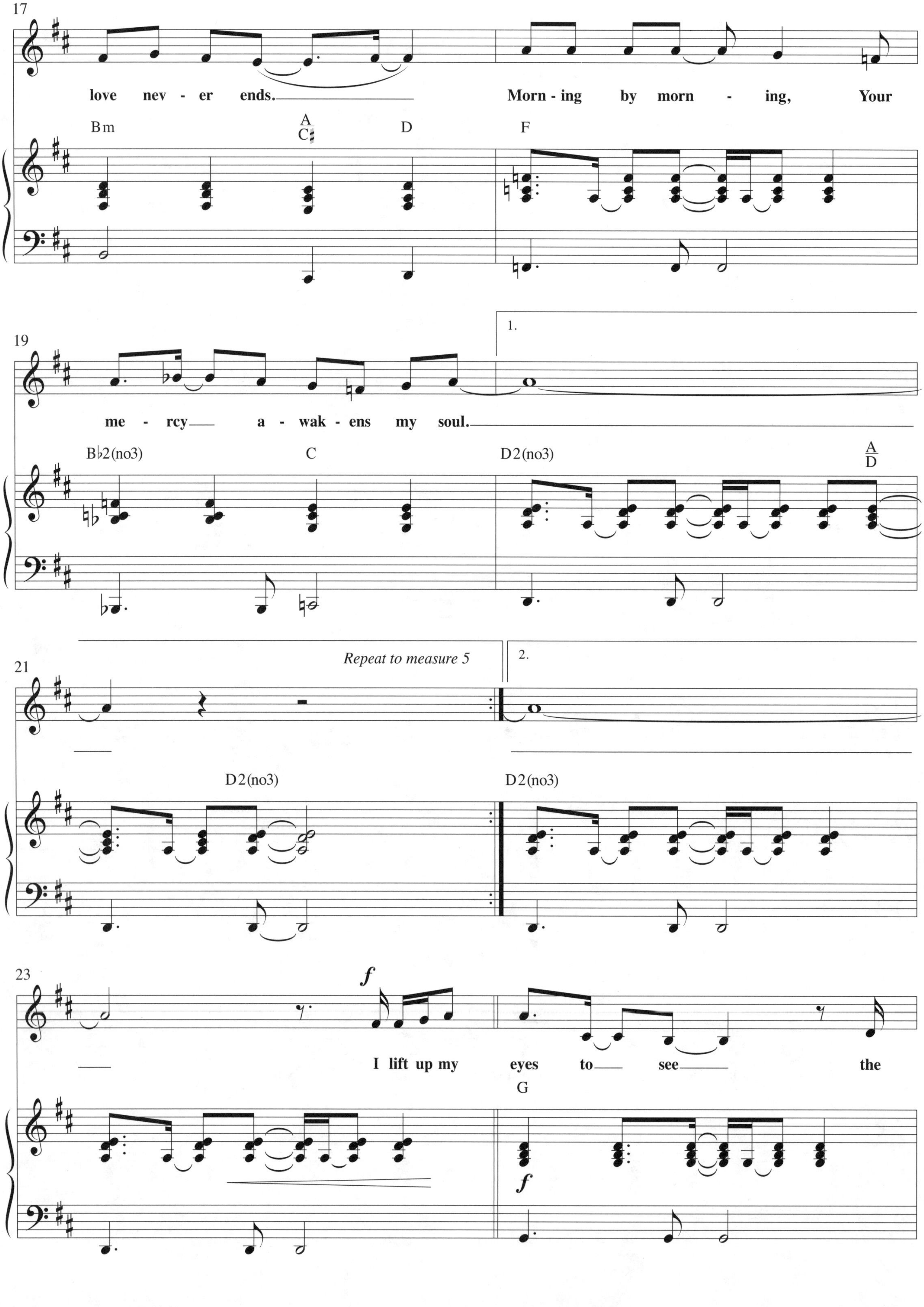
17
love nev - er ends.
Morn - ing by morn - ing, Your
Bm
A
C♯
D
F
19
1.
me - rcy a - wak - ens my soul.
B♭2(no3)
C
D2(no3)
A
D
21
Repeat to measure 5
2.
D2(no3)
D2(no3)
23
f
I lift up my eyes to see the
G
f

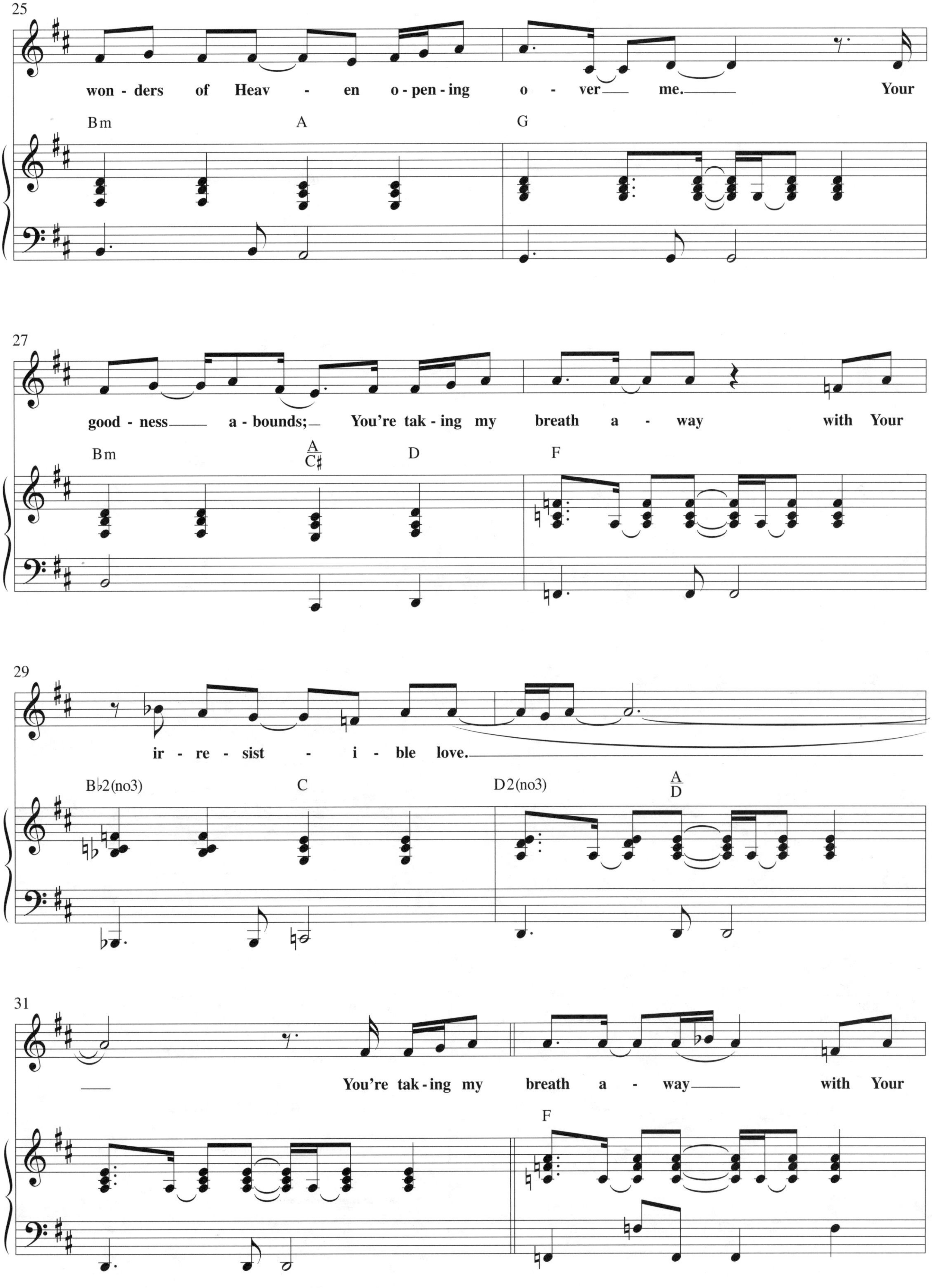
25
wonders of Heav - en o - pen - ing o - ver me. Your
Bm A G
27
good - ness a - bounds; You're tak - ing my breath a - way with Your
Bm A/C♯ D F
29
ir - re - sist - i - ble love.
B♭2(no3) C D2(no3) A/D
31
You're tak - ing my breath a - way with Your
F

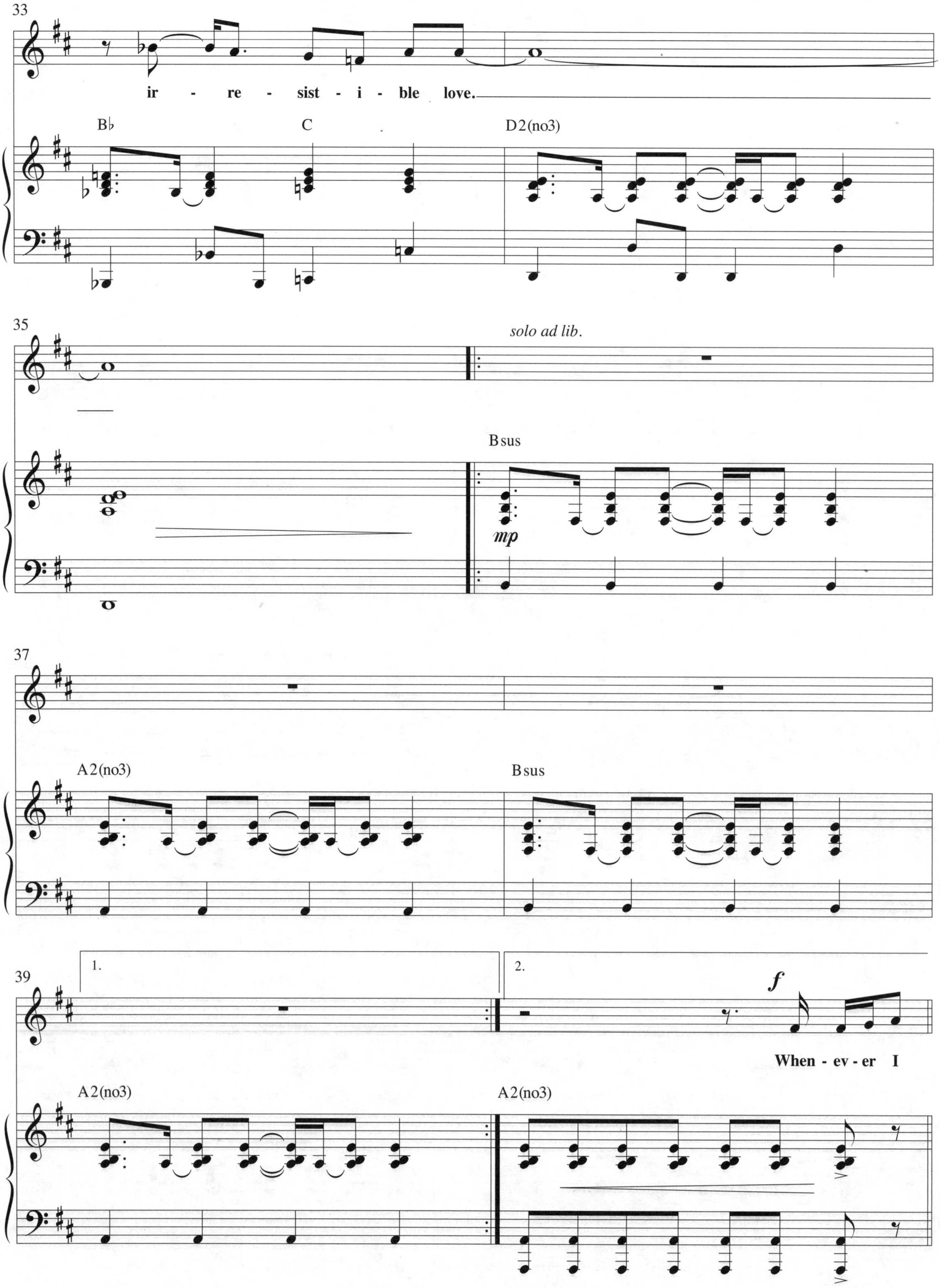
33
ir - re - sist - i - ble love.
B♭
C
D2(no3)
35
solo ad lib.
Bsus
mp
37
A2(no3)
Bsus
39
1.
2.
f
When - ev - er I
A2(no3)
A2(no3)

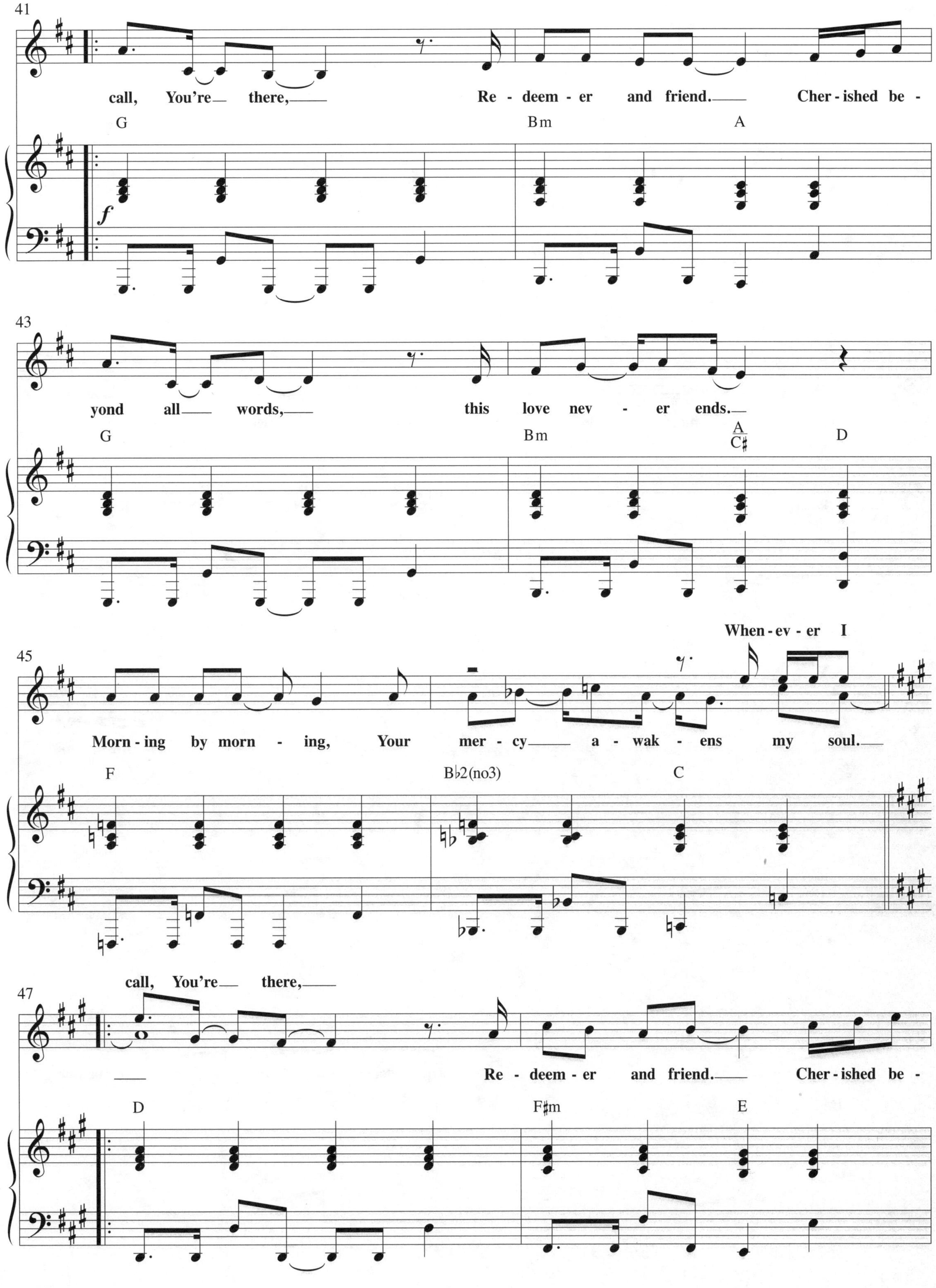
41
call, You're there, Re - deem - er and friend. Cher - ished be -
G
Bm
A
f
43
yond all words, this love nev - er ends.
G
Bm
A
C♯
D
When - ev - er I
45
Morn - ing by morn - ing, Your mer - cy a - wak - ens my soul.
F
B♭2(no3)
C
call, You're there,
47
Re - deem - er and friend. Cher - ished be -
D
F♯m
E

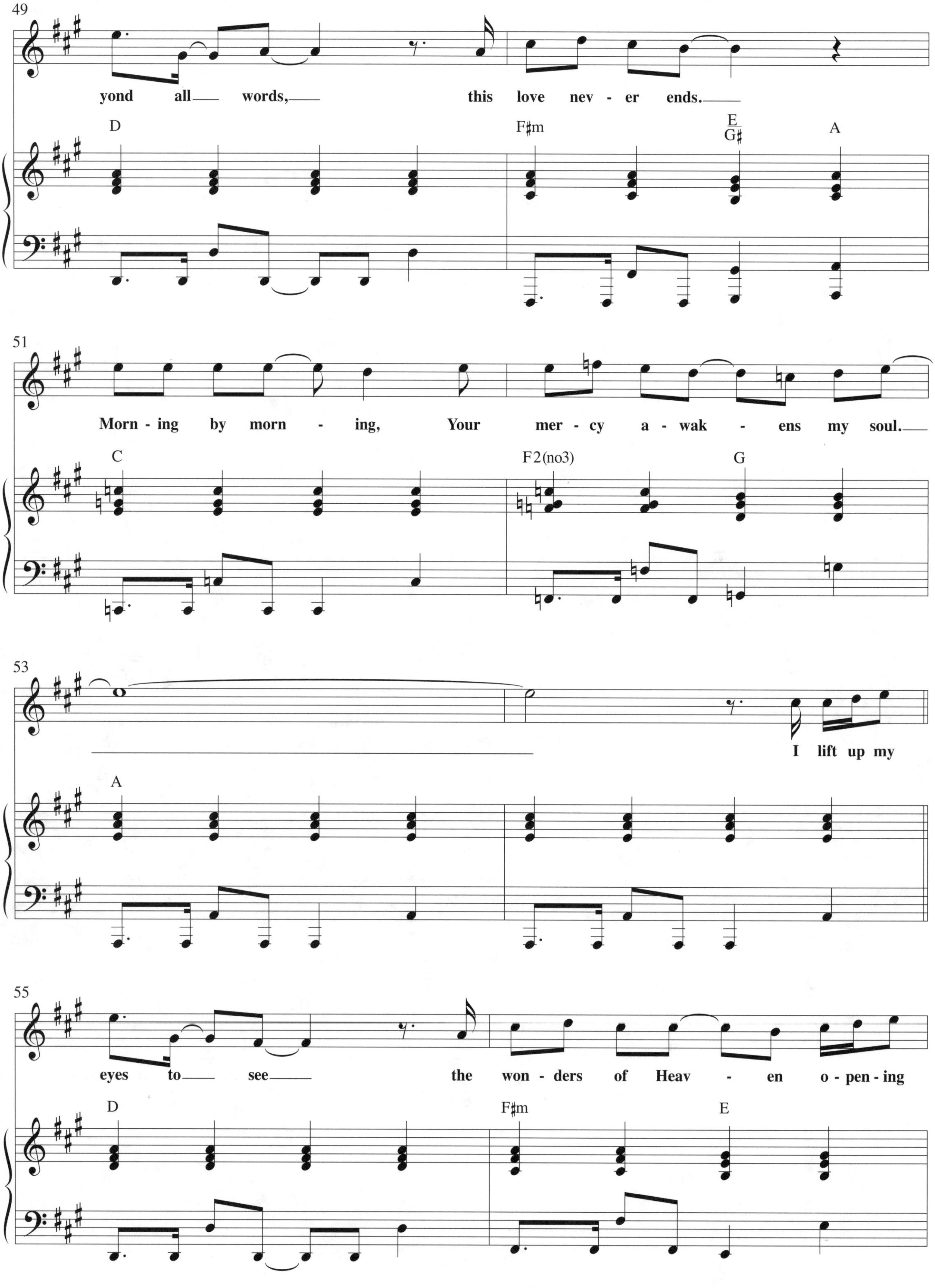
49
yond all words, this love nev - er ends.
D
F♯m
E/G♯
A
51
Morn - ing by morn - ing, Your mer - cy a - wak - ens my soul.
C
F2(no3)
G
53
I lift up my
A
55
eyes to see the won - ders of Heav - en o - pen - ing
D
F♯m
E

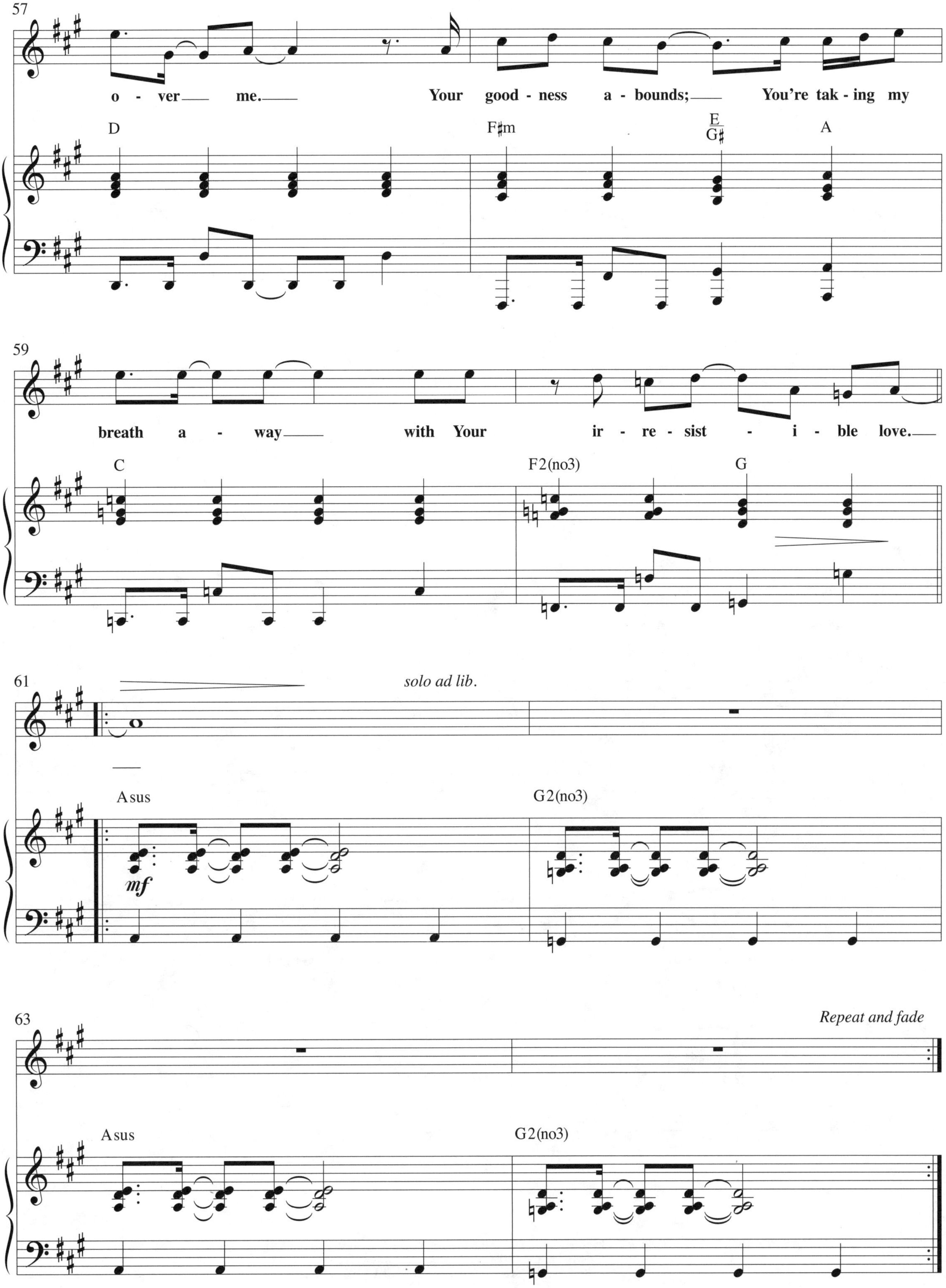
57
o - ver me. Your good - ness a - bounds; You're tak - ing my
D F♯m E/G♯ A
59
breath a - way with Your ir - re - sist - i - ble love.
C F2(no3) G
61
solo ad lib.
Asus G2(no3)
mf
63
Repeat and fade
Asus G2(no3)

Kiss Of Heaven

Words and Music by
DARLENE ZSCHECH
and DAVID MOYES

Joyfully ♩ = 100

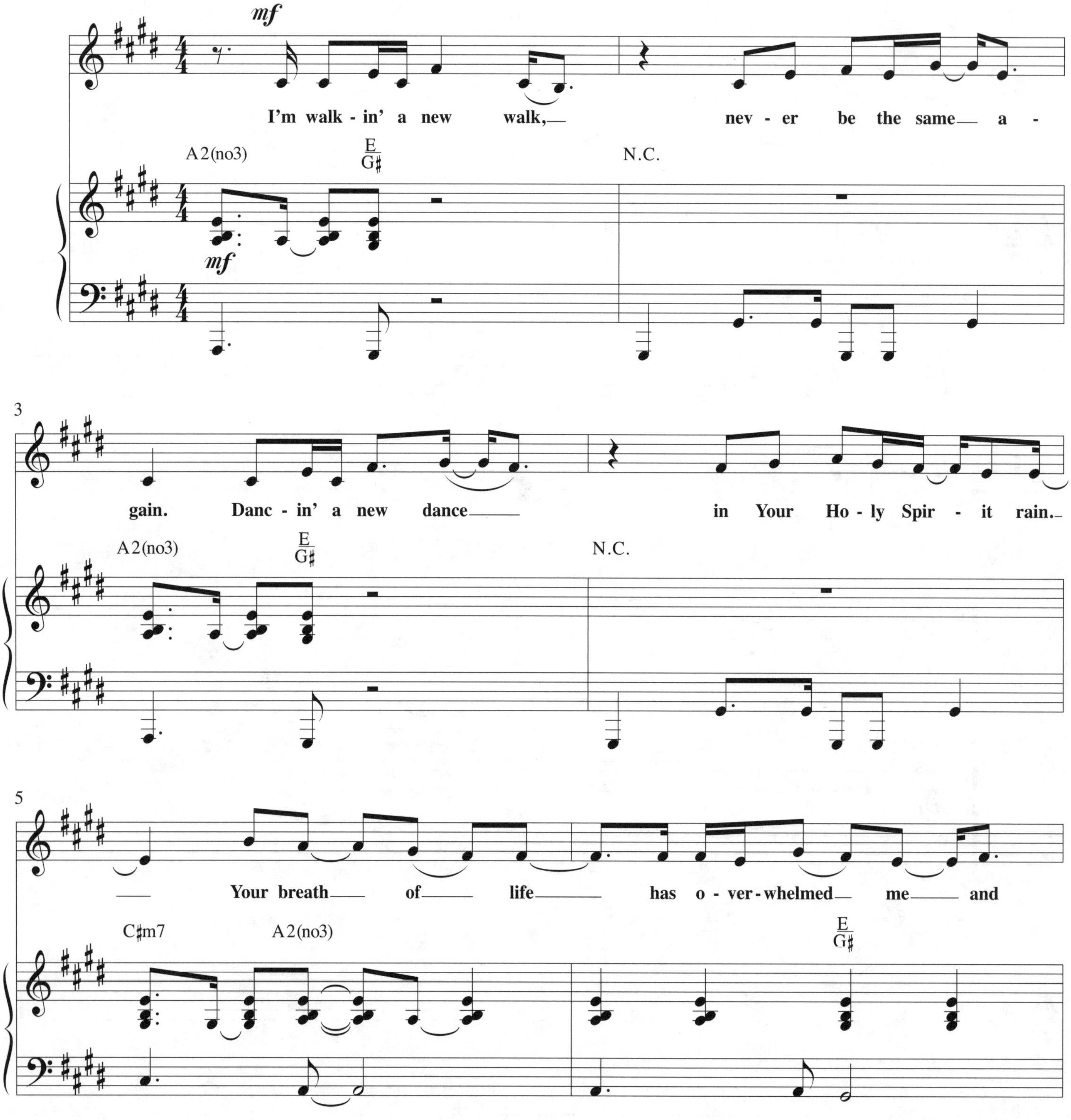

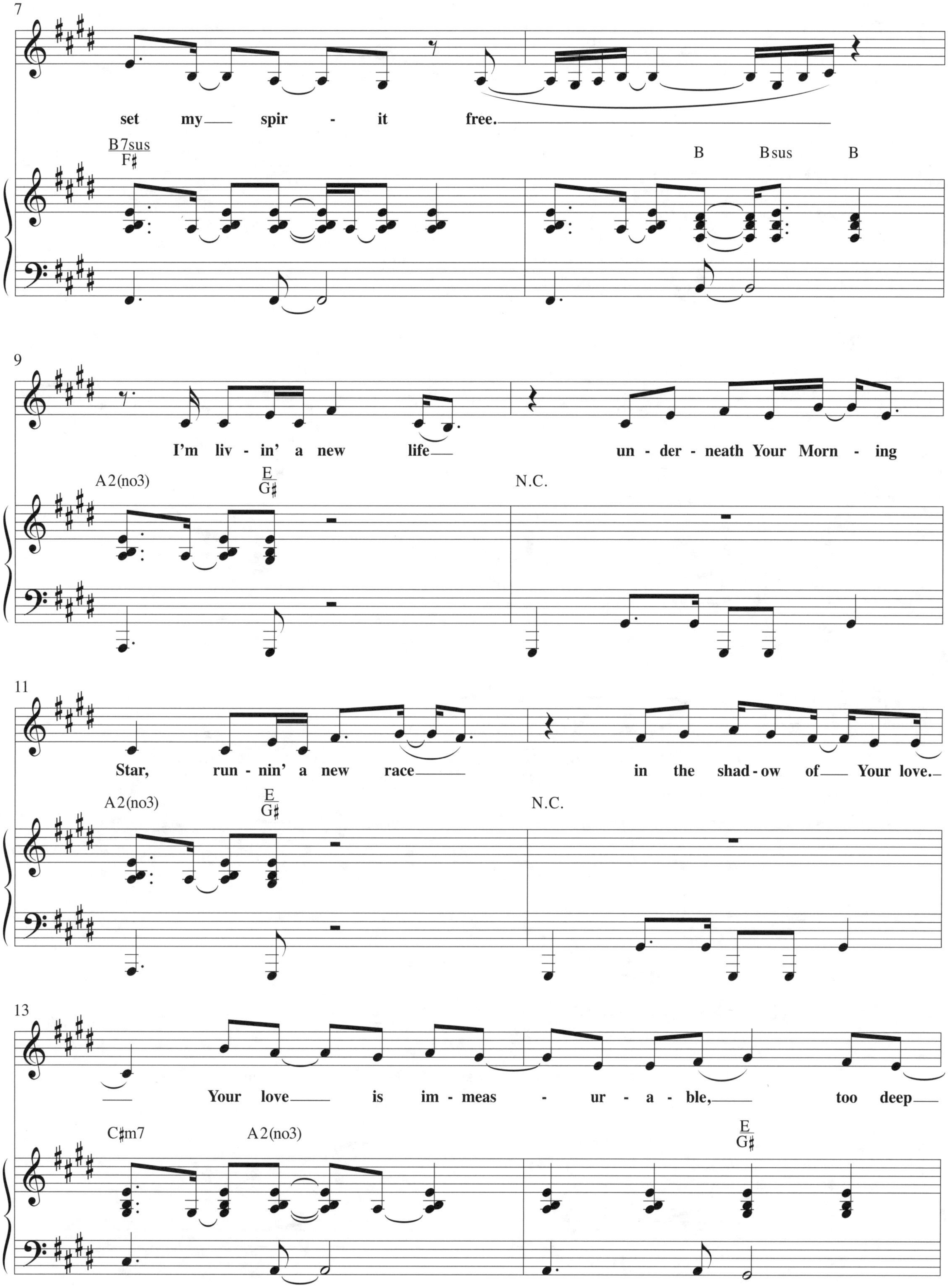
7
set my spir - it free.
B7sus/F♯
B Bsus B
9
I'm liv - in' a new life un - der - neath Your Morn - ing
A2(no3) E/G♯ N.C.
11
Star, run - nin' a new race in the shad - ow of Your love.
A2(no3) E/G♯ N.C.
13
Your love is im - meas - ur - a - ble, too deep
C♯m7 A2(no3) E/G♯

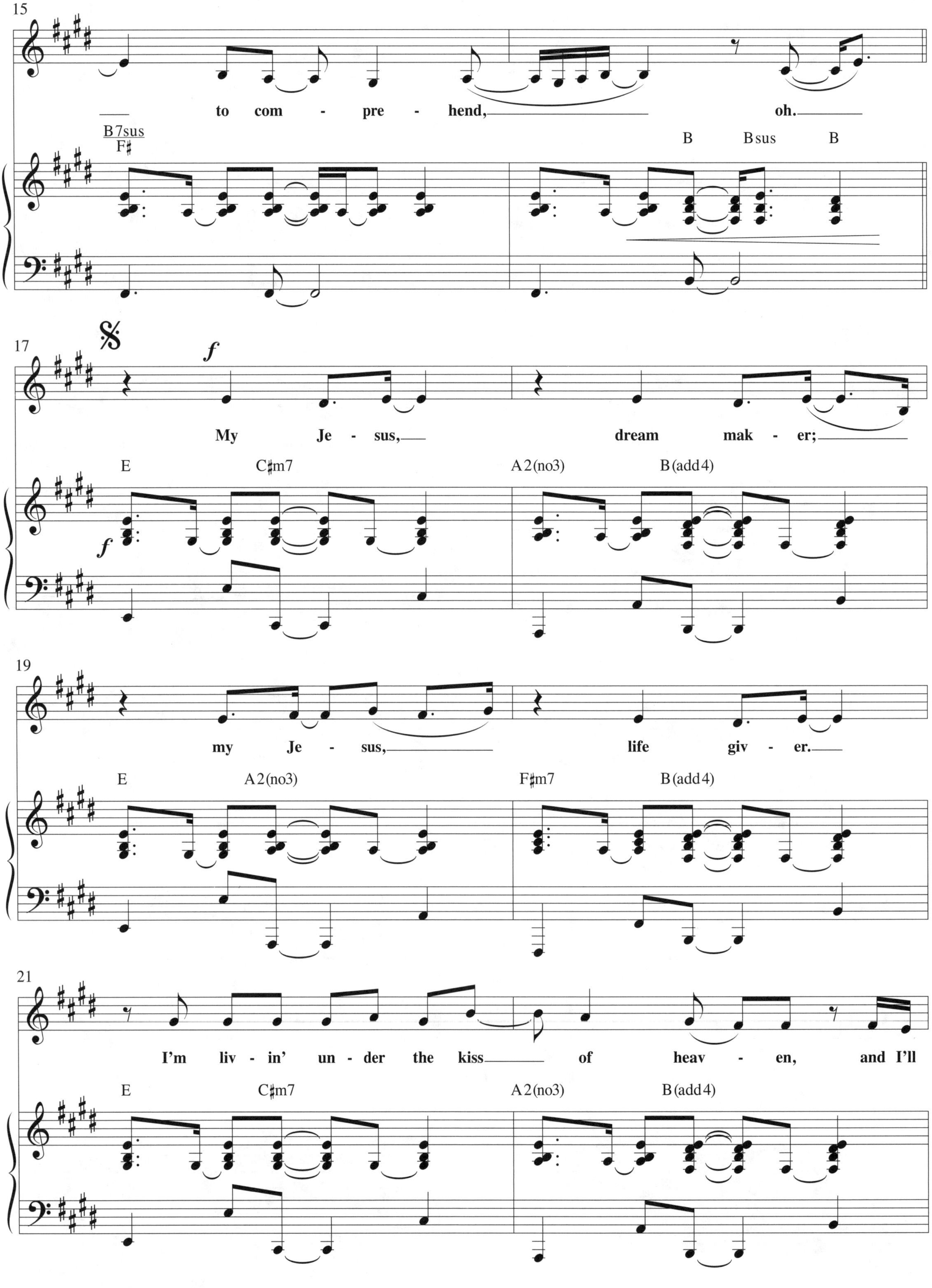
15
to com - pre - hend,
oh.
B7sus/F♯
B Bsus B
17
My Je - sus,
dream mak - er;
E C♯m7 A2(no3) B(add4)
19
my Je - sus,
life giv - er.
E A2(no3) F♯m7 B(add4)
21
I'm liv - in' un - der the kiss of heav - en, and I'll
E C♯m7 A2(no3) B(add4)

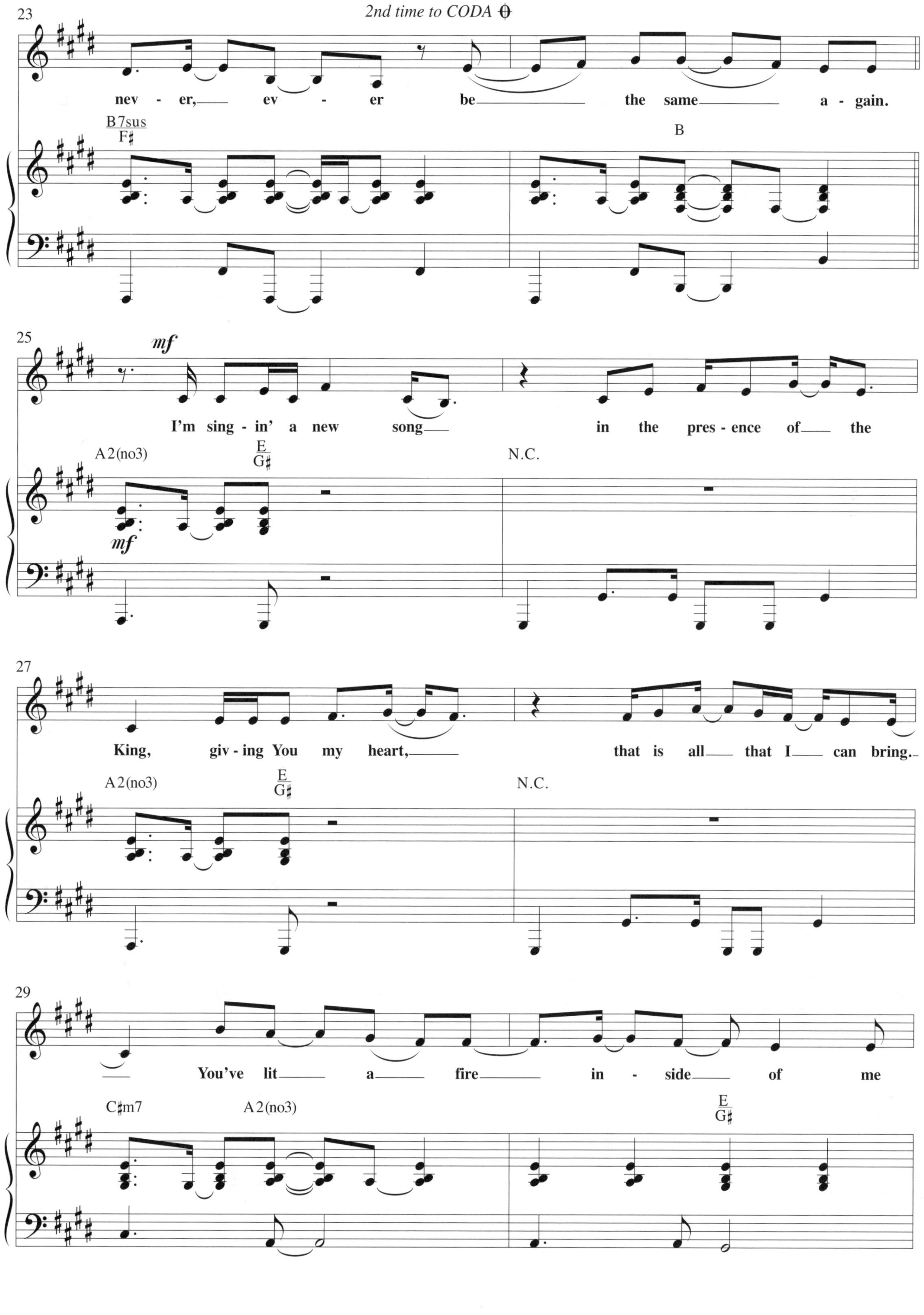
23
2nd time to CODA
never, ever be the same again.
B7sus/F♯
B
25
mf
I'm singin' a new song in the presence of the
A2(no3)
E/G♯
N.C.
mf
27
King, giving You my heart, that is all that I can bring.
A2(no3)
E/G♯
N.C.
29
You've lit a fire inside of me
C♯m7
A2(no3)
E/G♯

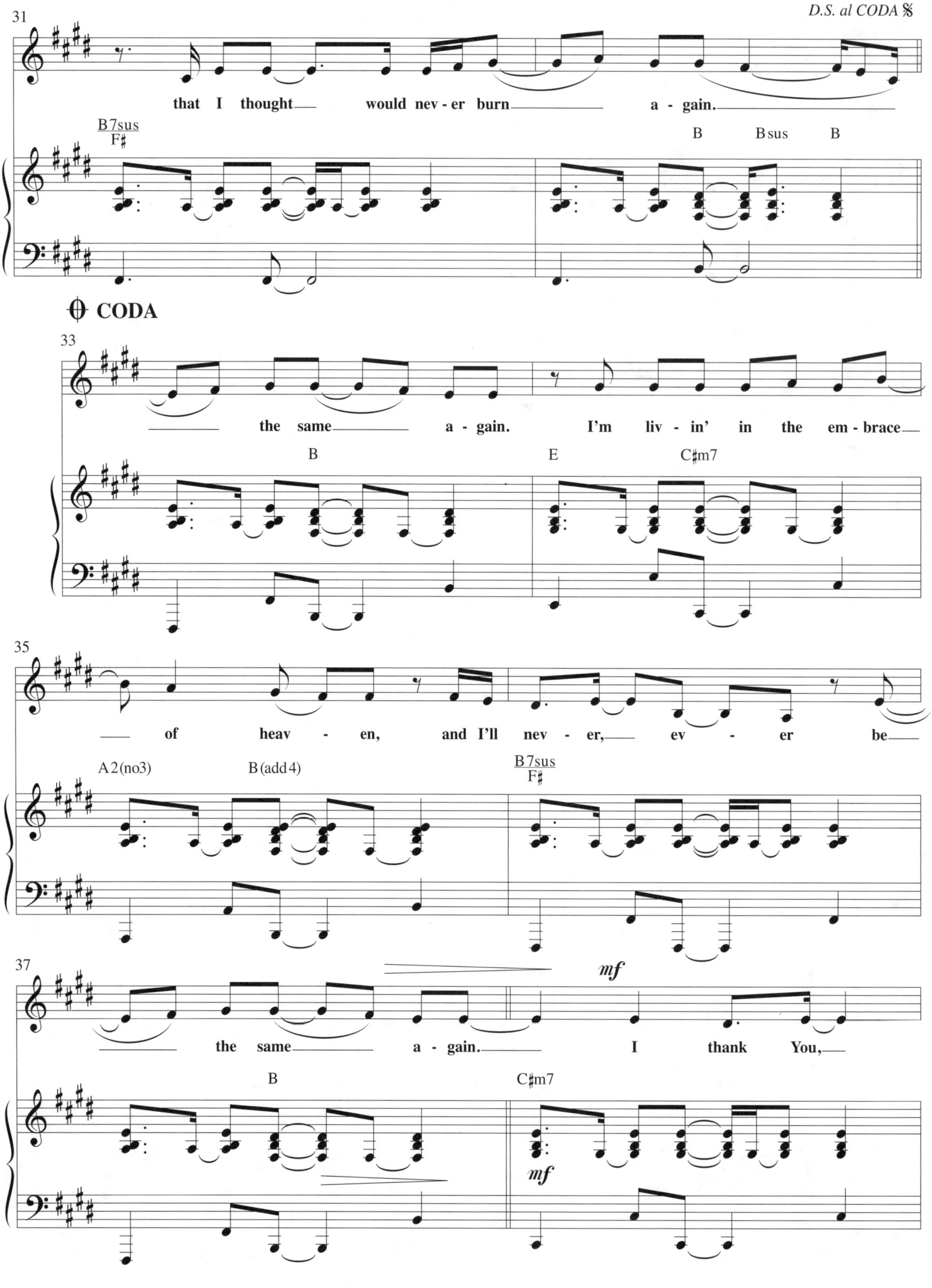
D.S. al CODA 𝄋
31
that I thought would nev - er burn a - gain.
B7sus/F♯
B Bsus B
CODA
33
the same a - gain. I'm liv - in' in the em - brace
B
E C♯m7
35
of heav - en, and I'll nev - er, ev - er be
A2(no3) B(add4)
B7sus/F♯
37
the same a - gain. I thank You,
mf
B
C♯m7
mf

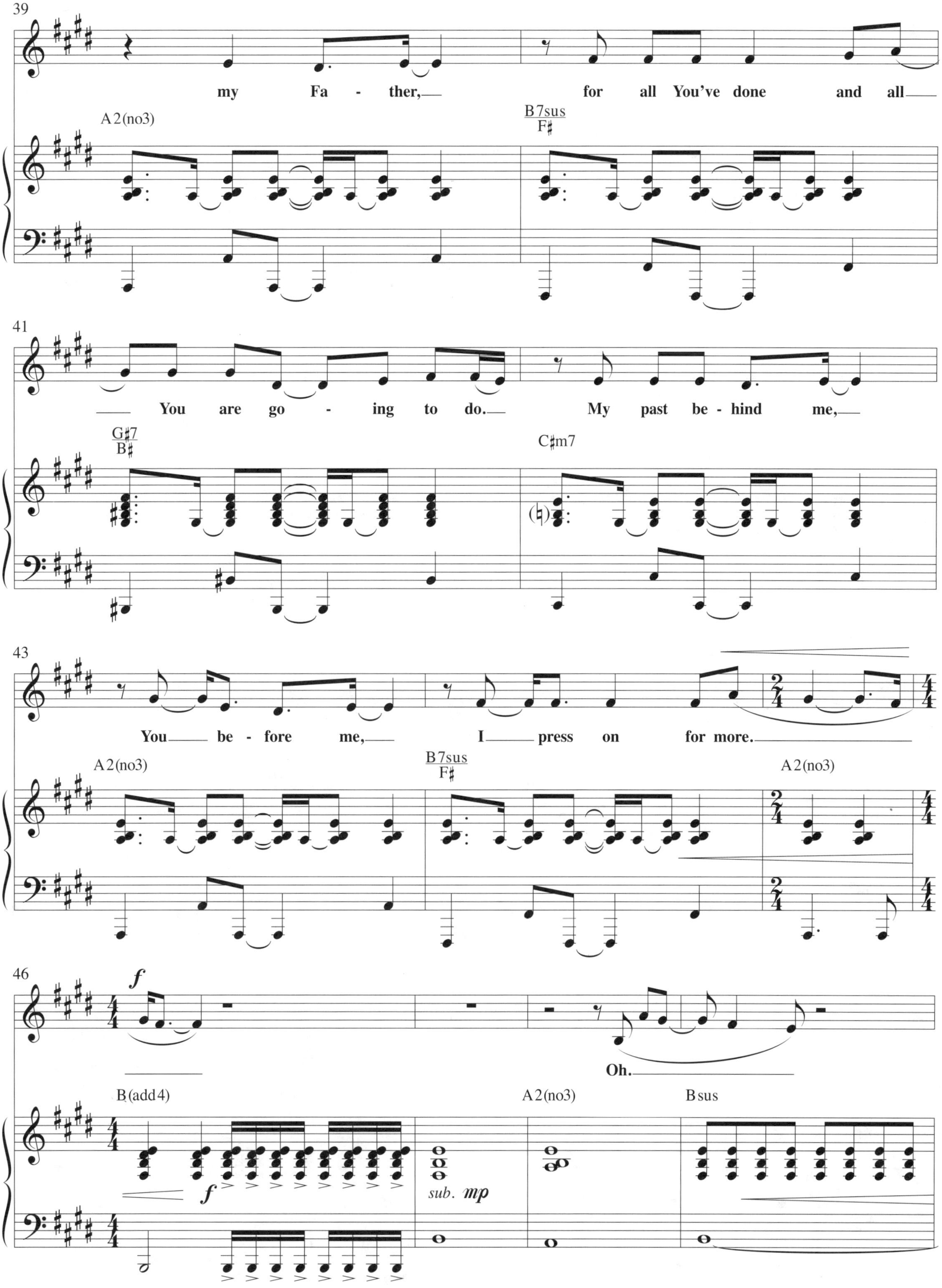
39
my Fa - ther, for all You've done and all
A2(no3)
B7sus/F♯
41
You are go - ing to do. My past be - hind me,
G♯7/B♯
C♯m7
43
You be - fore me, I press on for more.
A2(no3)
B7sus/F♯
A2(no3)
46
f
Oh.
B(add4)
f
sub. mp
A2(no3)
Bsus

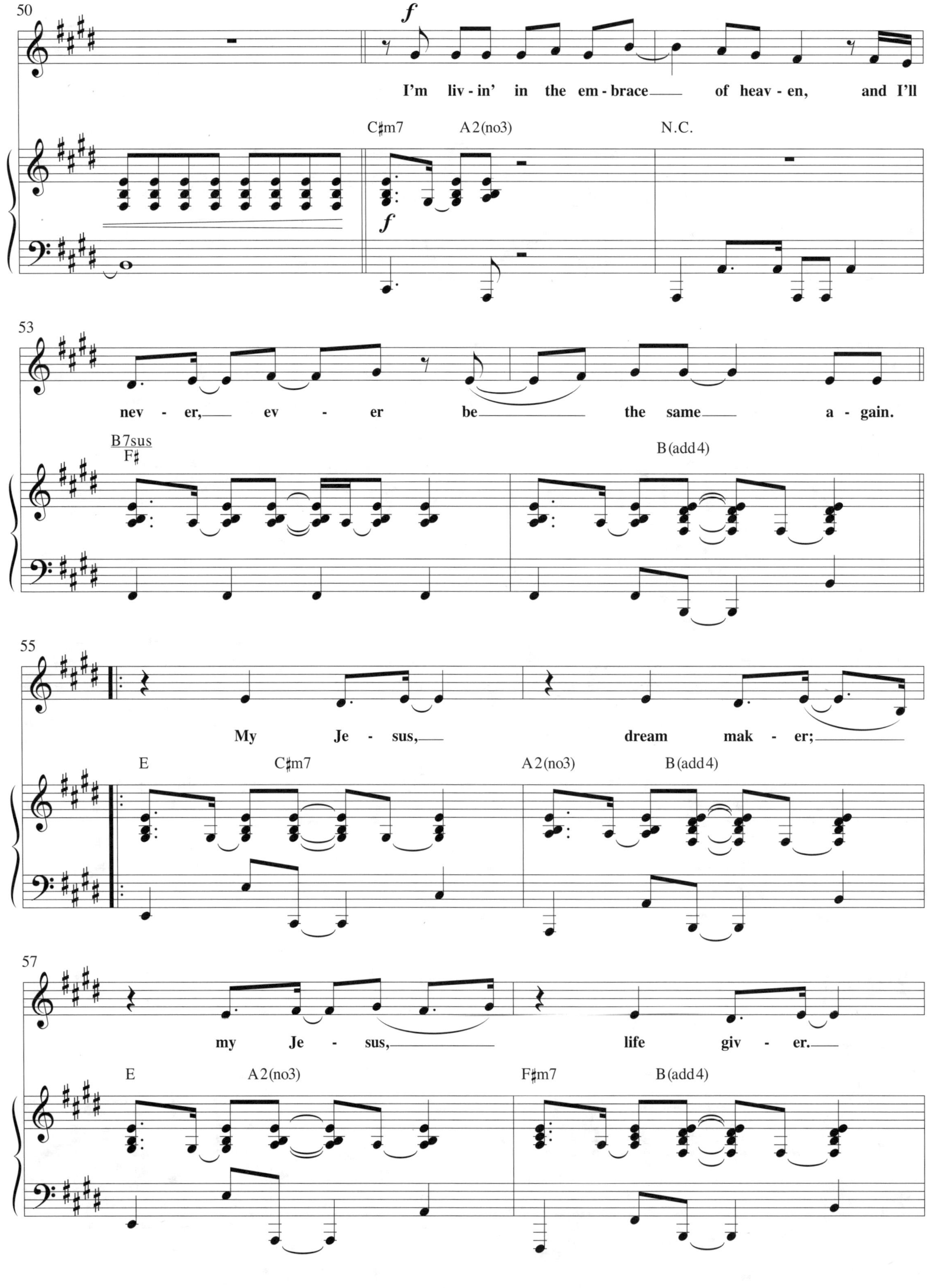
50
f
I'm liv - in' in the em - brace of heav - en, and I'll
C♯m7
A2(no3)
N.C.
53
nev - er, ev - er be the same a - gain.
B7sus
F♯
B(add4)
55
My Je - sus, dream mak - er;
E
C♯m7
A2(no3)
B(add4)
57
my Je - sus, life giv - er.
E
A2(no3)
F♯m7
B(add4)

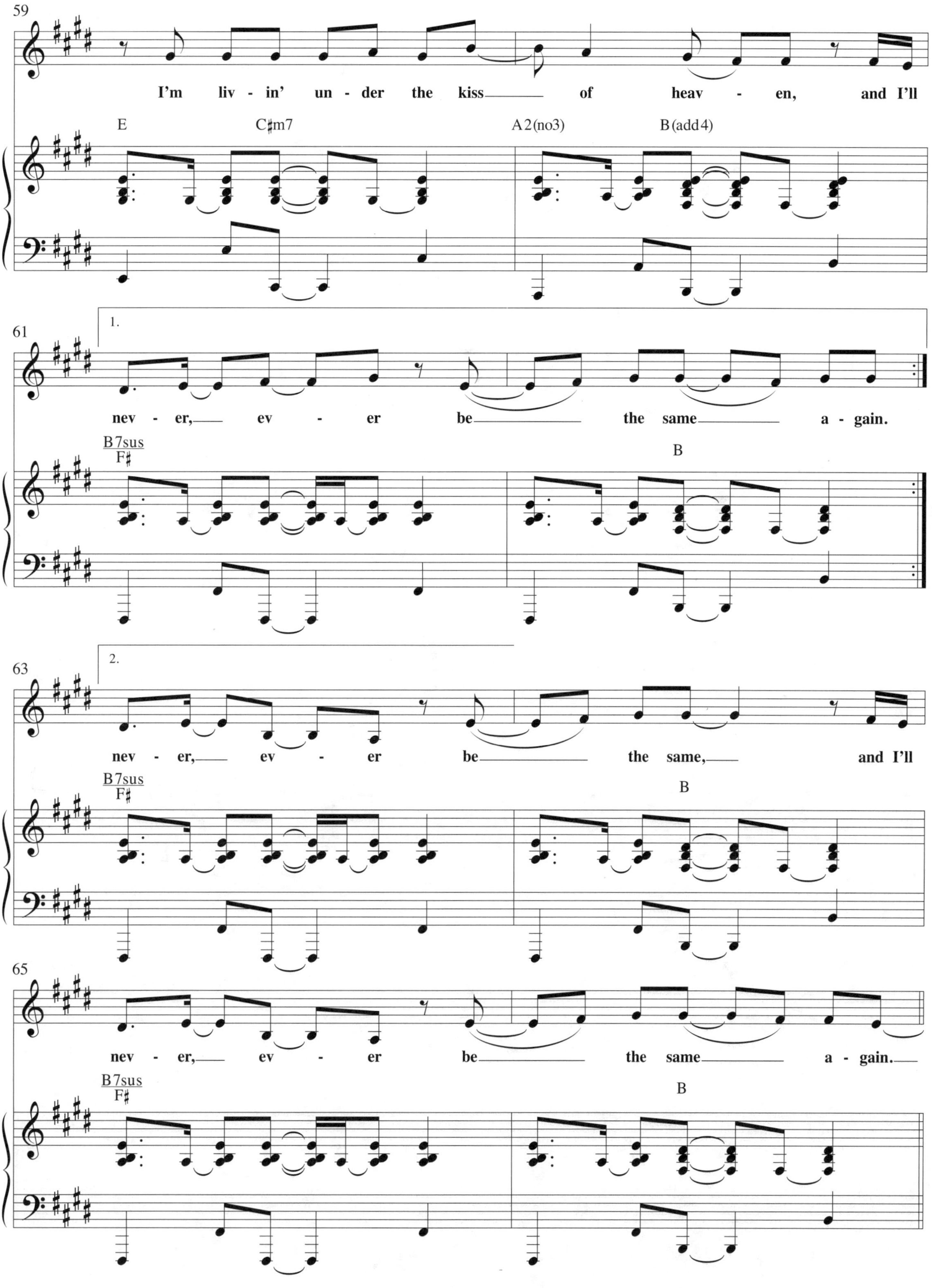
59
I'm liv - in' un - der the kiss of heav - en, and I'll
E C♯m7 A2(no3) B(add4)
61
1.
nev - er, ev - er be the same a - gain.
B7sus/F♯ B
63
2.
nev - er, ev - er be the same, and I'll
B7sus/F♯ B
65
nev - er, ev - er be the same a - gain.
B7sus/F♯ B

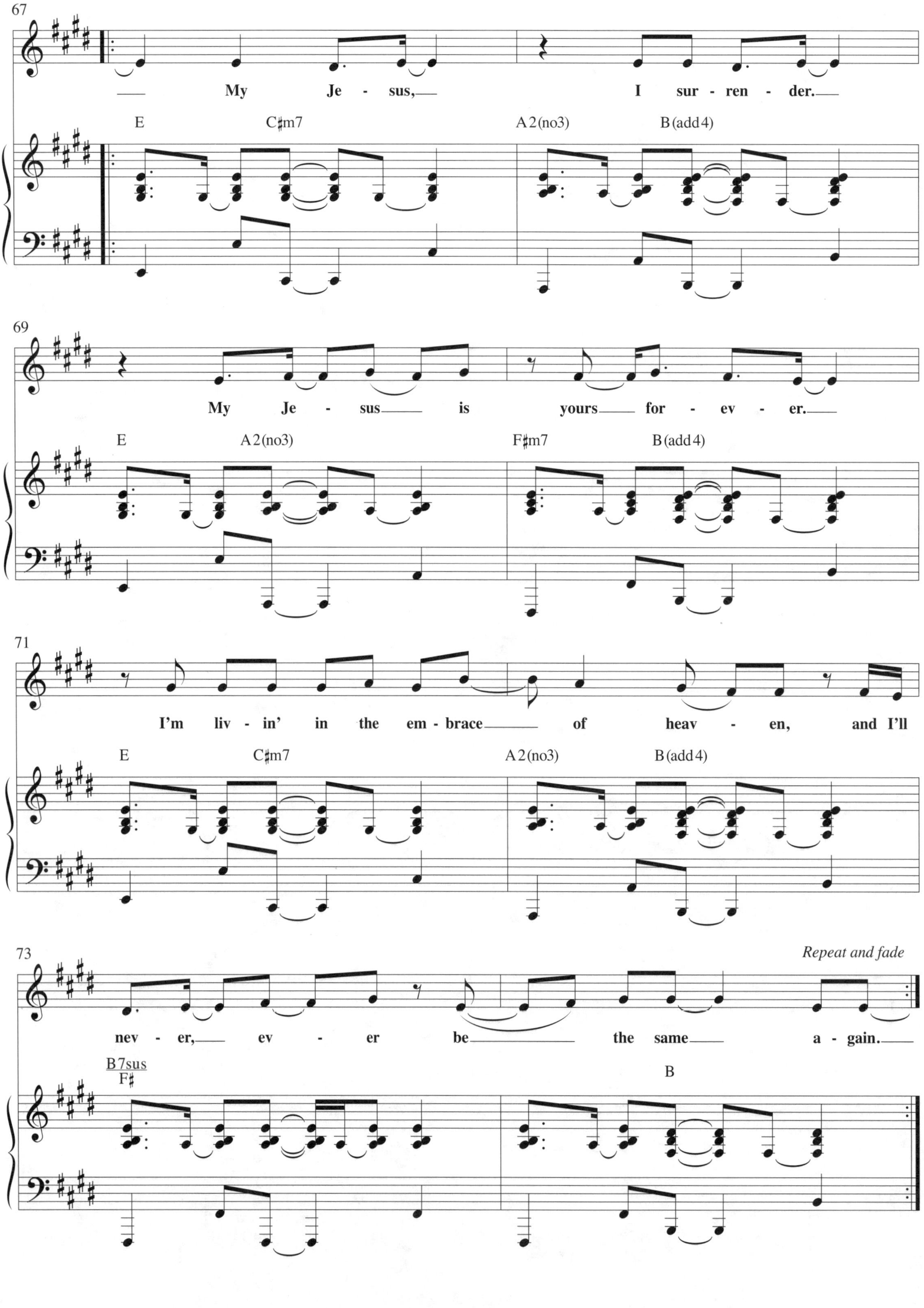
67
My Je - sus,
I sur - ren - der.
E
C♯m7
A2(no3)
B(add4)
69
My Je - sus is yours for - ev - er.
E
A2(no3)
F♯m7
B(add4)
71
I'm liv - in' in the em - brace of heav - en, and I'll
E
C♯m7
A2(no3)
B(add4)
73
Repeat and fade
nev - er, ev - er be the same a - gain.
B7sus/F♯
B

Everlasting

Words and Music by
DAVID HOLMES, MARTY SAMPSON
and DARLENE ZSCHECH

Steady four ♩ = 72

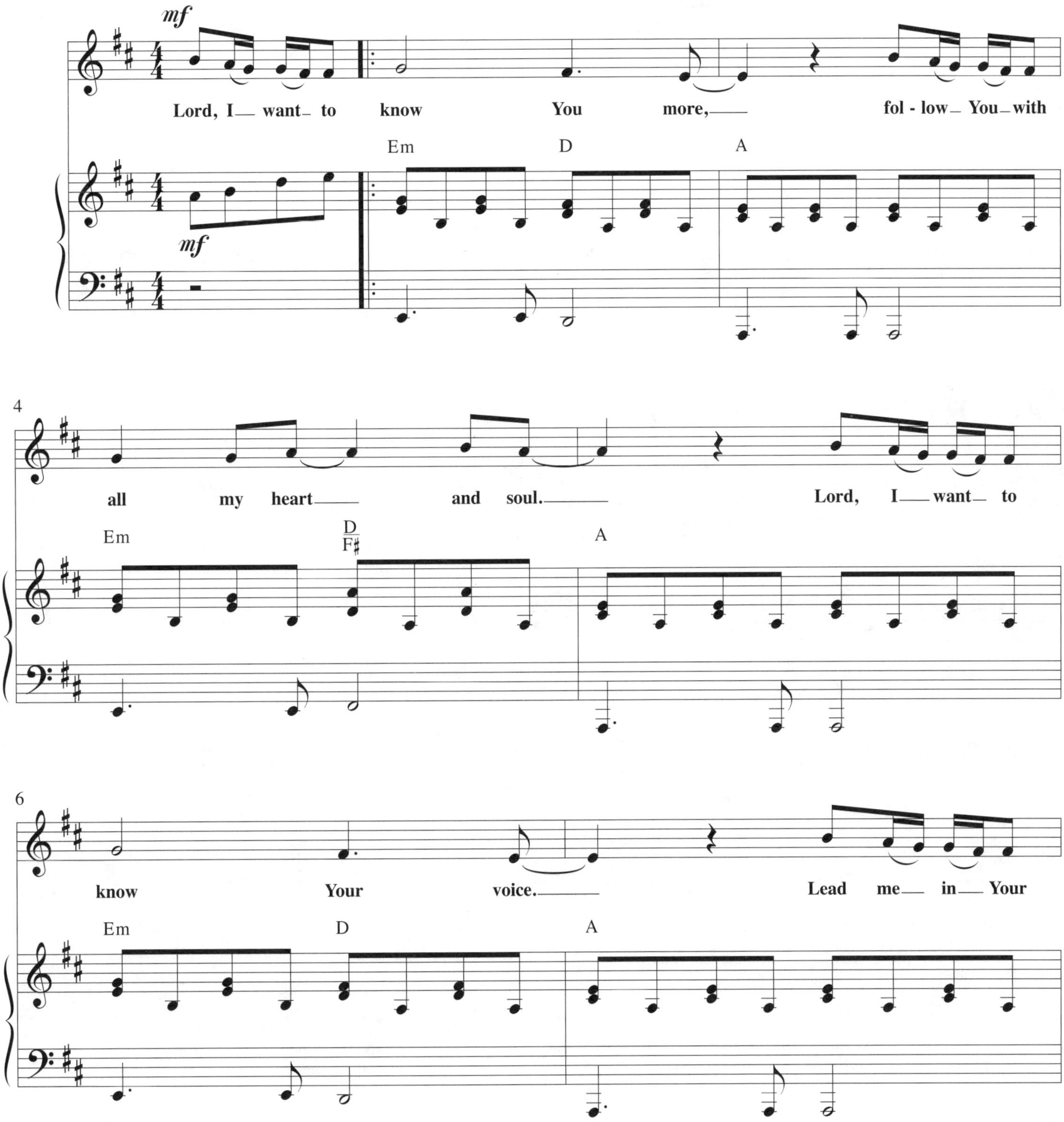

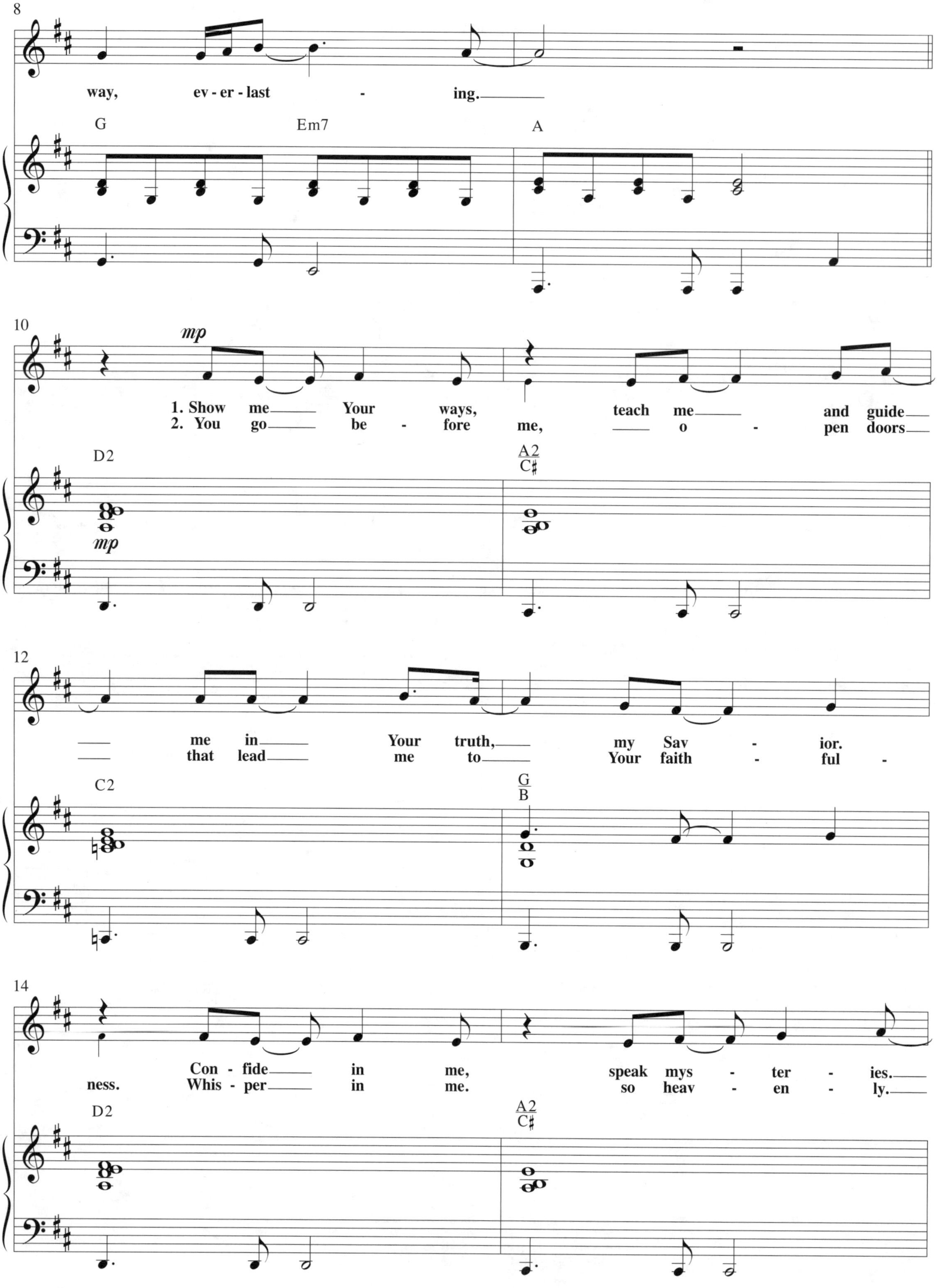
8
way, ev - er - last - ing.
G
Em7
A
10
mp
1. Show me Your ways, teach me and guide
2. You go be - fore me, o - pen doors
D2
A2
C♯
mp
12
me in Your truth, my Sav - ior.
that lead me to Your faith - ful -
C2
G
B
14
Con - fide in me, speak mys - ter - ies.
ness. Whis - per in me. so heav - en - ly.
D2
A2
C♯

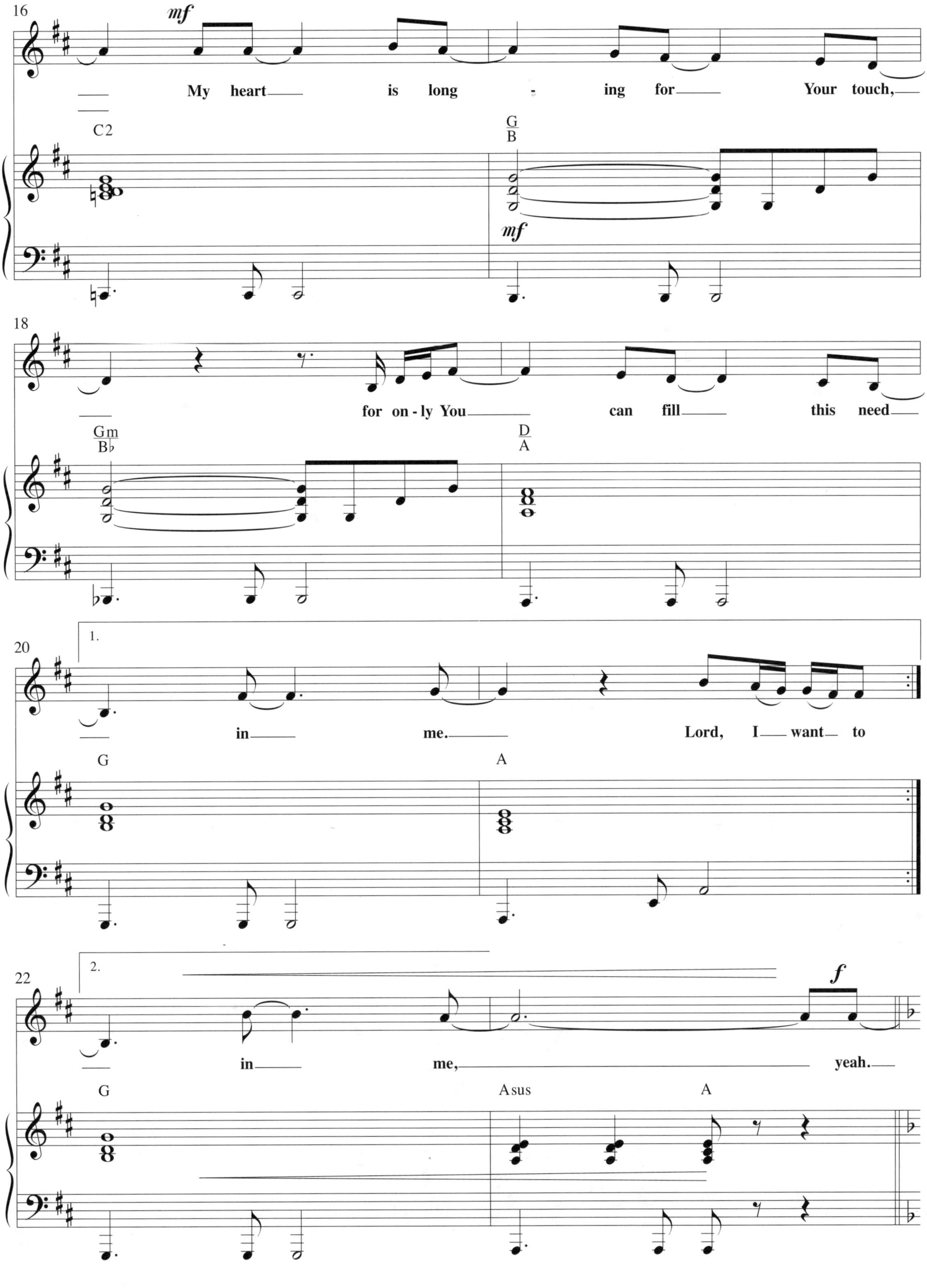
16
mf
My heart is long - ing for Your touch,
C2
G
B
mf
18
for on - ly You can fill this need
Gm
B♭
D
A
20
1.
in me. Lord, I want to
G
A
22
2.
f
in me, yeah.
G
Asus
A

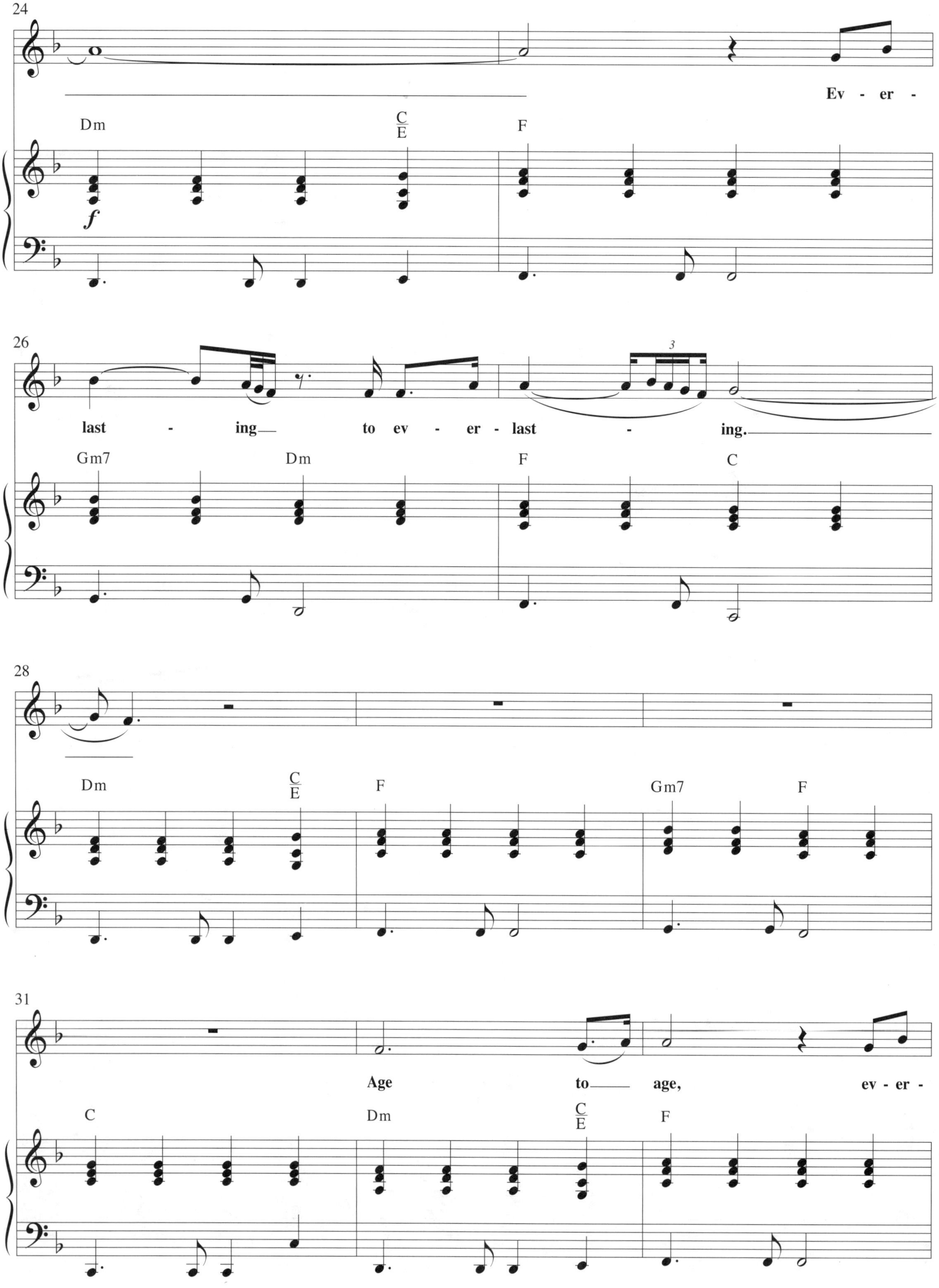
24
Ev - er -
Dm
C
E
F
f
26
last - ing to ev - er - last - ing.
Gm7
Dm
F
C
28
Dm
C
E
F
Gm7
F
31
Age to age, ev - er -
C
Dm
C
E
F

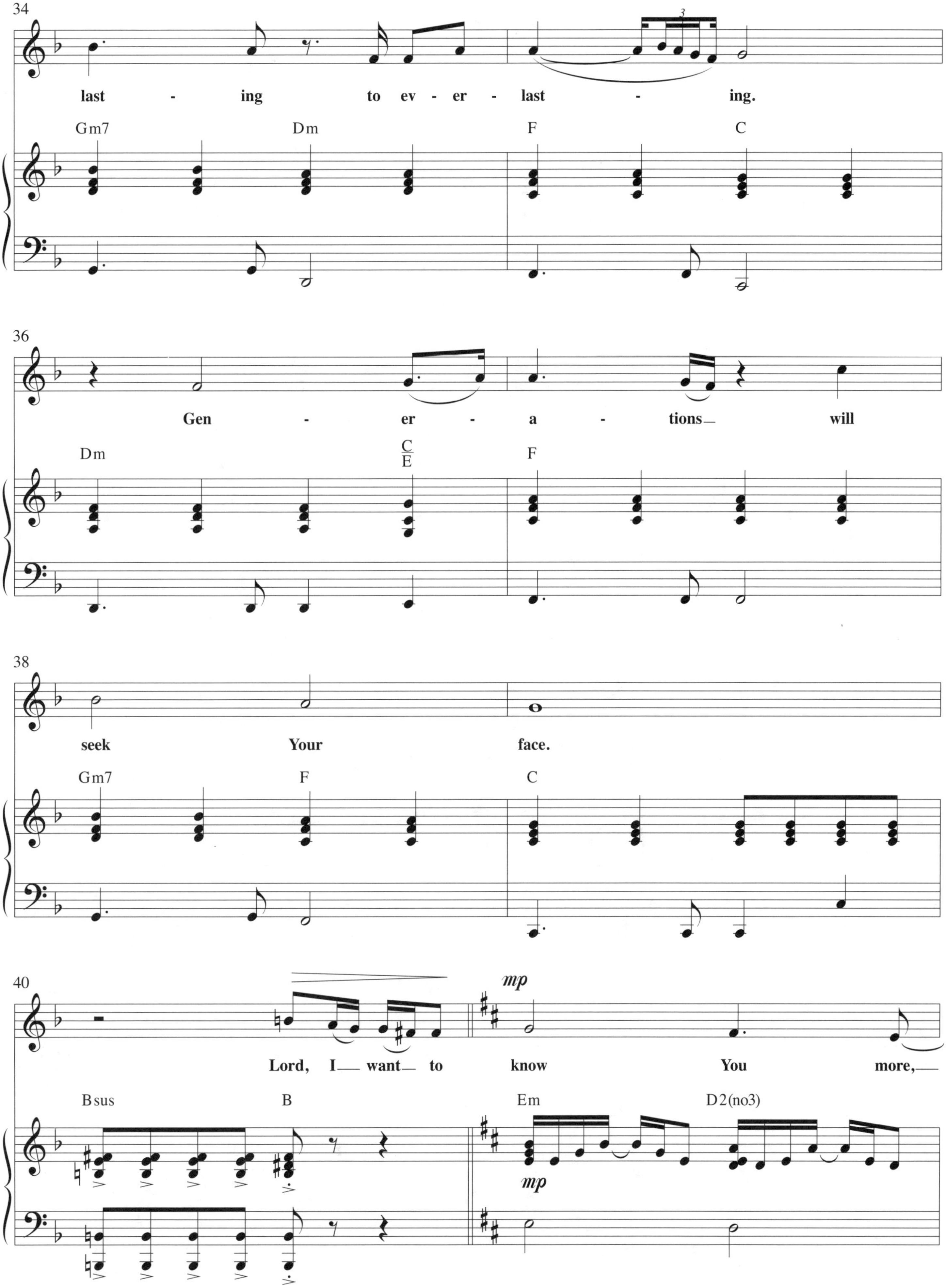
34
last - ing to ev - er - last - ing.
Gm7 Dm F C
36
Gen - er - a - tions will
Dm C/E F
38
seek Your face.
Gm7 F C
40
mp
Lord, I want to know You more,
Bsus B Em D2(no3)
mp

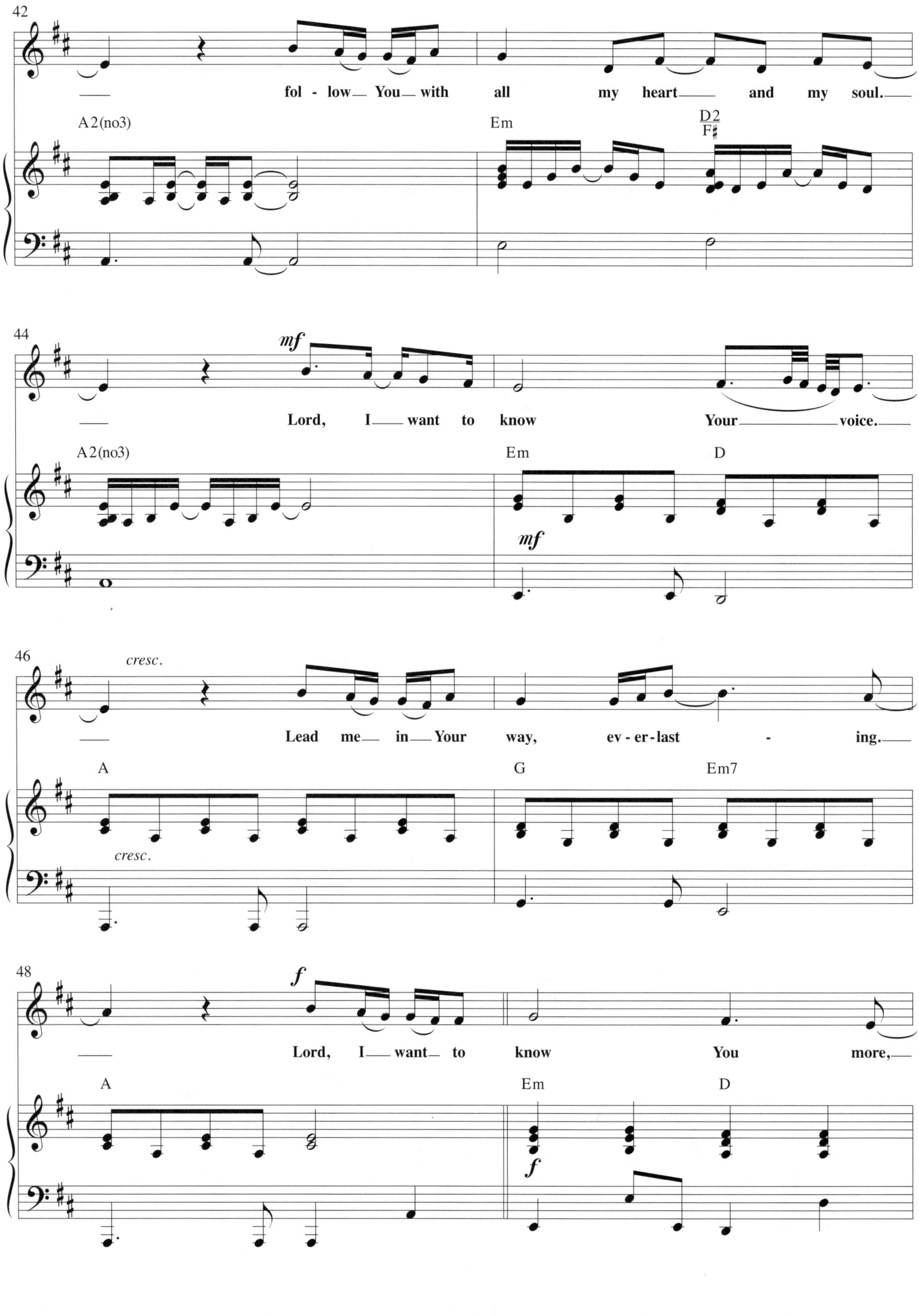
42
fol - low You with all my heart and my soul.
A2(no3)
Em
D2/F♯
44
mf
Lord, I want to know Your voice.
A2(no3)
Em
D
mf
46
cresc.
Lead me in Your way, ev - er - last - ing.
A
G
Em7
cresc.
48
f
Lord, I want to know You more,
A
Em
D
f

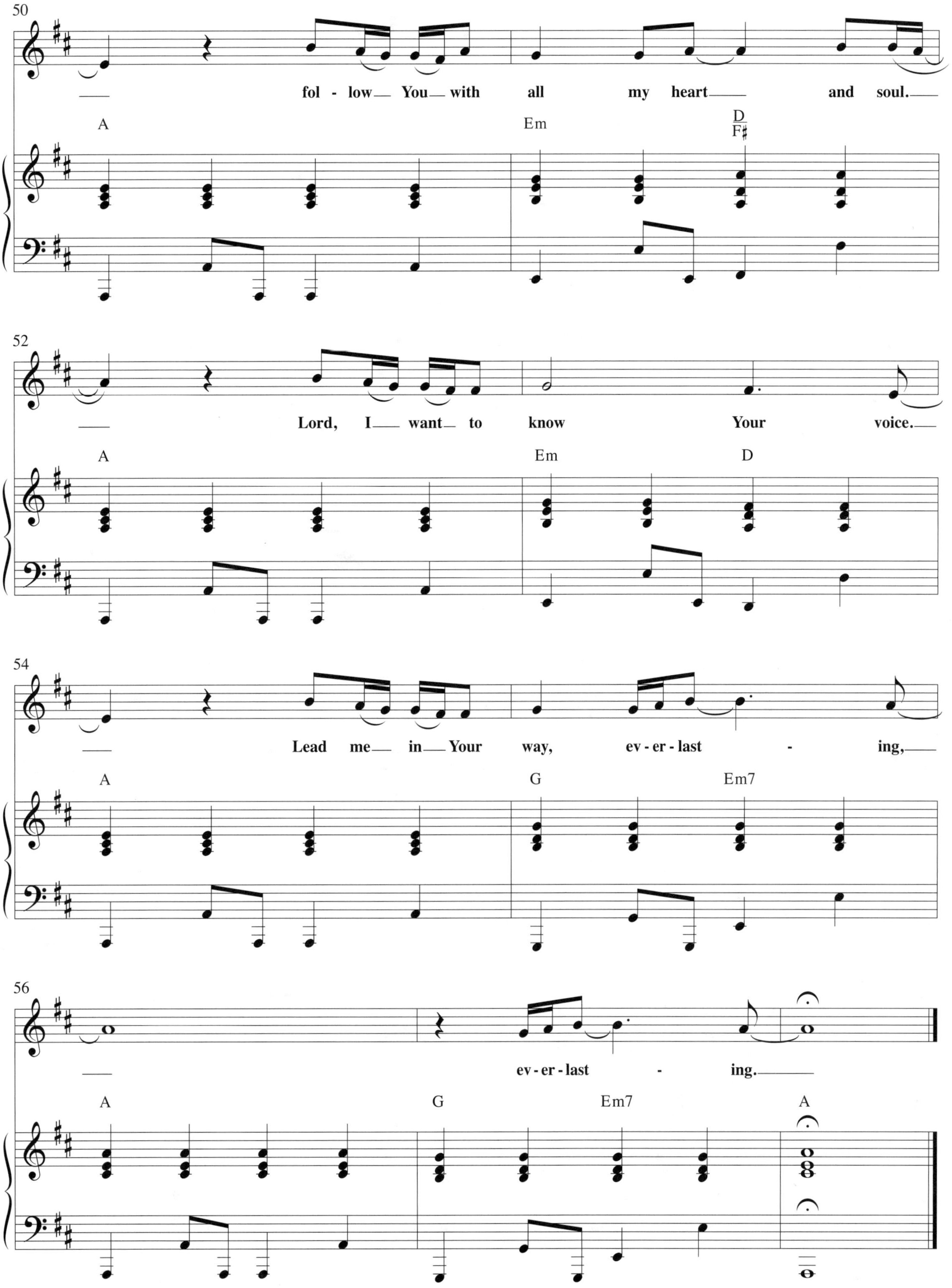
50
fol - low You with all my heart and soul.
A Em D/F♯
52
Lord, I want to know Your voice.
A Em D
54
Lead me in Your way, ev - er - last - ing,
A G Em7
56
ev - er - last - ing.
A G Em7 A

Shout To The Lord

Words and Music by
DARLENE ZSCHECH

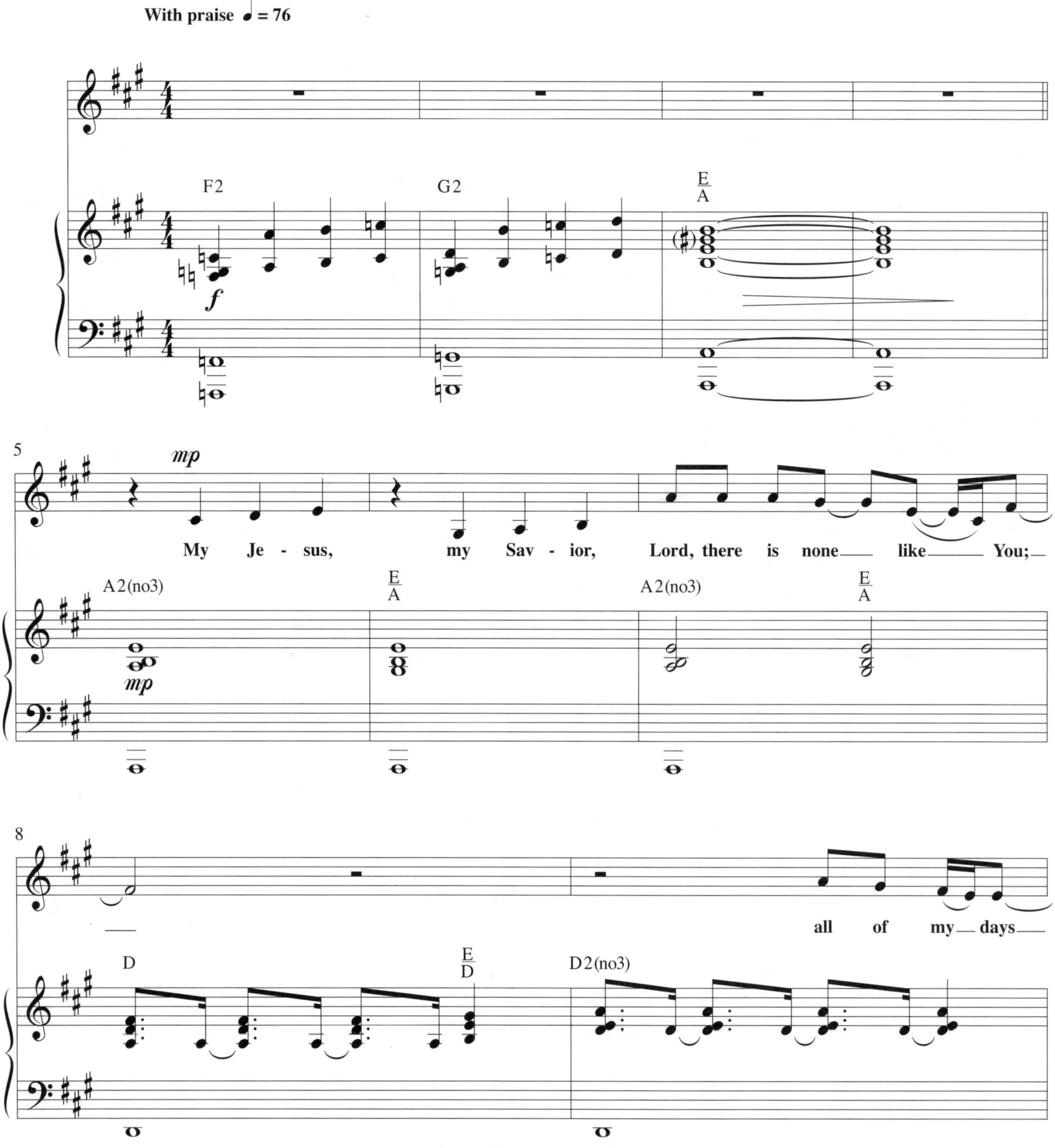

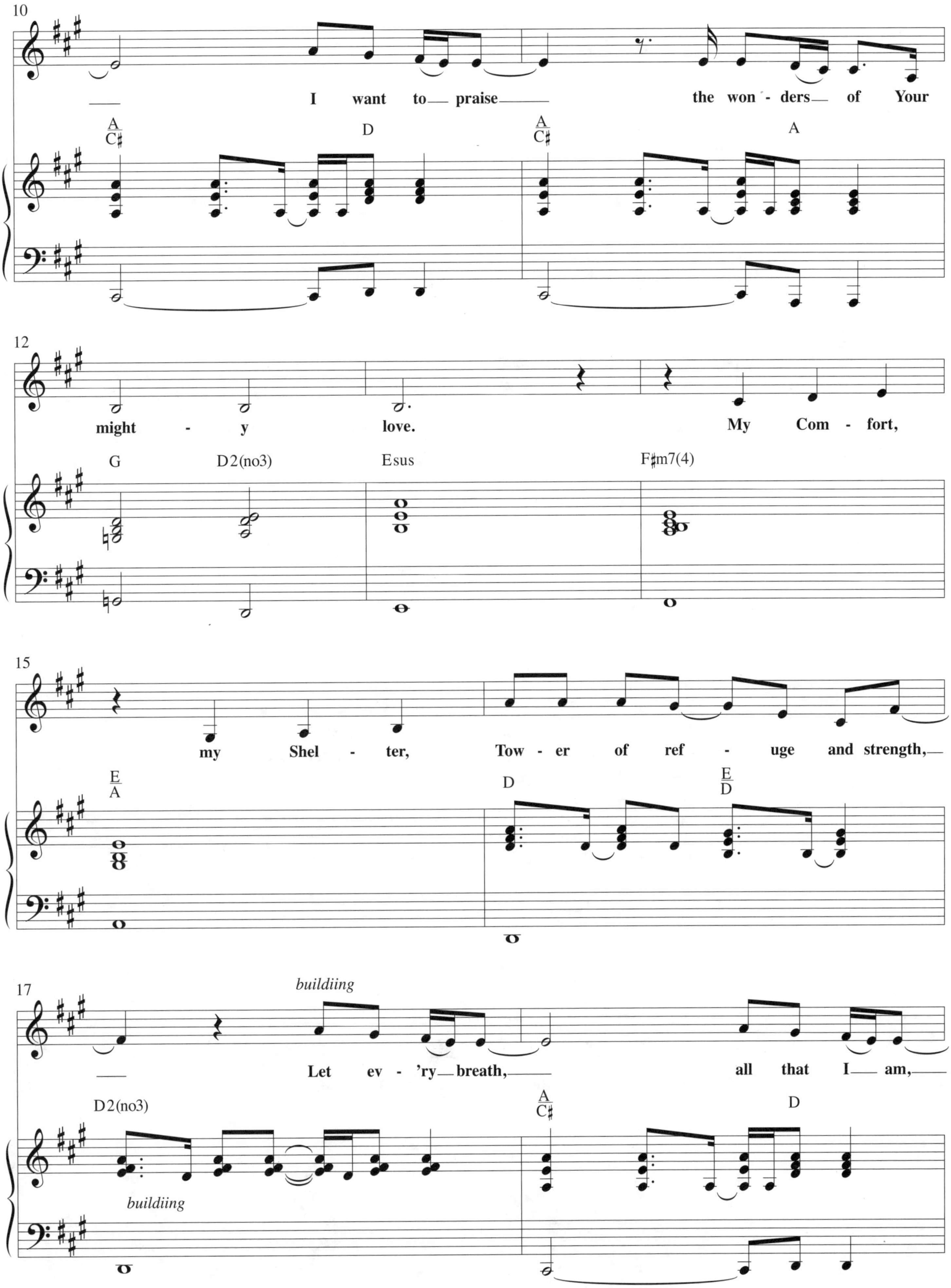
10
I want to praise the won-ders of Your
A/C♯ D A/C♯ A
12
might-y love. My Com-fort,
G D2(no3) Esus F♯m7(4)
15
my Shel-ter, Tow-er of ref-uge and strength,
E/A D E/D
17
buildiing
Let ev-'ry breath, all that I am,
D2(no3) A/C♯ D
buildiing

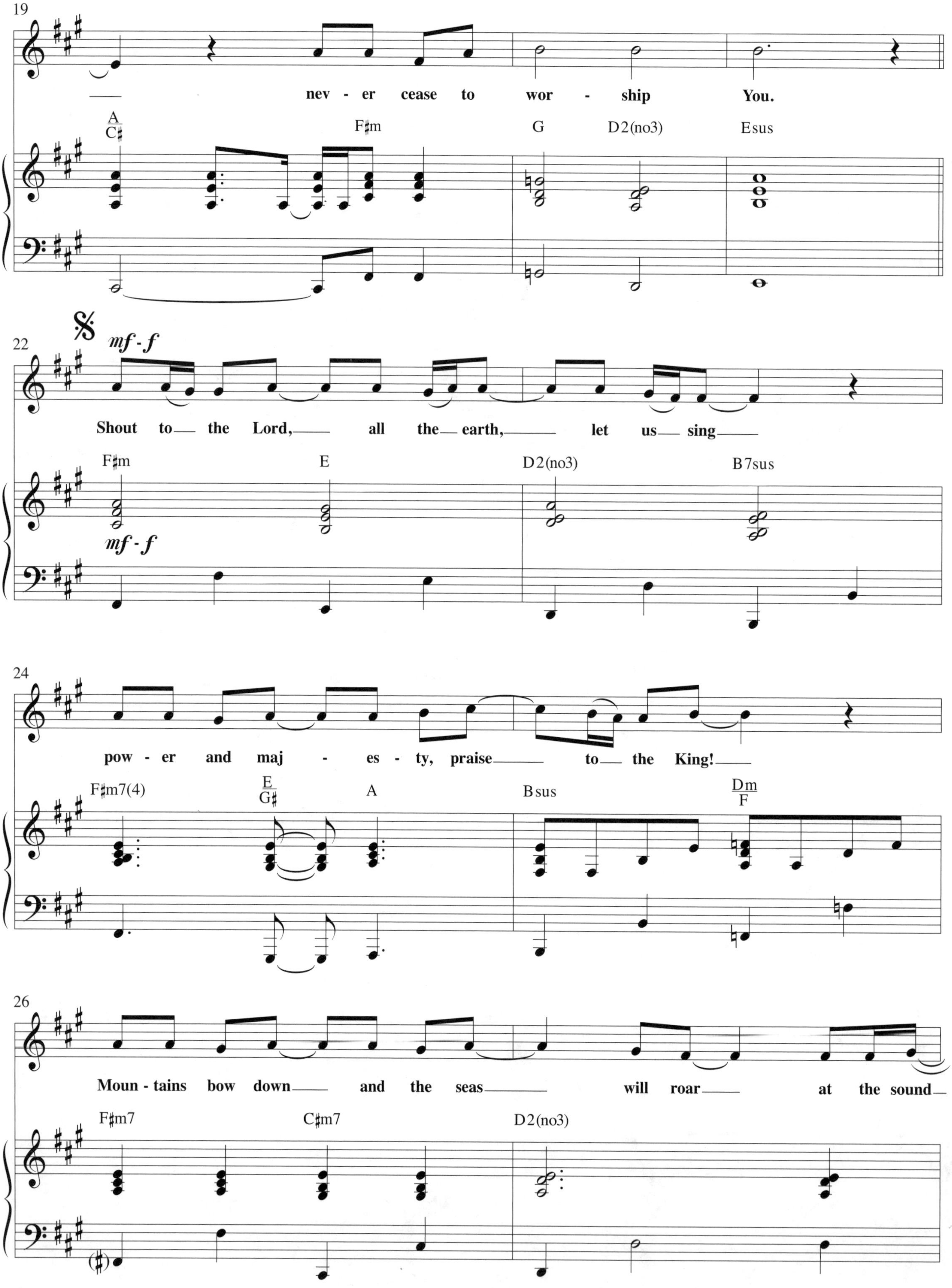
19
never cease to worship You.
A/C♯ F♯m G D2(no3) Esus
22
mf - f
Shout to the Lord, all the earth, let us sing
F♯m E D2(no3) B7sus
24
power and majesty, praise to the King!
F♯m7(4) E/G♯ A Bsus Dm/F
26
Mountains bow down and the seas will roar at the sound
F♯m7 C♯m7 D2(no3)

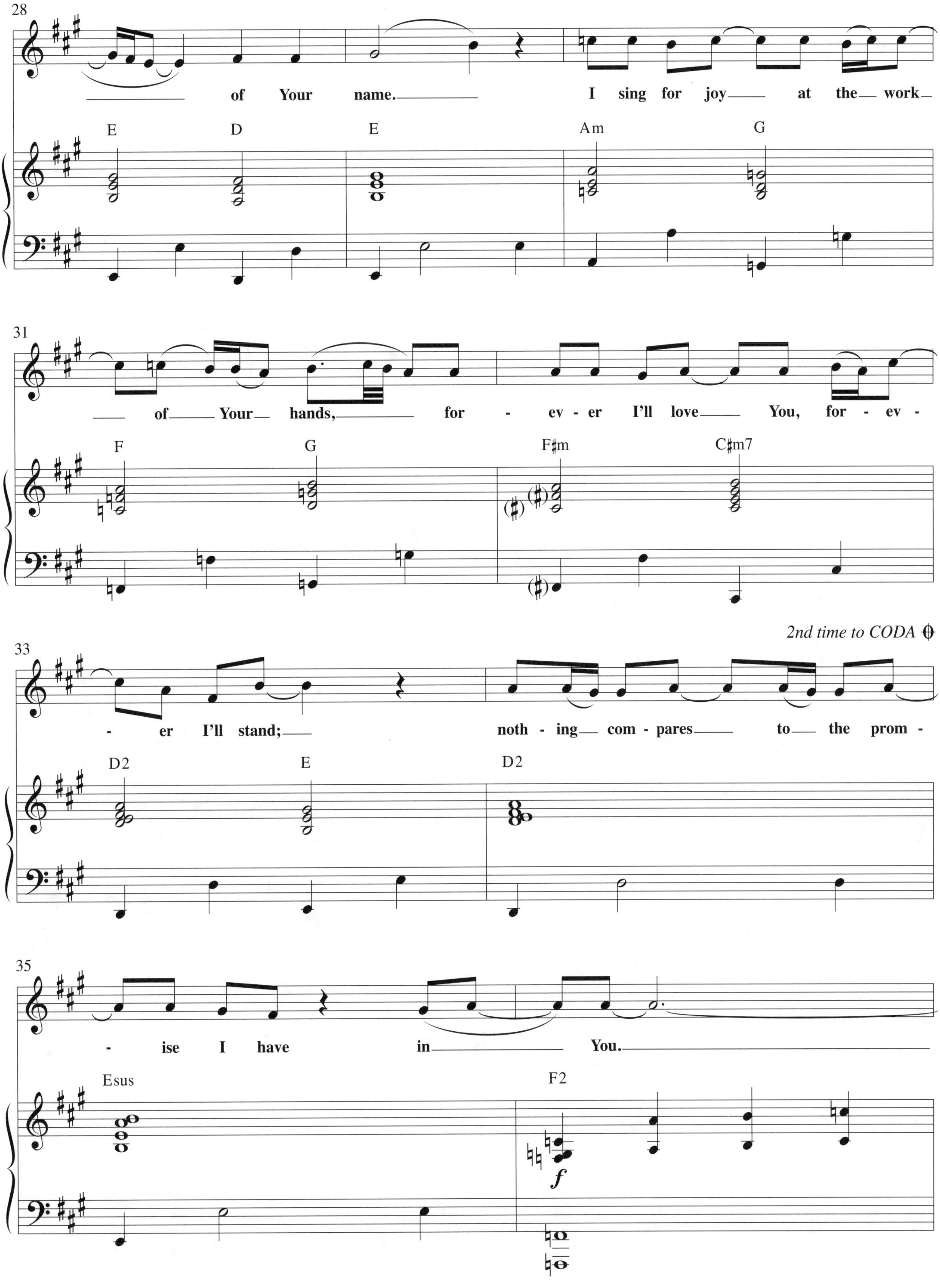
28
of Your name. I sing for joy at the work
E D E Am G
31
of Your hands, for - ev - er I'll love You, for - ev -
F G F♯m C♯m7
2nd time to CODA
33
- er I'll stand; nothing - ing com - pares to the prom -
D2 E D2
35
- ise I have in You.
Esus F2
f

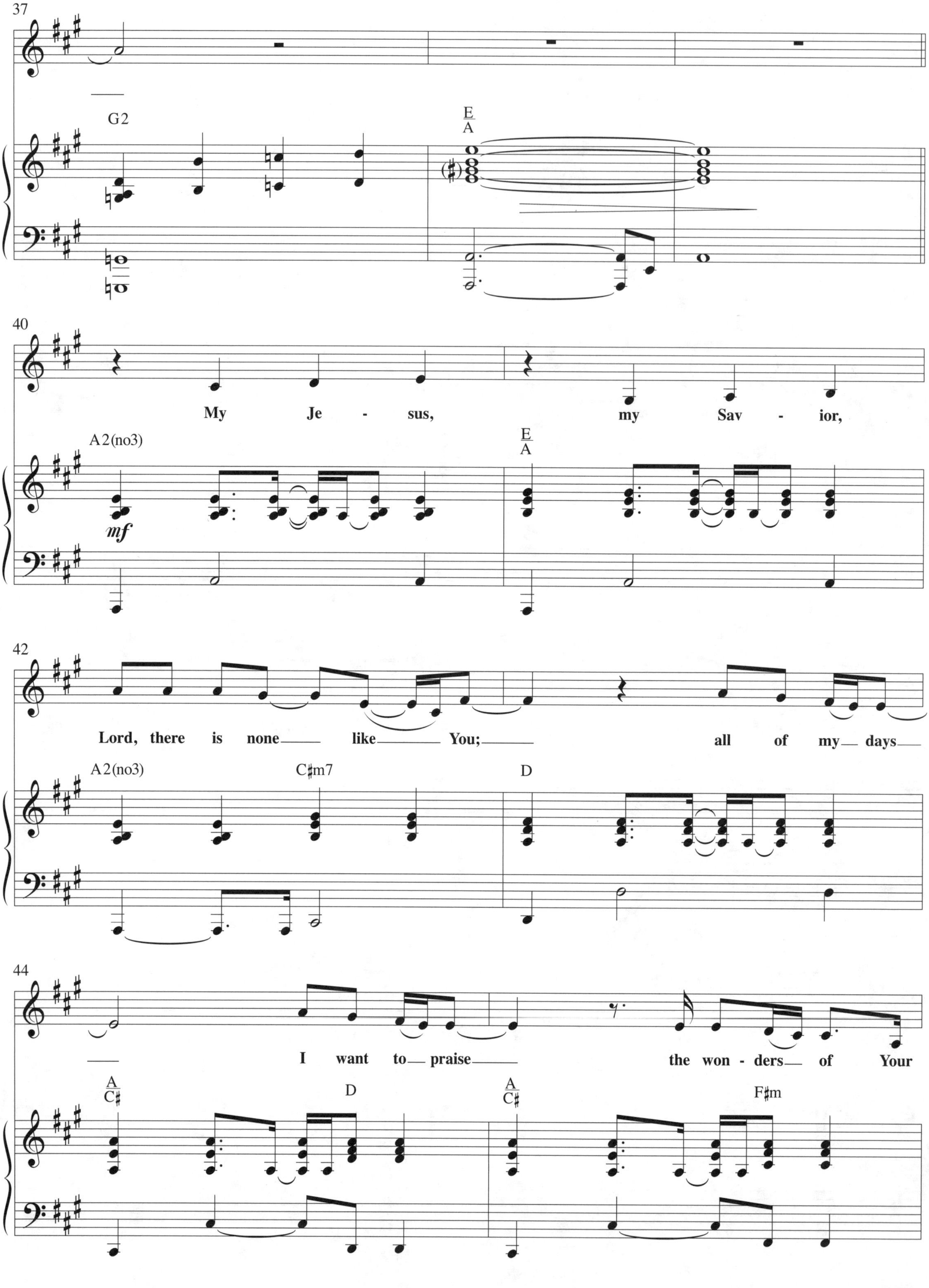
37
G2
E/A
40
My Je - sus, my Sav - ior,
A2(no3)
mf
E/A
42
Lord, there is none like You; all of my days
A2(no3)
C♯m7
D
44
I want to praise the won - ders of Your
A/C♯
D
A/C♯
F♯m

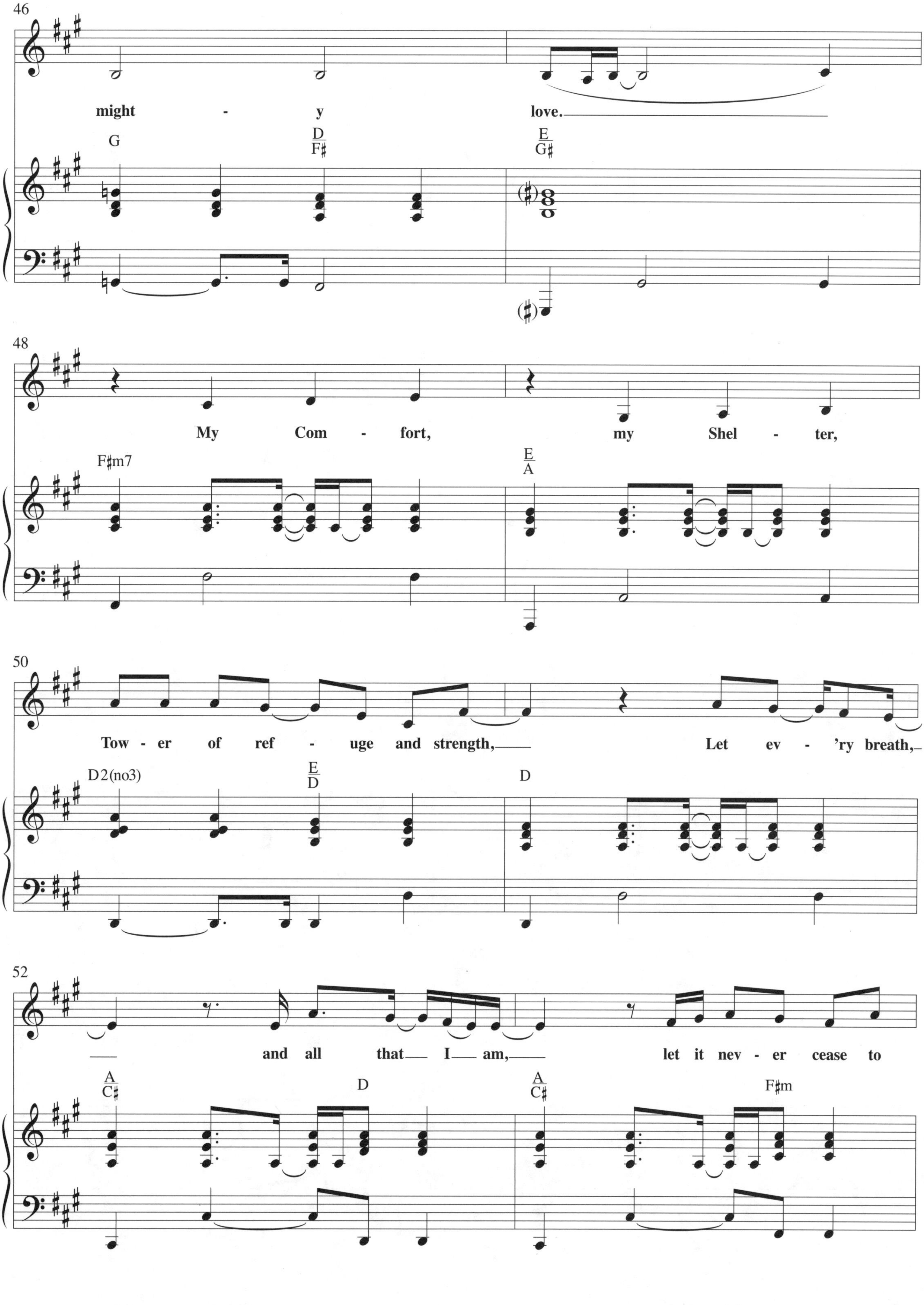
46
might - y love.
G D/F♯ E/G♯
48
My Com - fort, my Shel - ter,
F♯m7 E/A
50
Tow - er of ref - uge and strength, Let ev - 'ry breath,
D2(no3) E/D D
52
and all that I am, let it nev - er cease to
A/C♯ D A/C♯ F♯m

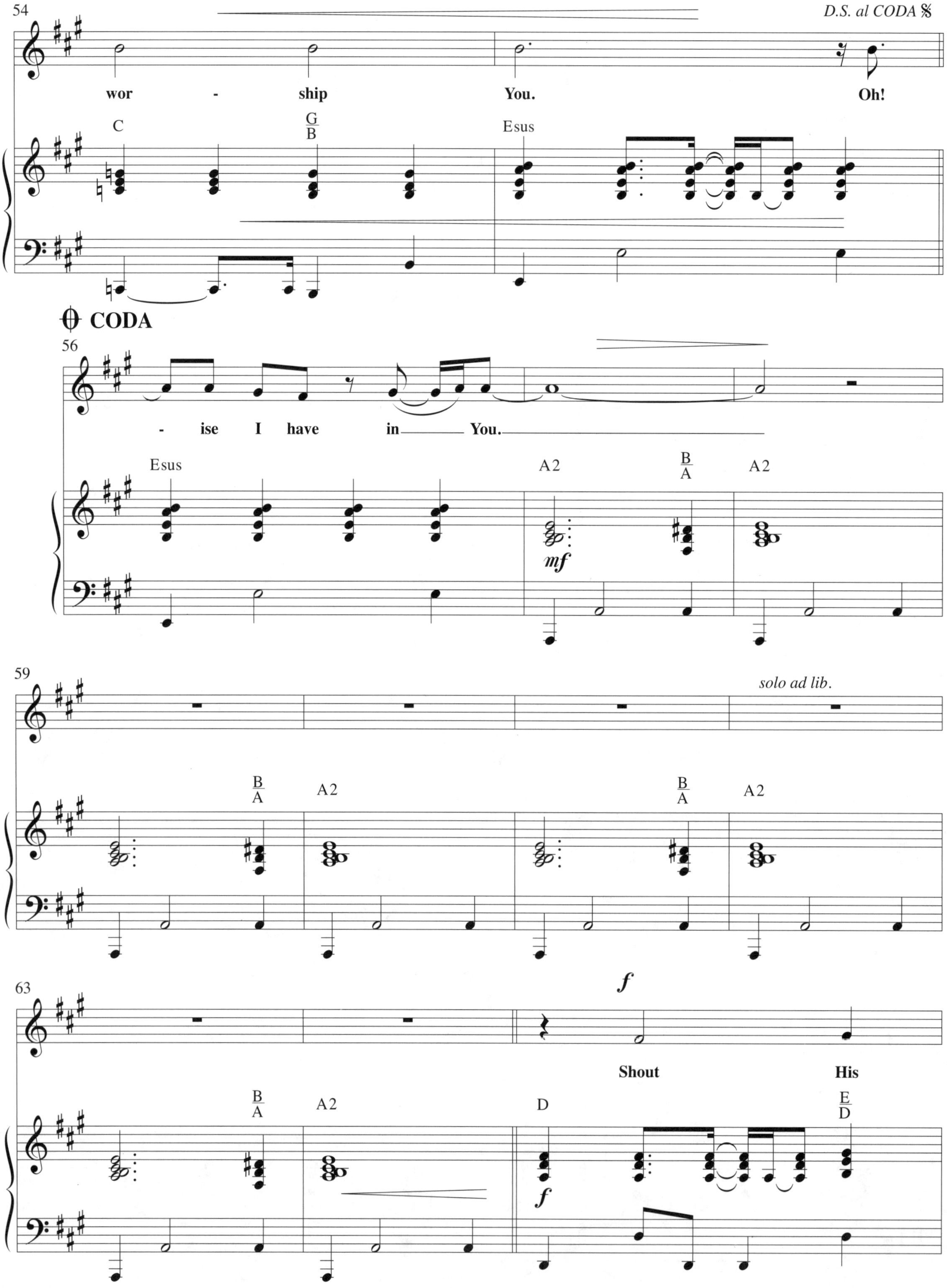
54
D.S. al CODA
wor - ship You. Oh!
C
G/B
Esus
CODA
56
- ise I have in You.
Esus
A2
B/A
A2
mf
59
solo ad lib.
B/A
A2
B/A
A2
63
f
Shout His
B/A
A2
D
E/D
f

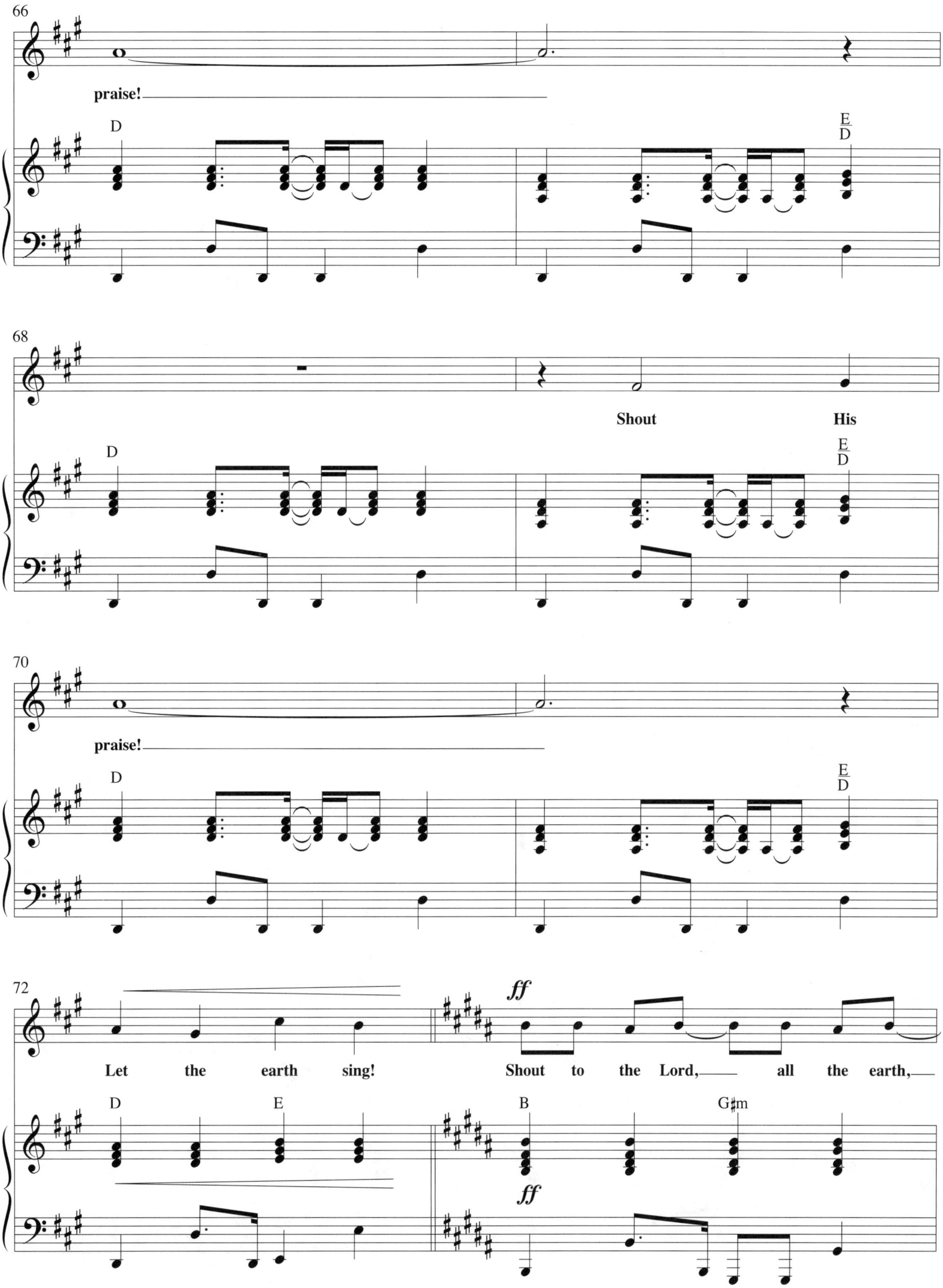
66
praise!
D
E/D
68
Shout His
D
E/D
70
praise!
D
E/D
72
Let the earth sing!
ff
Shout to the Lord, all the earth,
D E B G♯m
ff

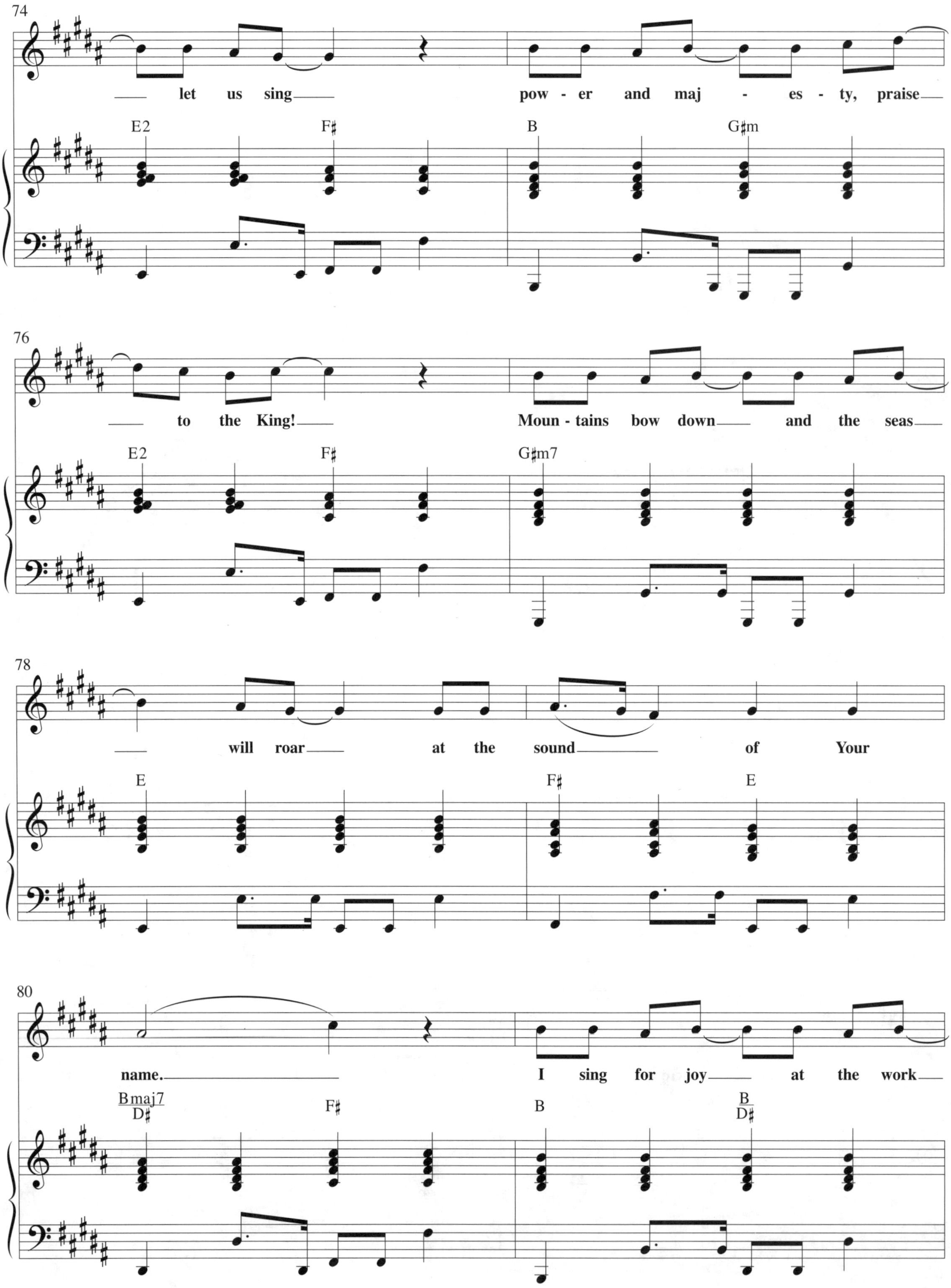
74
let us sing
pow - er and maj - es - ty, praise
E2 F♯ B G♯m
76
to the King!
Moun - tains bow down and the seas
E2 F♯ G♯m7
78
will roar at the sound of Your
E F♯ E
80
name.
I sing for joy at the work
Bmaj7/D♯ F♯ B B/D♯

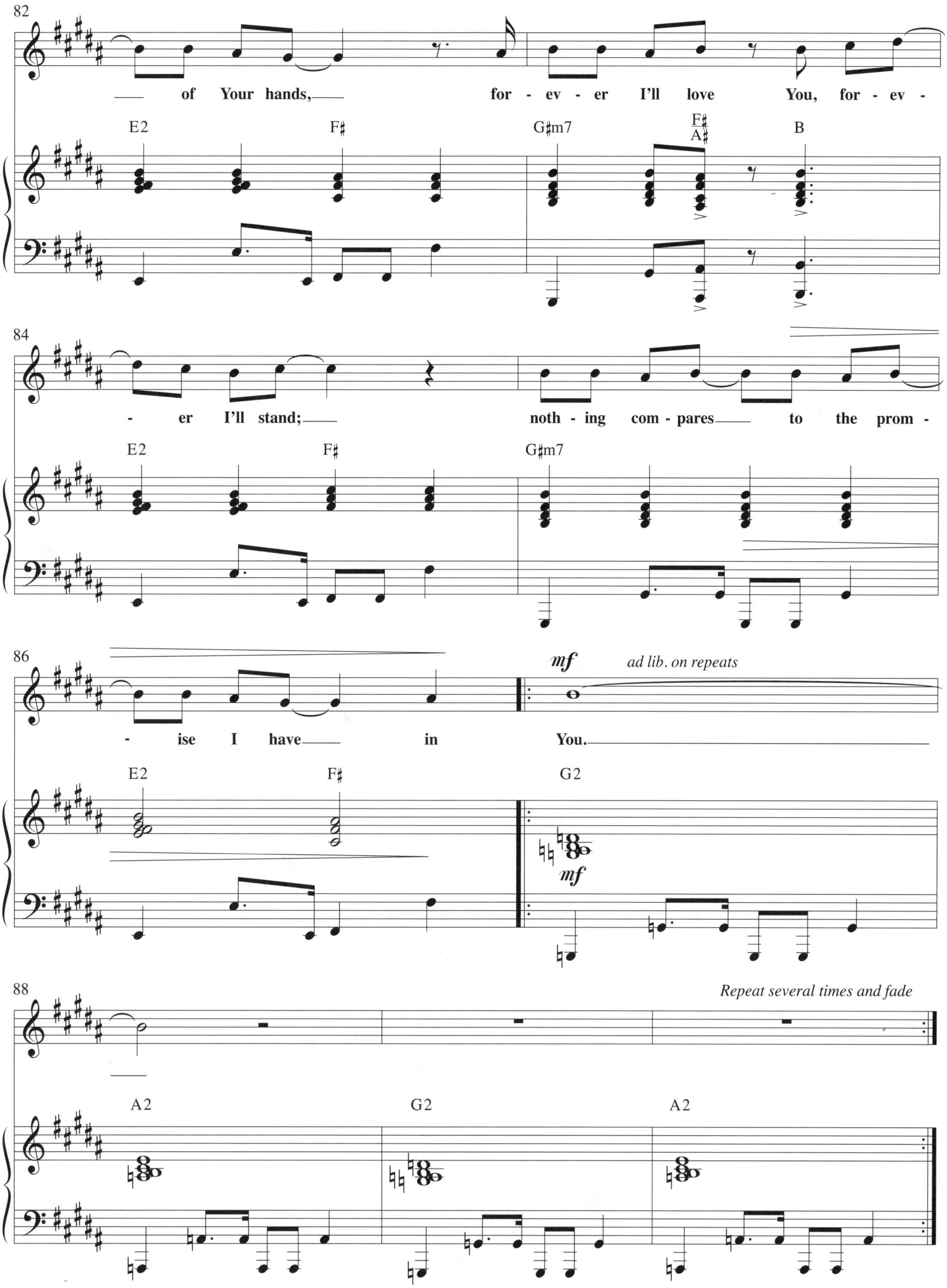
82
of Your hands, for - ev - er I'll love You, for - ev -
E2 F♯ G♯m7 F♯/A♯ B
84
- er I'll stand; noth - ing com - pares to the prom -
E2 F♯ G♯m7
86
- ise I have in You.
mf
ad lib. on repeats
E2 F♯ G2
88
Repeat several times and fade
A2 G2 A2

Dreams

Words and Music by
DARLENE ZSCHECH
and DAVID HOLMES

Prayerfully ♩ = 89

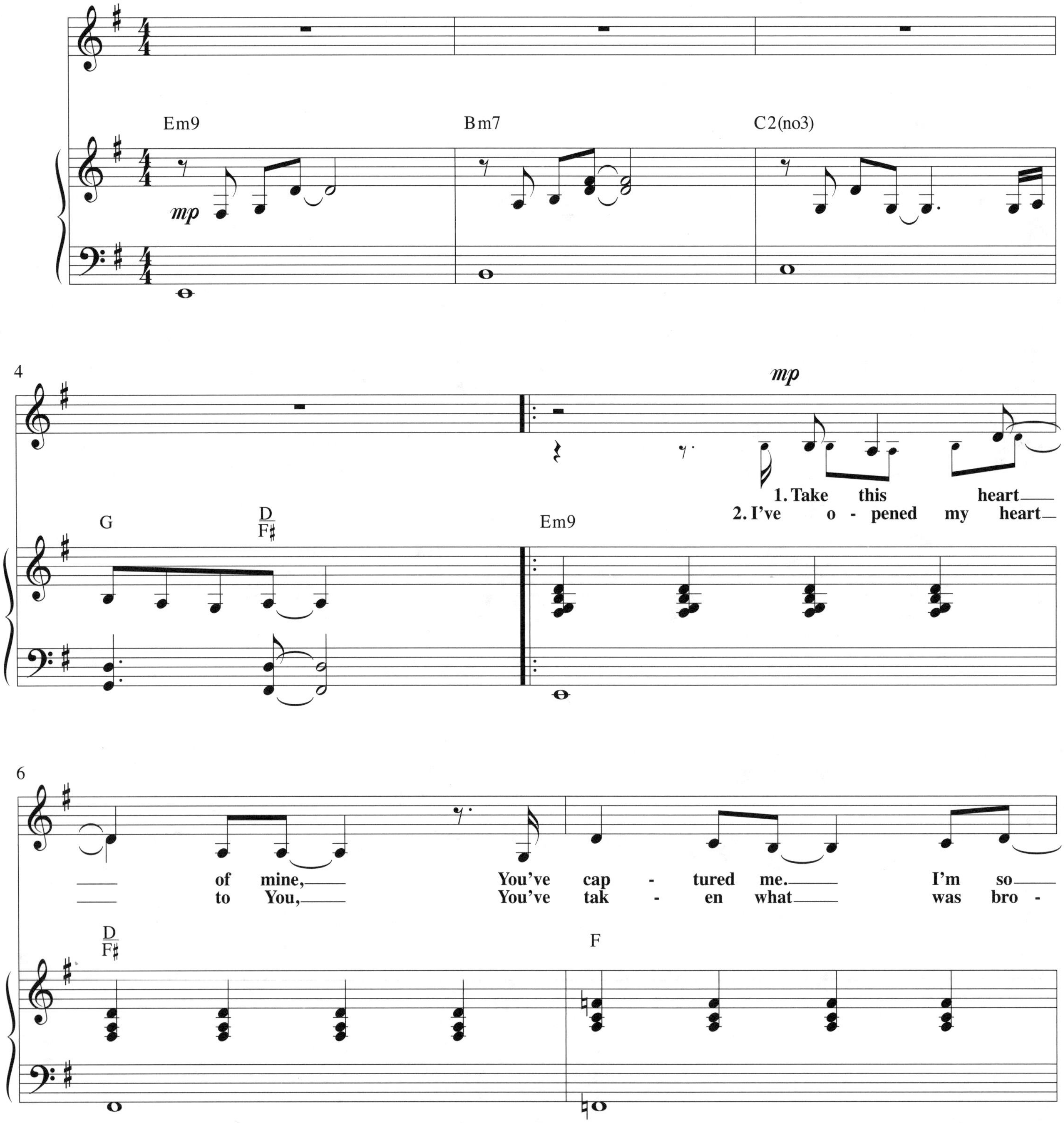

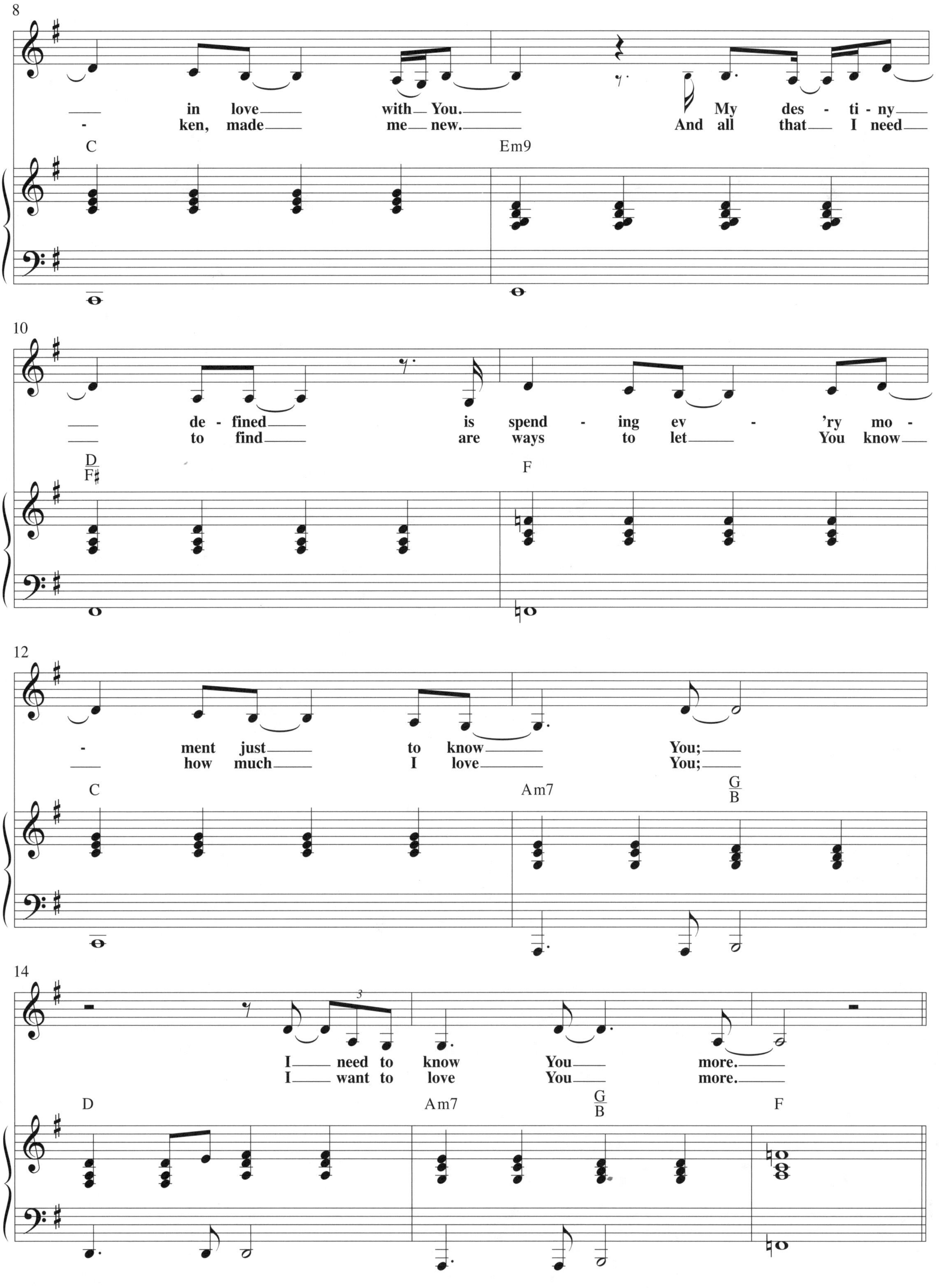
8
in love with You. My des - ti - ny
- ken, made me new. And all that I need
C
Em9
10
de - fined is spend - ing ev - 'ry mo -
to find are ways to let You know
D/F♯
F
12
- ment just to know You;
how much I love You;
C
Am7
G/B
14
I need to know You more.
I want to love You more.
D
Am7
G/B
F

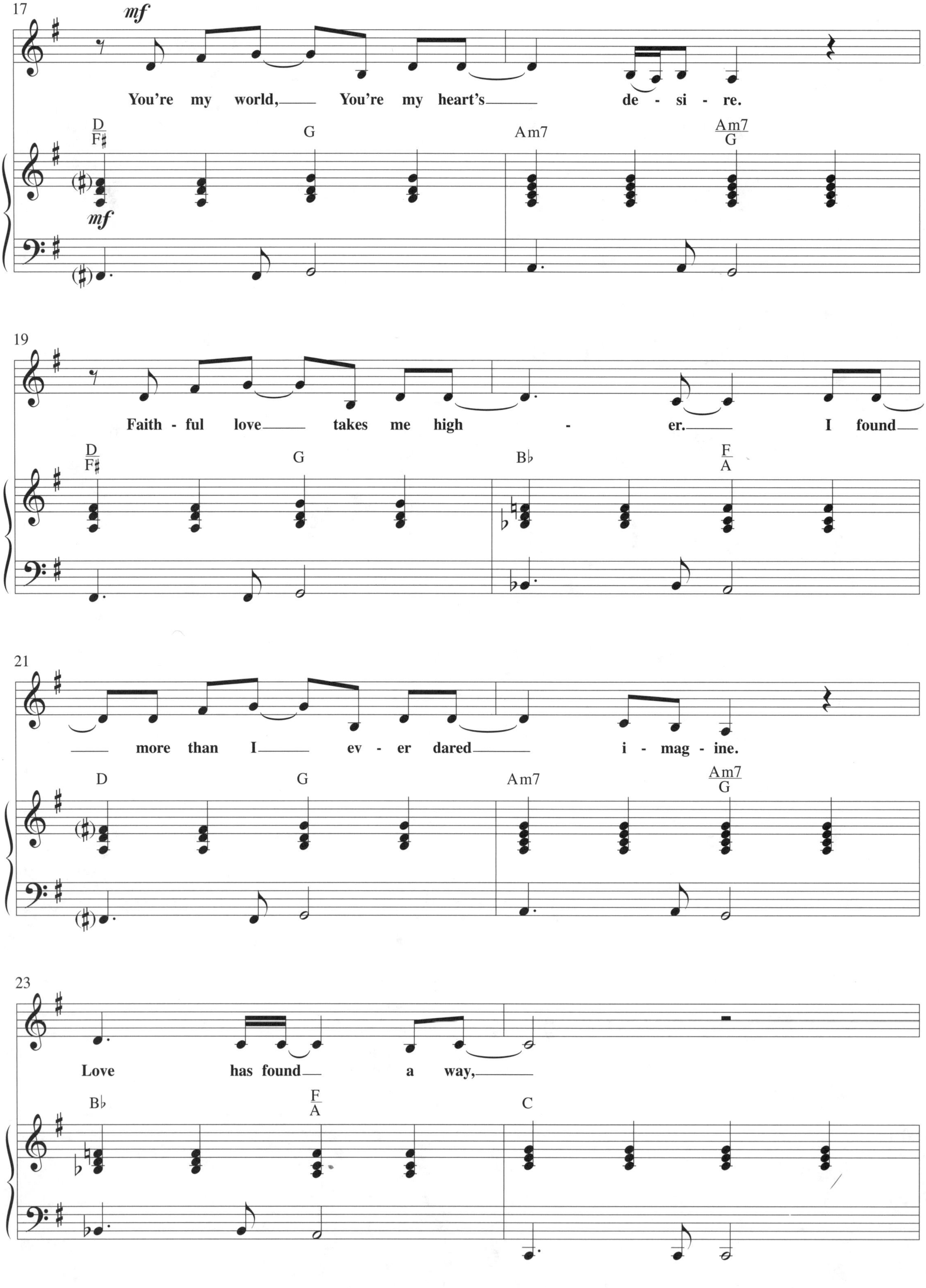
17
mf
You're my world, You're my heart's de - si - re.
D/F♯ G Am7 Am7/G
mf
19
Faith - ful love takes me high - er. I found
D/F♯ G B♭ F/A
21
more than I ev - er dared i - mag - ine.
D G Am7 Am7/G
23
Love has found a way,
B♭ F/A C

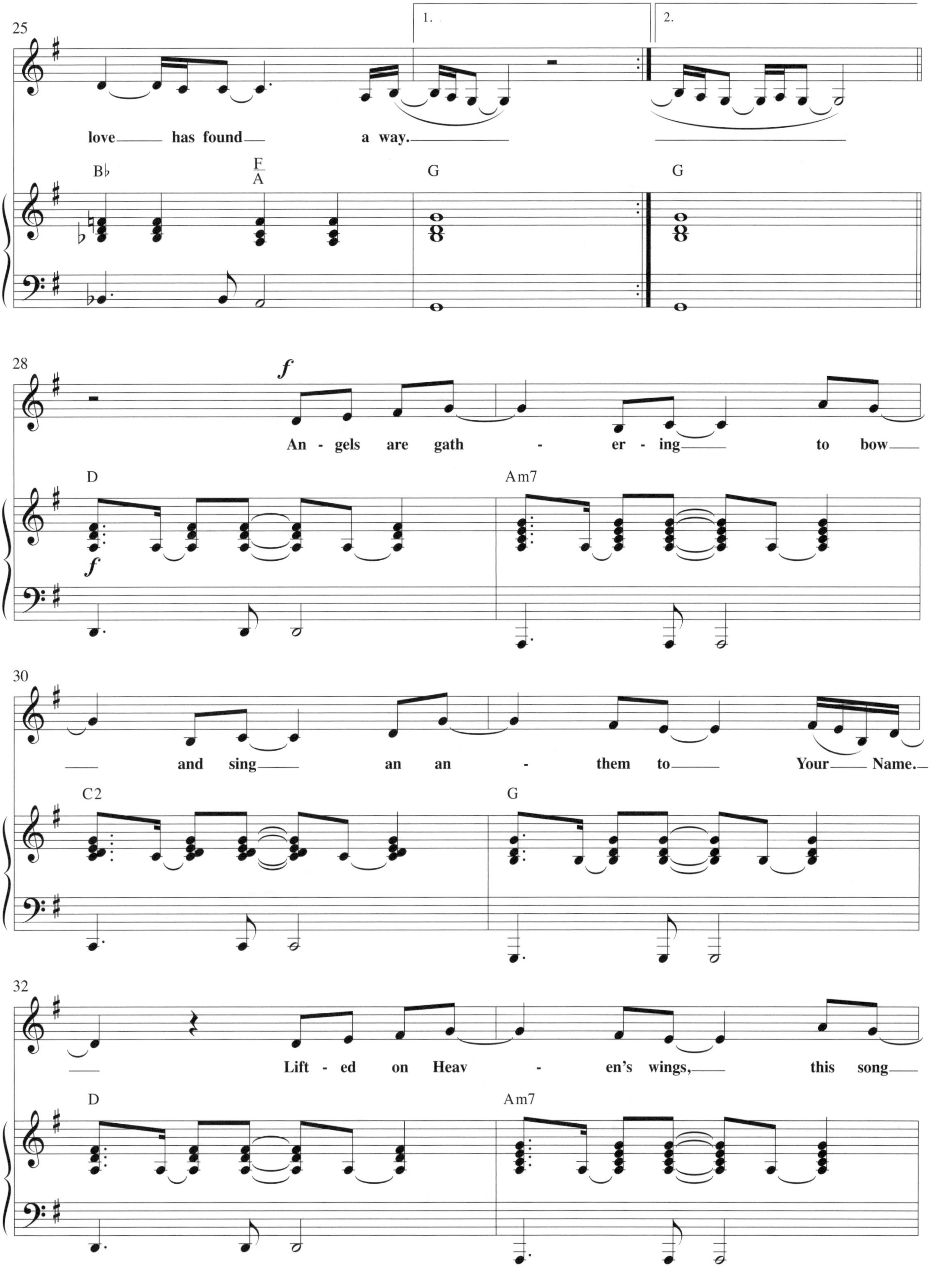
25
1.
2.
love has found a way.
B♭
F/A
G
G
28
f
An - gels are gath - er - ing to bow
D
Am7
f
30
and sing an an - them to Your Name.
C2
G
32
Lift - ed on Heav - en's wings, this song
D
Am7

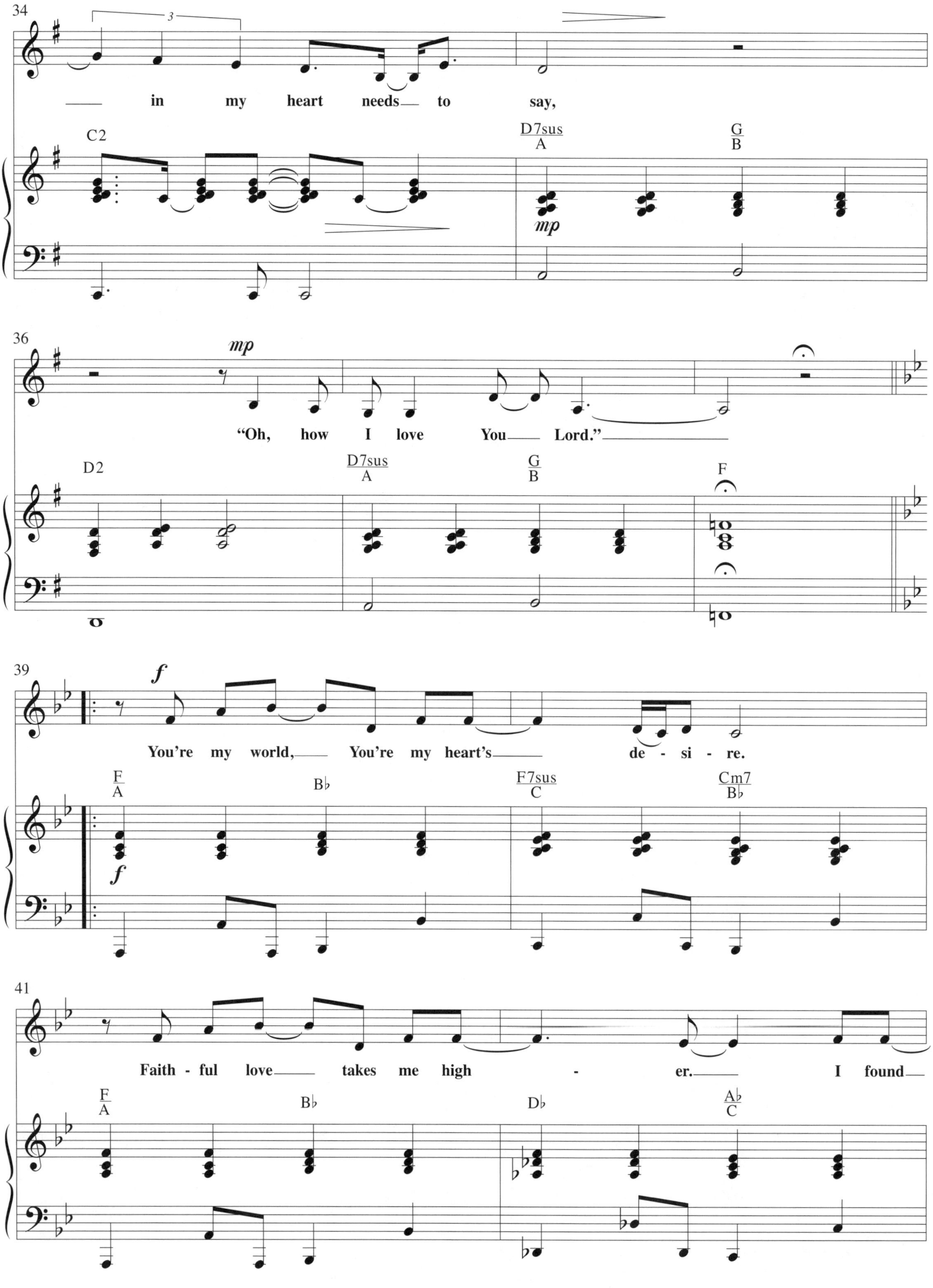
34
in my heart needs to say,
C2
D7sus/A
G/B
mp
36
mp
"Oh, how I love You Lord."
D2
D7sus/A
G/B
F
39
f
You're my world, You're my heart's de - si - re.
F/A
B♭
F7sus/C
Cm7/B♭
f
41
Faith - ful love takes me high - er. I found
F/A
B♭
D♭
A♭/C

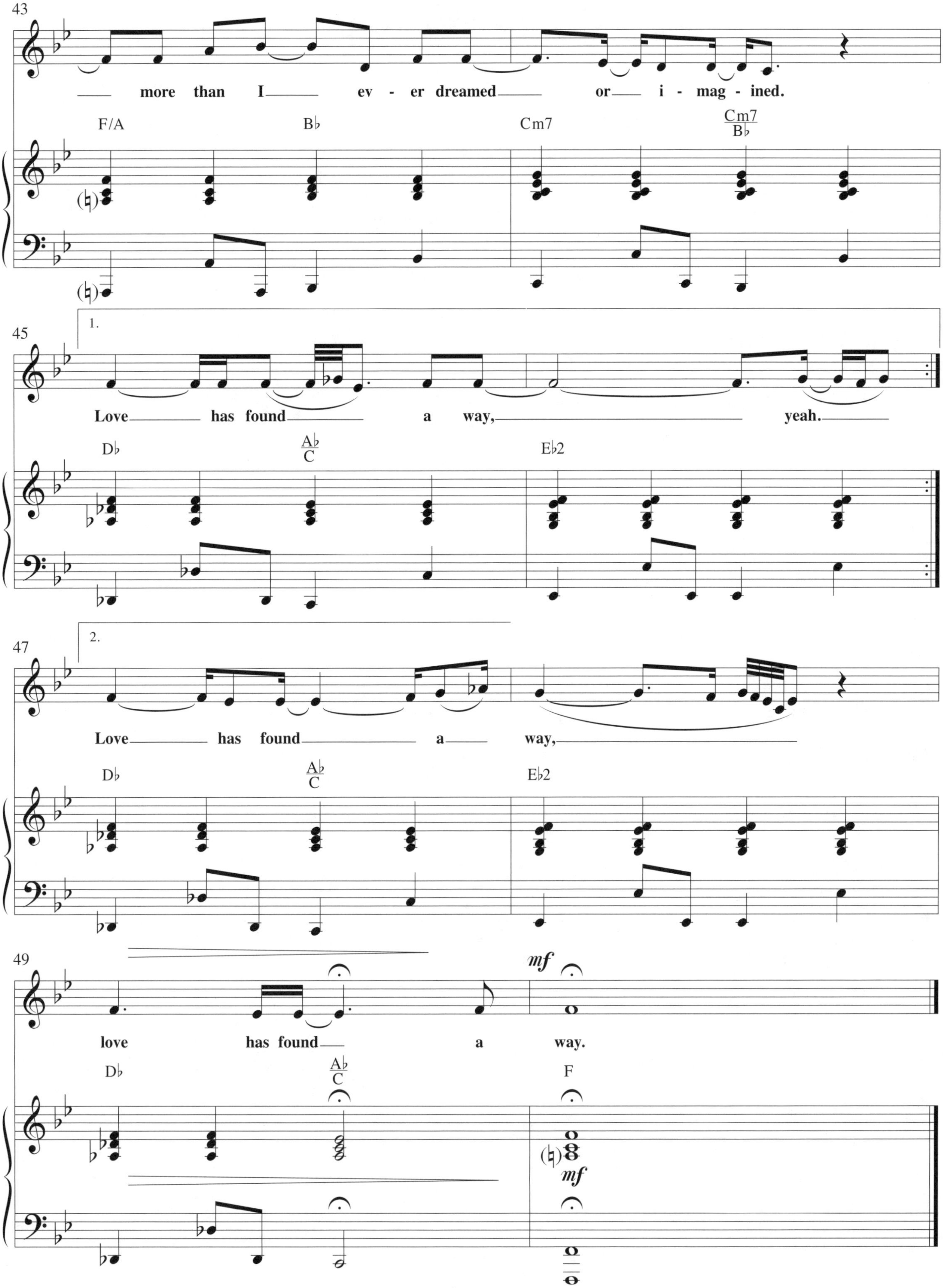
43
more than I ev - er dreamed or i - mag - ined.
F/A
B♭
Cm7
Cm7/B♭
45
1.
Love has found a way, yeah.
D♭
A♭/C
E♭2
47
2.
Love has found a way,
D♭
A♭/C
E♭2
49
love has found a way.
mf
D♭
A♭/C
F
mf

Wonderful You

Words and Music by
DAVID HOLMES and
DARLENE ZSCHECH

Happily ♩ = 92

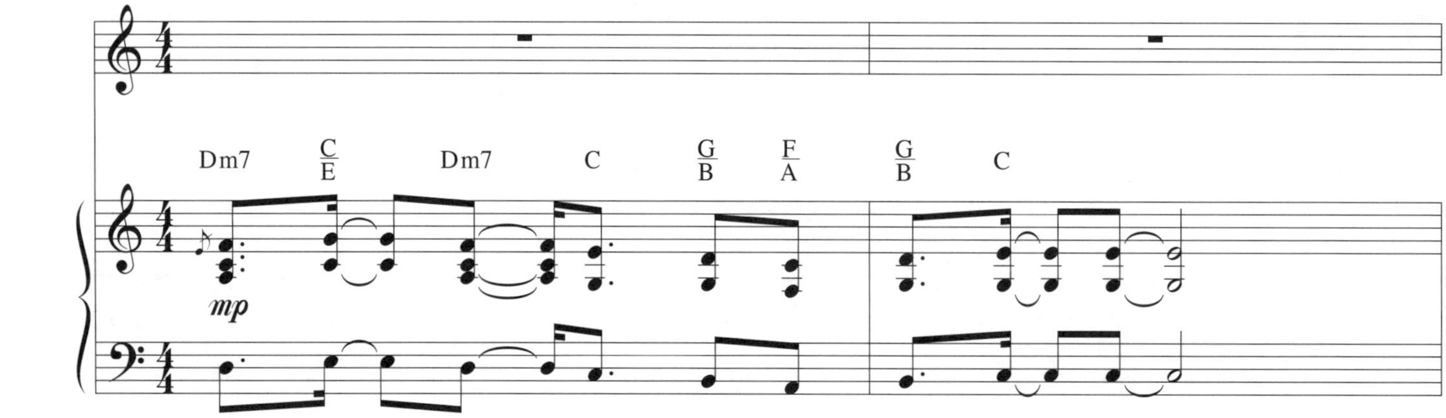

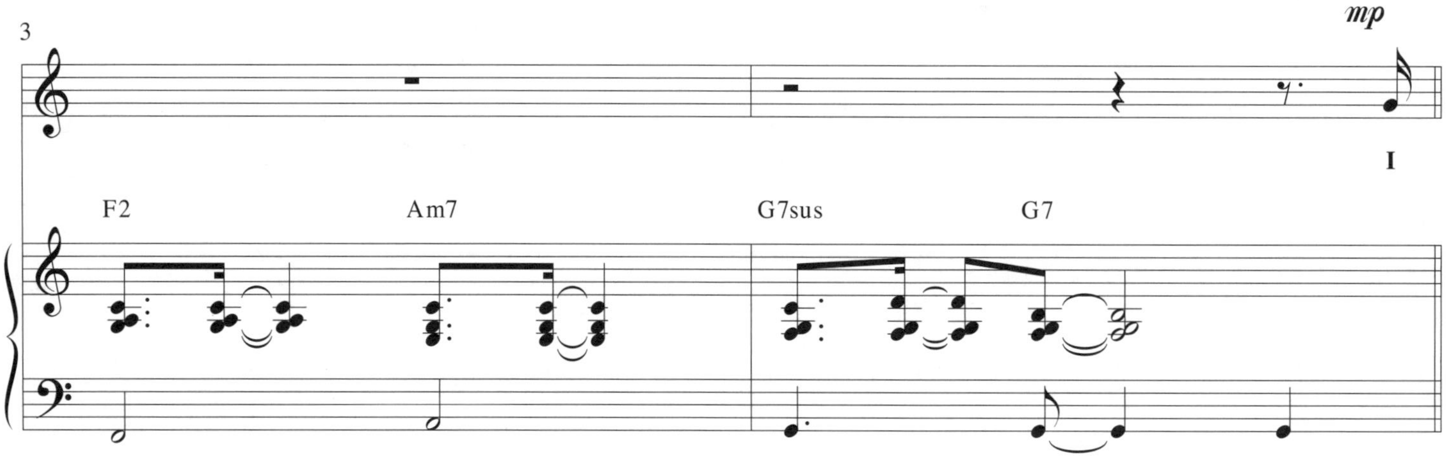

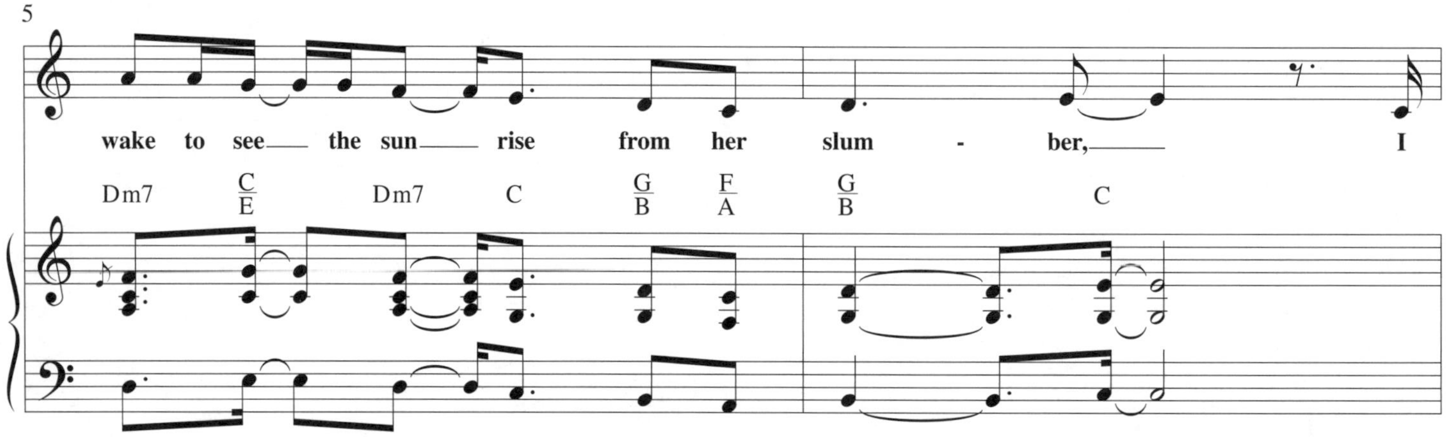

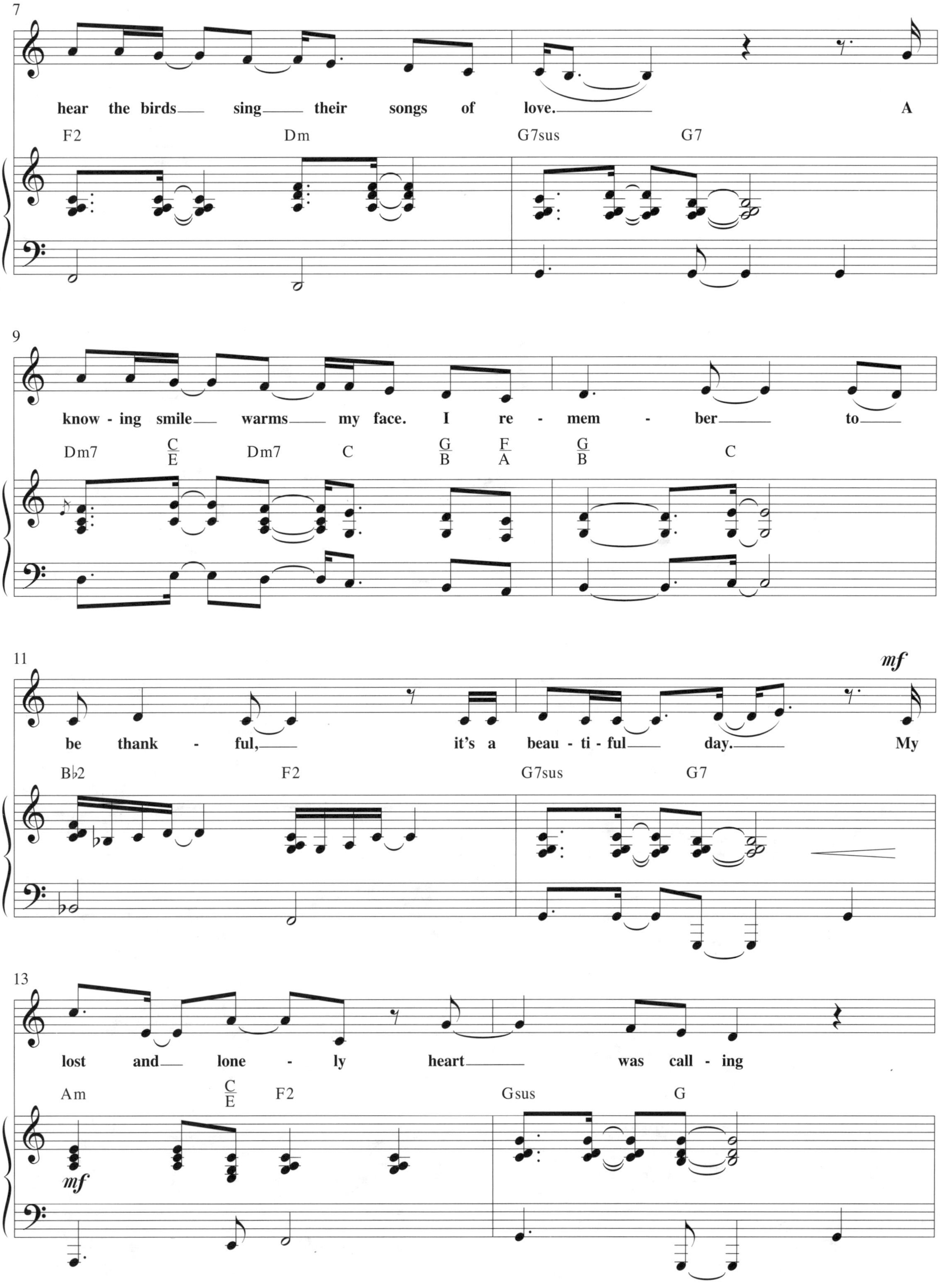
hear the birds sing their songs of love. A
F2 Dm G7sus G7
know - ing smile warms my face. I re - mem - ber to
Dm7 C/E Dm7 C G/B F/A G/B C
be thank - ful, it's a beau - ti - ful day. My
mf
B♭2 F2 G7sus G7
lost and lone - ly heart was call - ing
Am C/E F2 Gsus G
mf

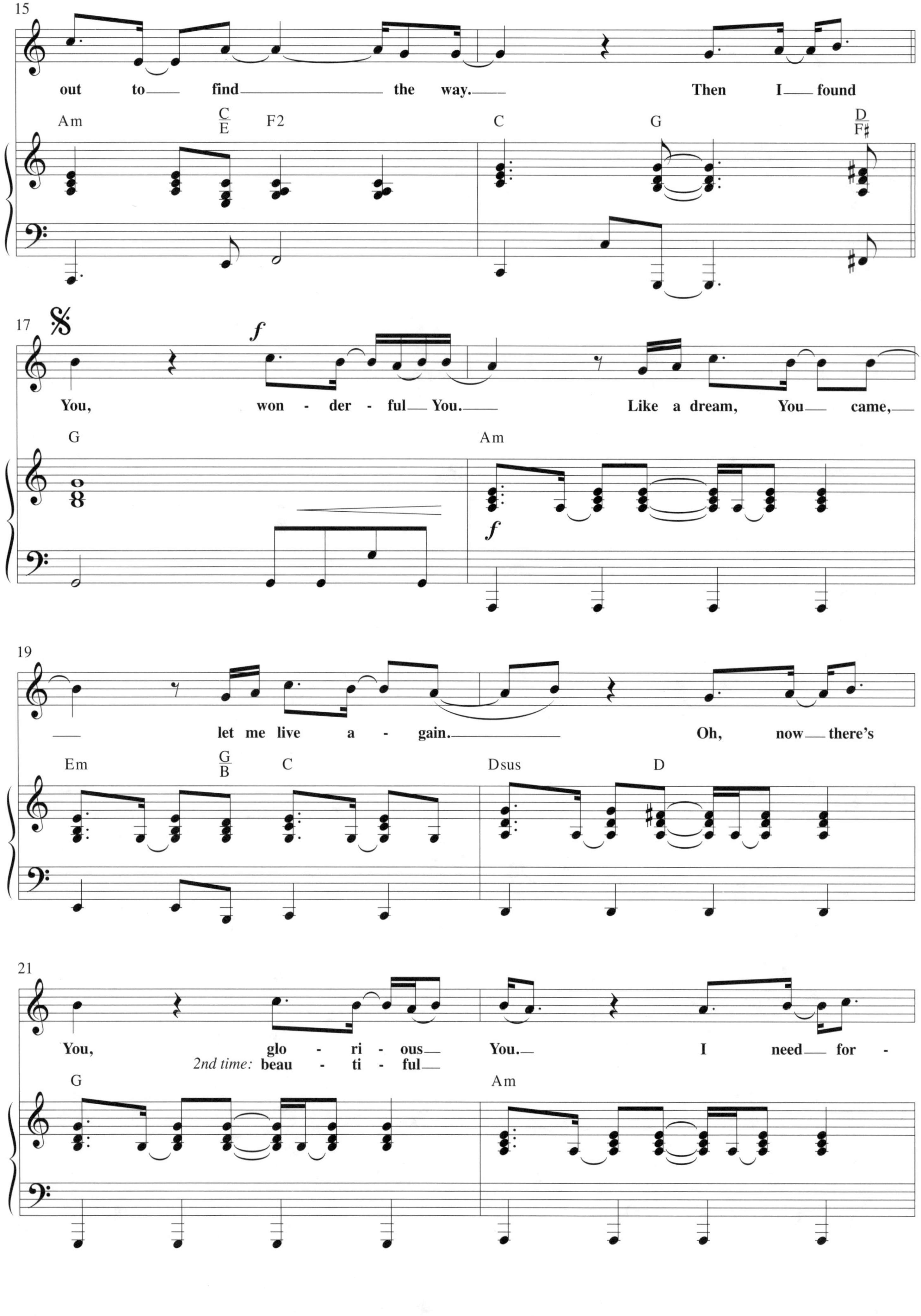
15
out to find the way. Then I found
Am C/E F2 C G D/F♯
17
f
You, won - der - ful You. Like a dream, You came,
G Am
f
19
let me live a - gain. Oh, now there's
Em G/B C Dsus D
21
You, glo - ri - ous You. I need for -
2nd time: beau - ti - ful
G Am

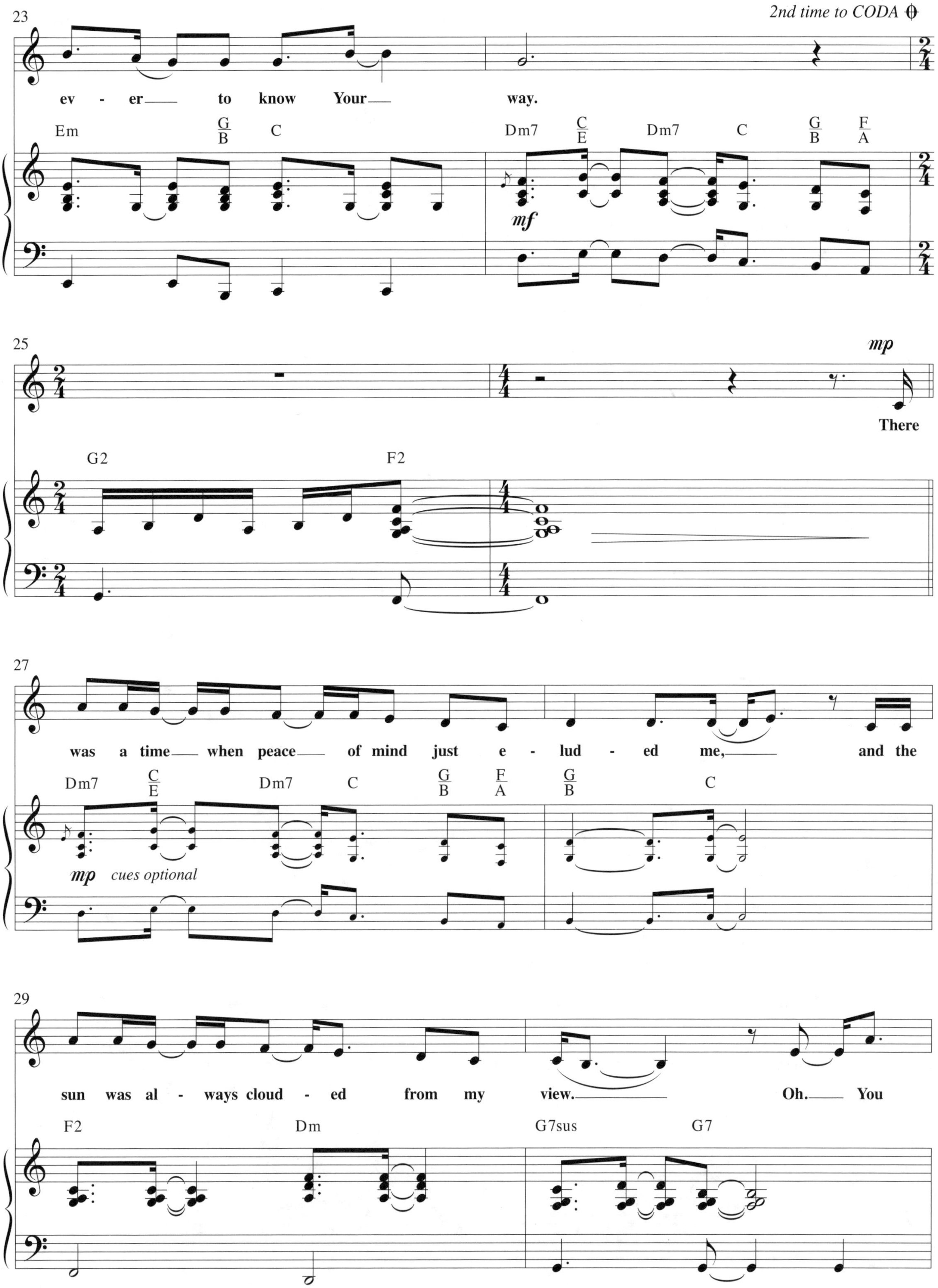
2nd time to CODA
23
ev - er to know Your way.
Em G/B C Dm7 C/E Dm7 C G/B F/A
mf
25
mp
There
G2 F2
27
was a time when peace of mind just e - lud - ed me, and the
Dm7 C/E Dm7 C G/B F/A G/B C
mp cues optional
29
sun was al - ways cloud - ed from my view. Oh. You
F2 Dm G7sus G7

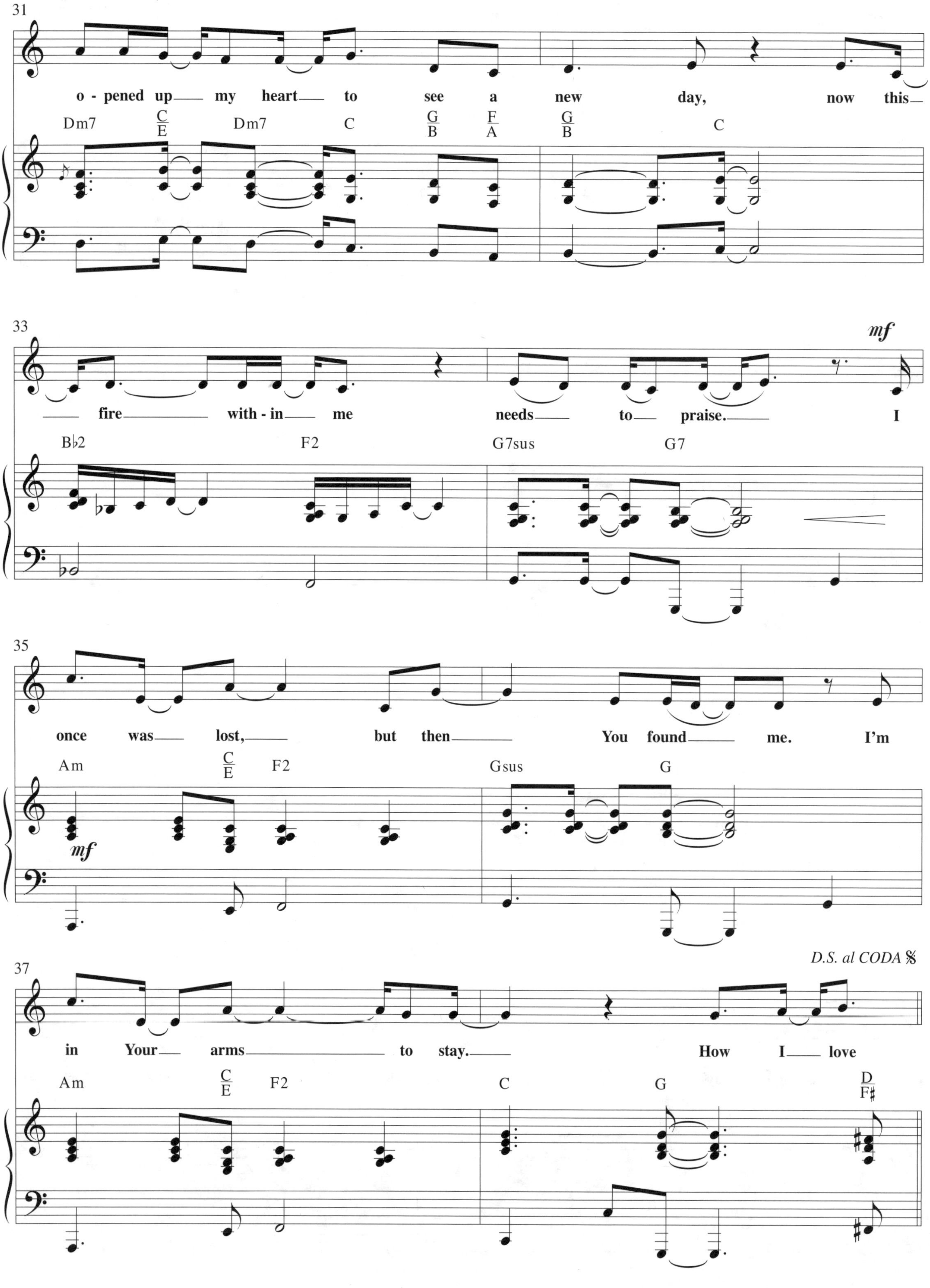
31
o - pened up my heart to see a new day, now this
Dm7 C/E Dm7 C G/B F/A G/B C
33
mf
fire with - in me needs to praise. I
B♭2 F2 G7sus G7
35
once was lost, but then You found me. I'm
Am C/E F2 Gsus G
mf
37
D.S. al CODA
in Your arms to stay. How I love
Am C/E F2 C G D/F♯

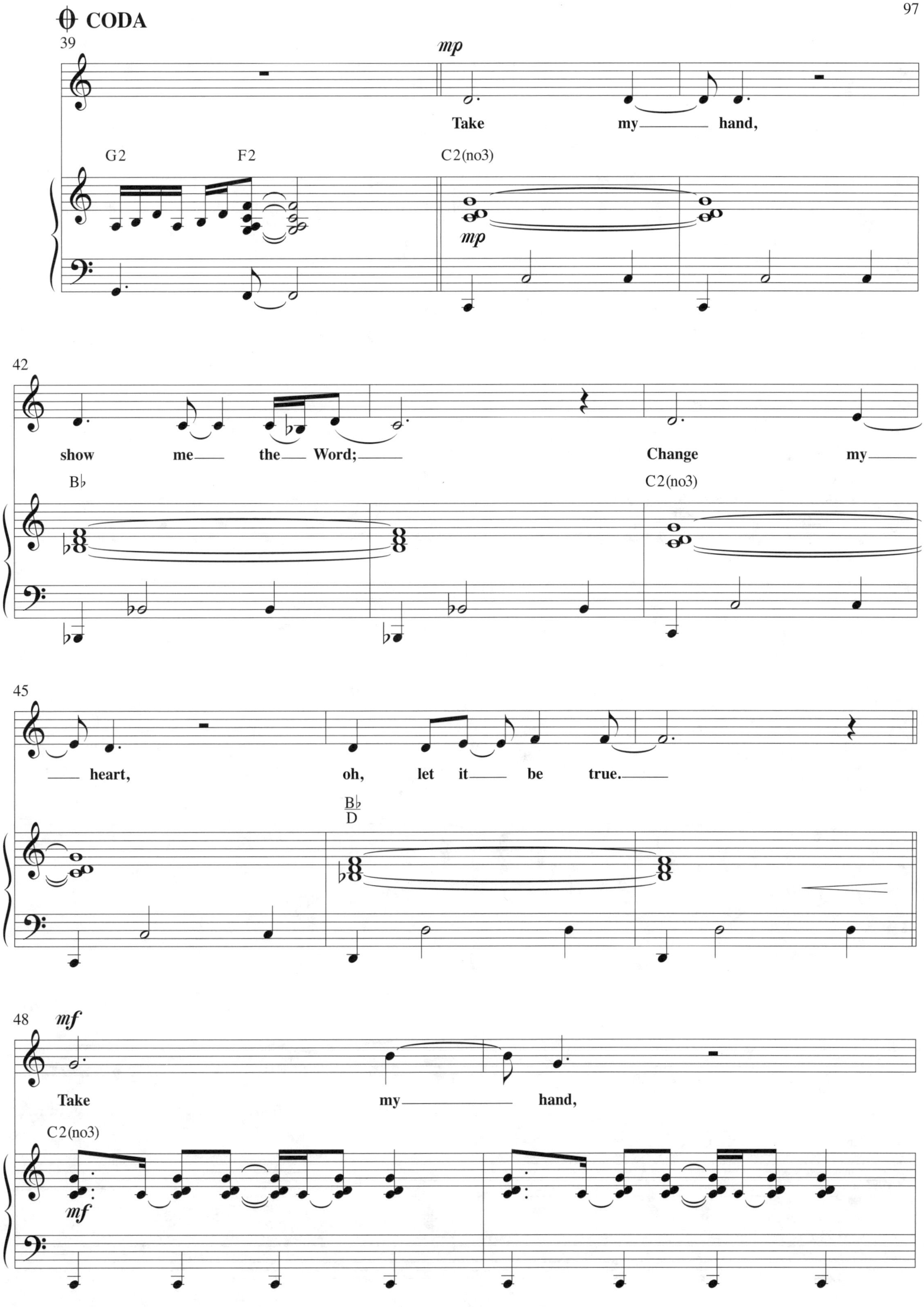
CODA
39
mp
Take my hand,
G2 F2 C2(no3)
mp
42
show me the Word; Change my
B♭ C2(no3)
45
heart, oh, let it be true.
B♭/D
48
mf
Take my hand,
C2(no3)
mf

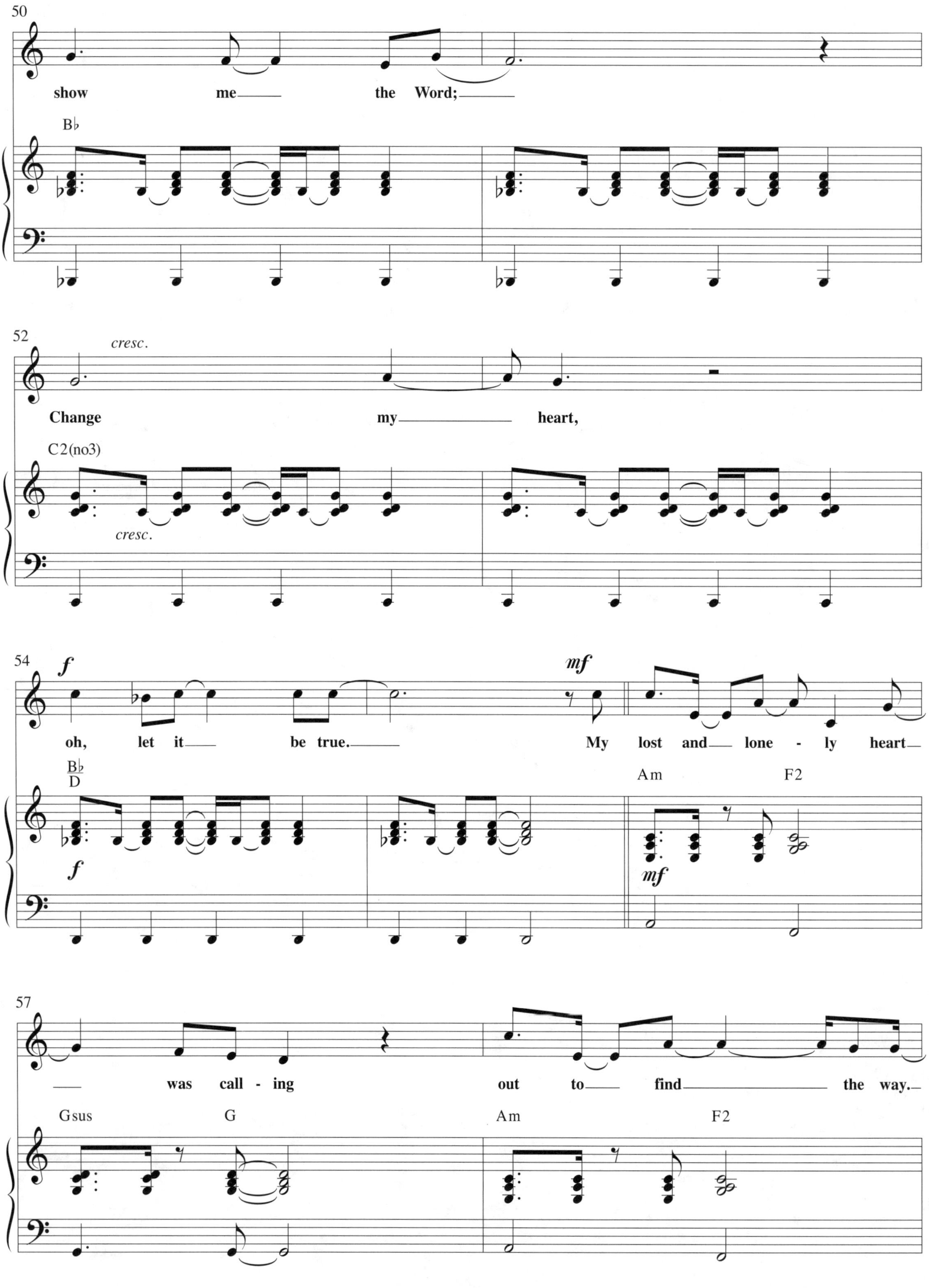
50
show me the Word;
B♭
52
cresc.
Change my heart,
C2(no3)
cresc.
54
f
oh, let it be true.
mf
My lost and lone - ly heart
B♭
D
Am
F2
f
mf
57
was call - ing out to find the way.
Gsus
G
Am
F2

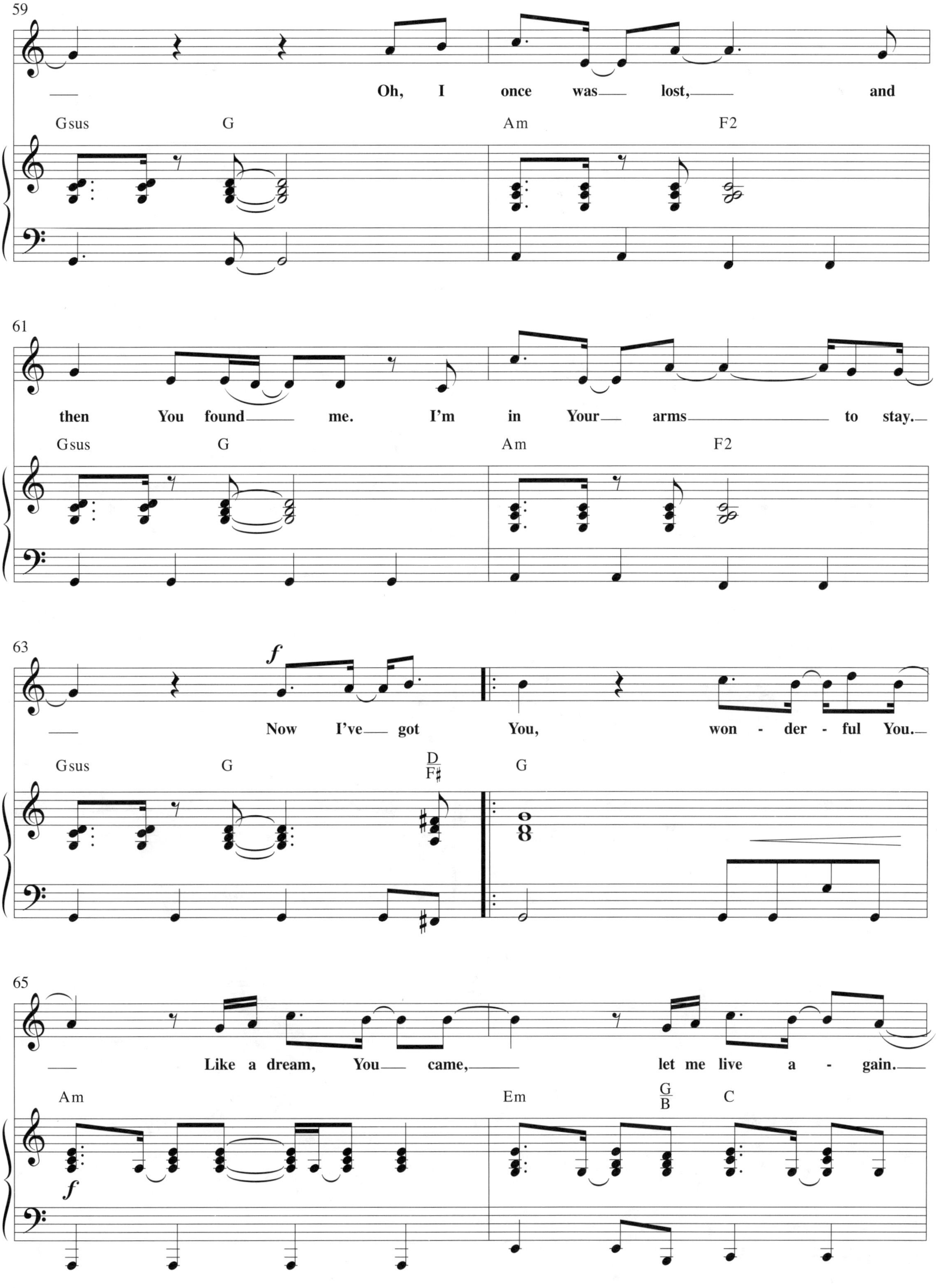
59
Oh, I once was lost, and
Gsus G Am F2
61
then You found me. I'm in Your arms to stay.
Gsus G Am F2
63
f
Now I've got You, won - der - ful You.
Gsus G D/F♯ G
65
Like a dream, You came, let me live a - gain.
Am Em G/B C
f

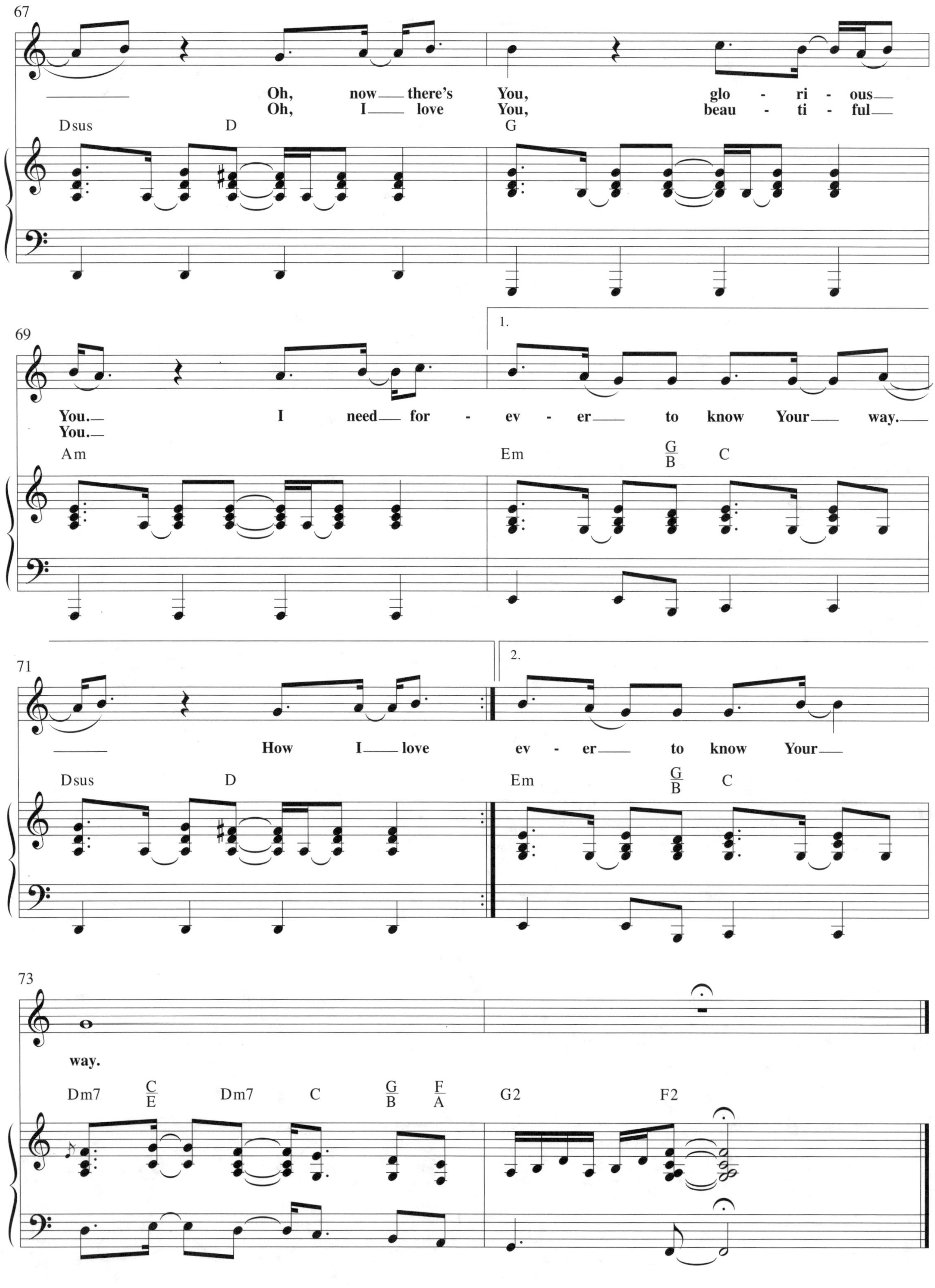
67
Oh, now there's You, glo - ri - ous
Oh, I love You, beau - ti - ful
Dsus
D
G
69
You. I need for - ev - er to know Your way.
You.
1.
Am
Em
G/B
C
71
How I love ev - er to know Your
2.
Dsus
D
Em
G/B
C
73
way.
Dm7
C/E
Dm7
C
G/B
F/A
G2
F2

Thankful

Words and Music by
DAVID HOLMES and
DARLENE ZSCHECH

Moderately ♩ = 69

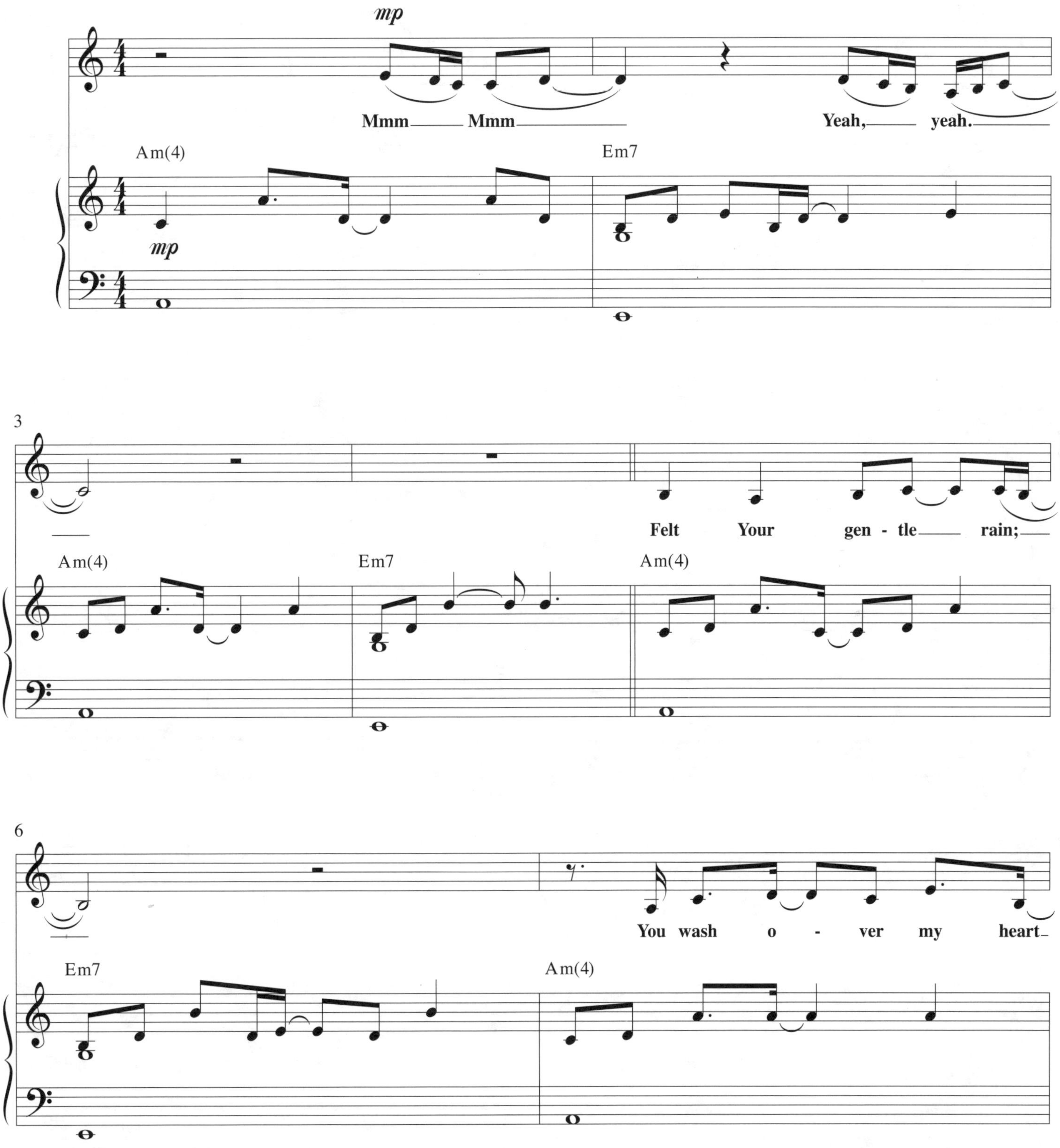

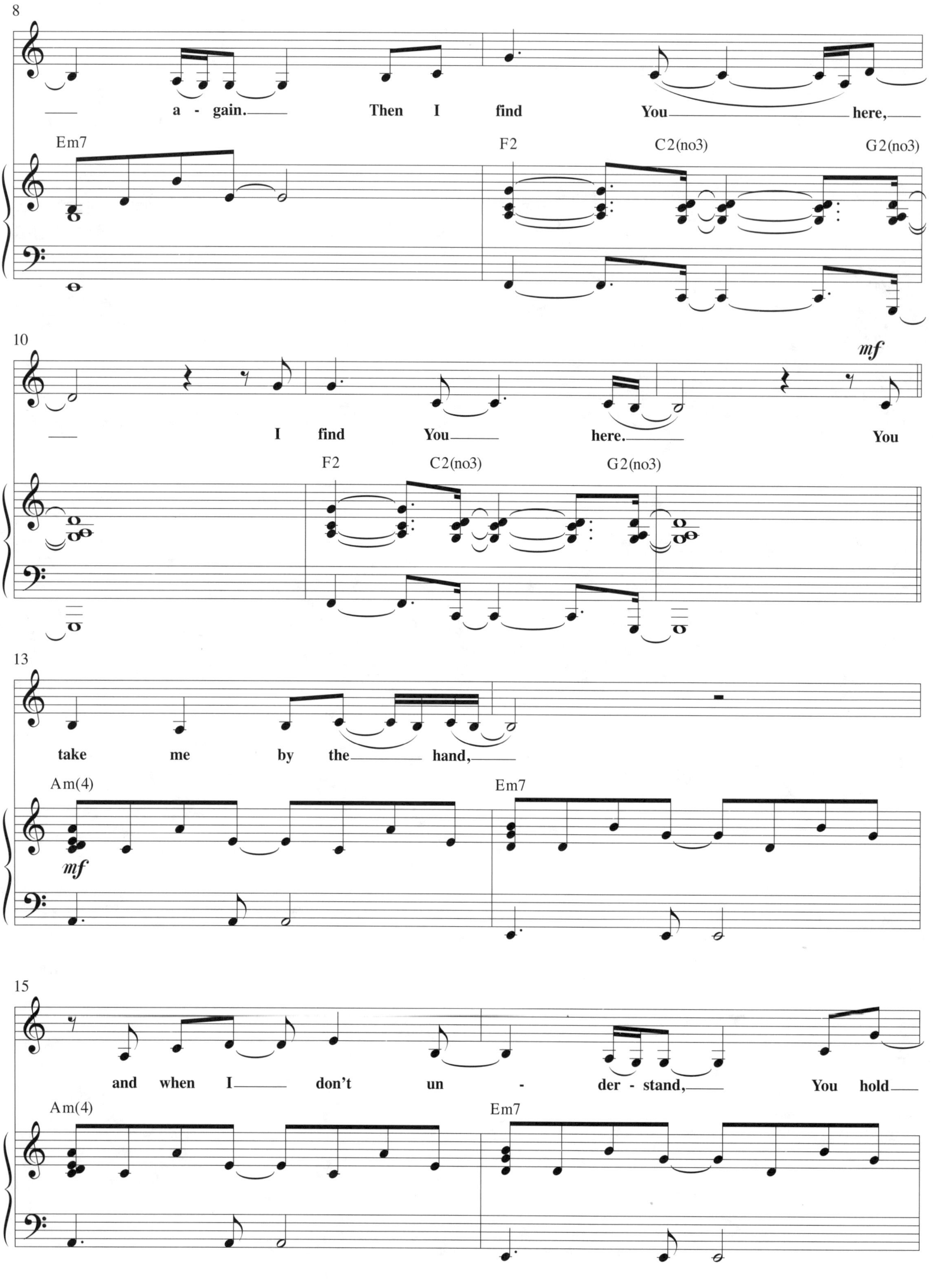
8
a - gain. Then I find You here,
Em7
F2
C2(no3)
G2(no3)
10
I find You here.
mf
You
F2
C2(no3)
G2(no3)
13
take me by the hand,
Am(4)
mf
Em7
15
and when I don't un - der - stand, You hold
Am(4)
Em7

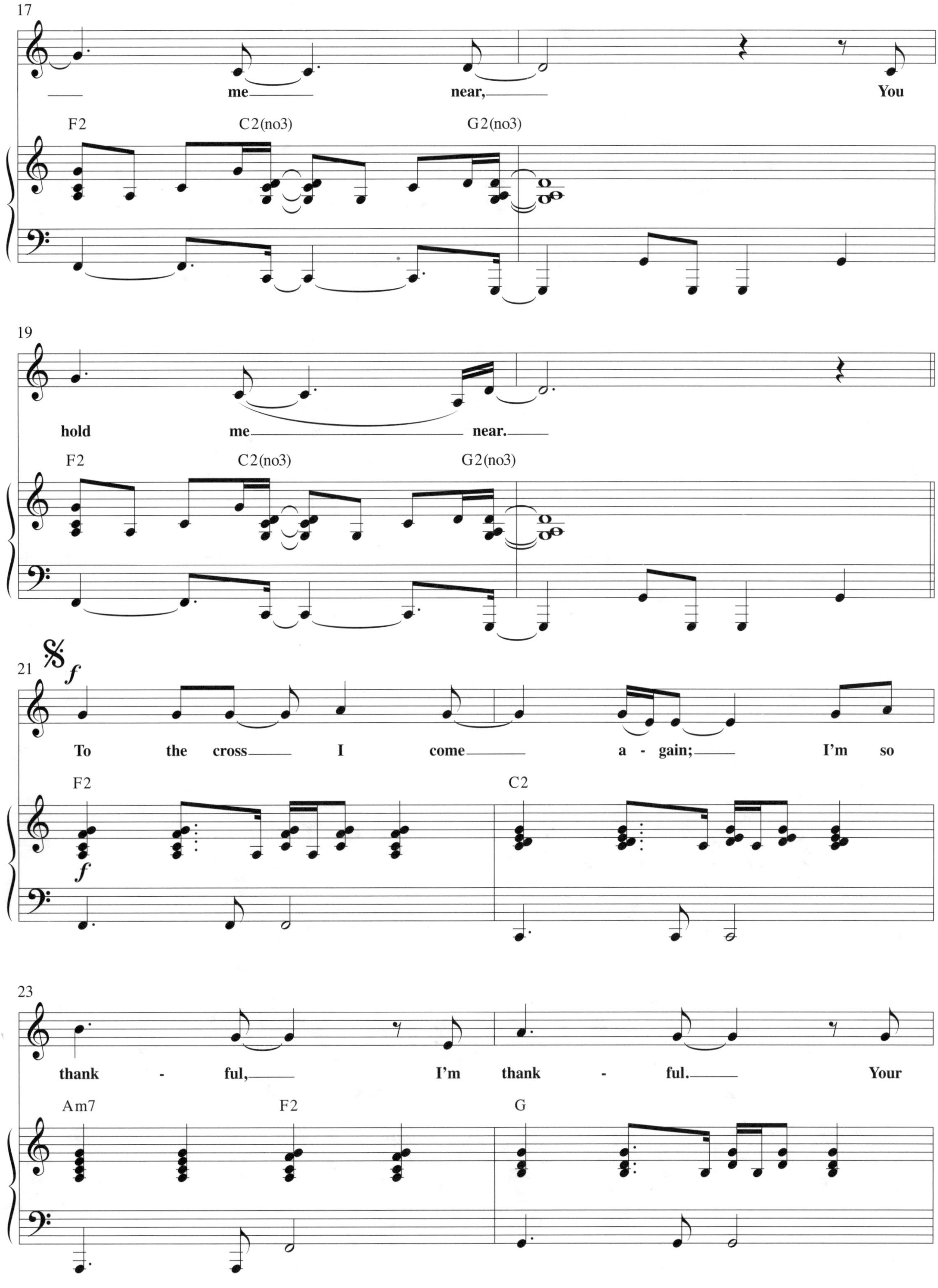
17
me near, You
F2 C2(no3) G2(no3)
19
hold me near.
F2 C2(no3) G2(no3)
21
To the cross I come a - gain; I'm so
F2 C2
23
thank - ful, I'm thank - ful. Your
Am7 F2 G

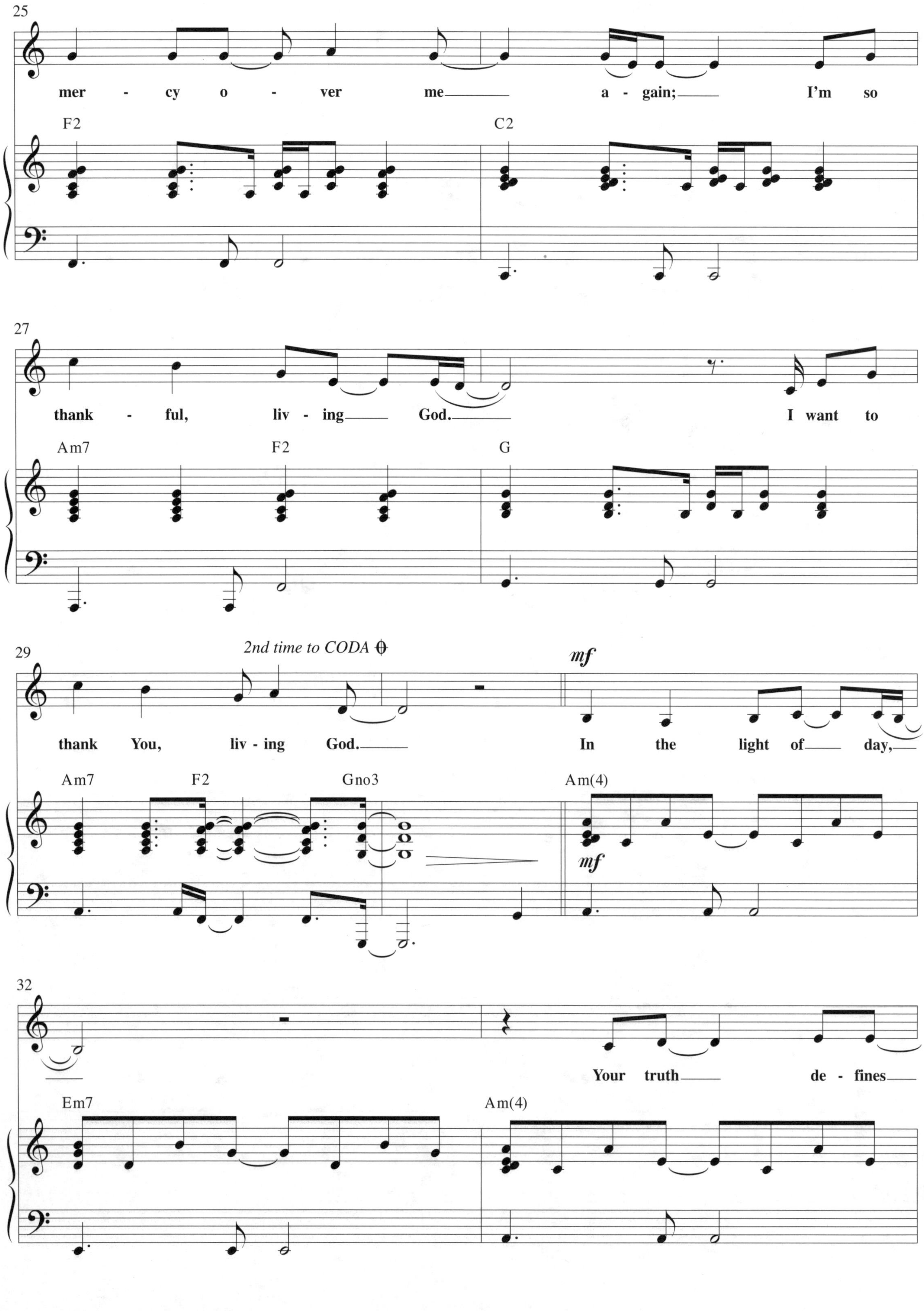
25
mer - cy o - ver me a - gain; I'm so
F2
C2
27
thank - ful, liv - ing God. I want to
Am7
F2
G
29
2nd time to CODA
mf
thank You, liv - ing God. In the light of day,
Am7
F2
Gno3
Am(4)
mf
32
Your truth de - fines
Em7
Am(4)

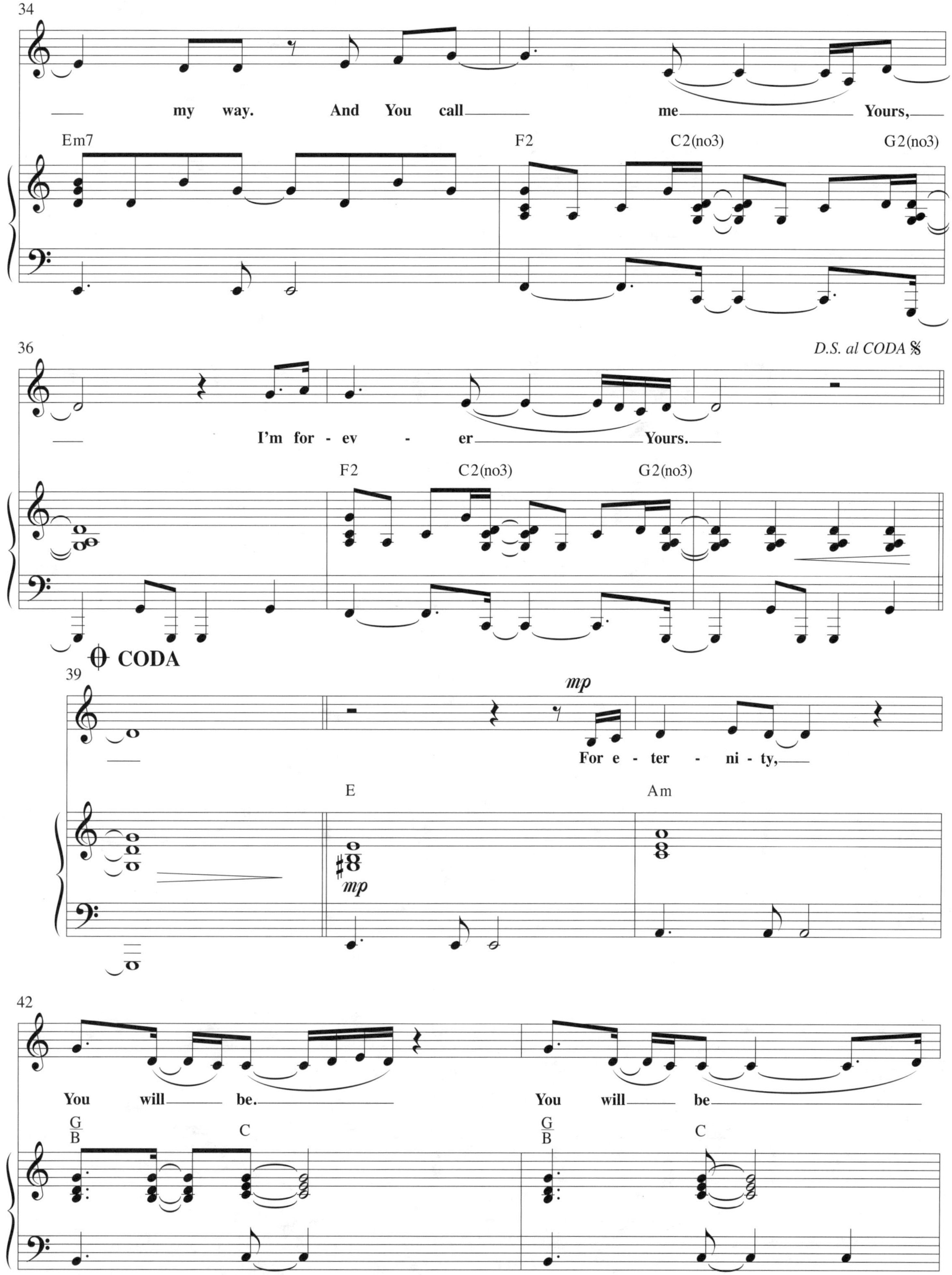
34
my way. And You call me Yours,
Em7
F2
C2(no3)
G2(no3)
36
D.S. al CODA 𝄋
I'm for - ev - er Yours.
F2
C2(no3)
G2(no3)
CODA
39
mp
For e - ter - ni - ty,
E
Am
mp
42
You will be. You will be
G
B
C
G
B
C

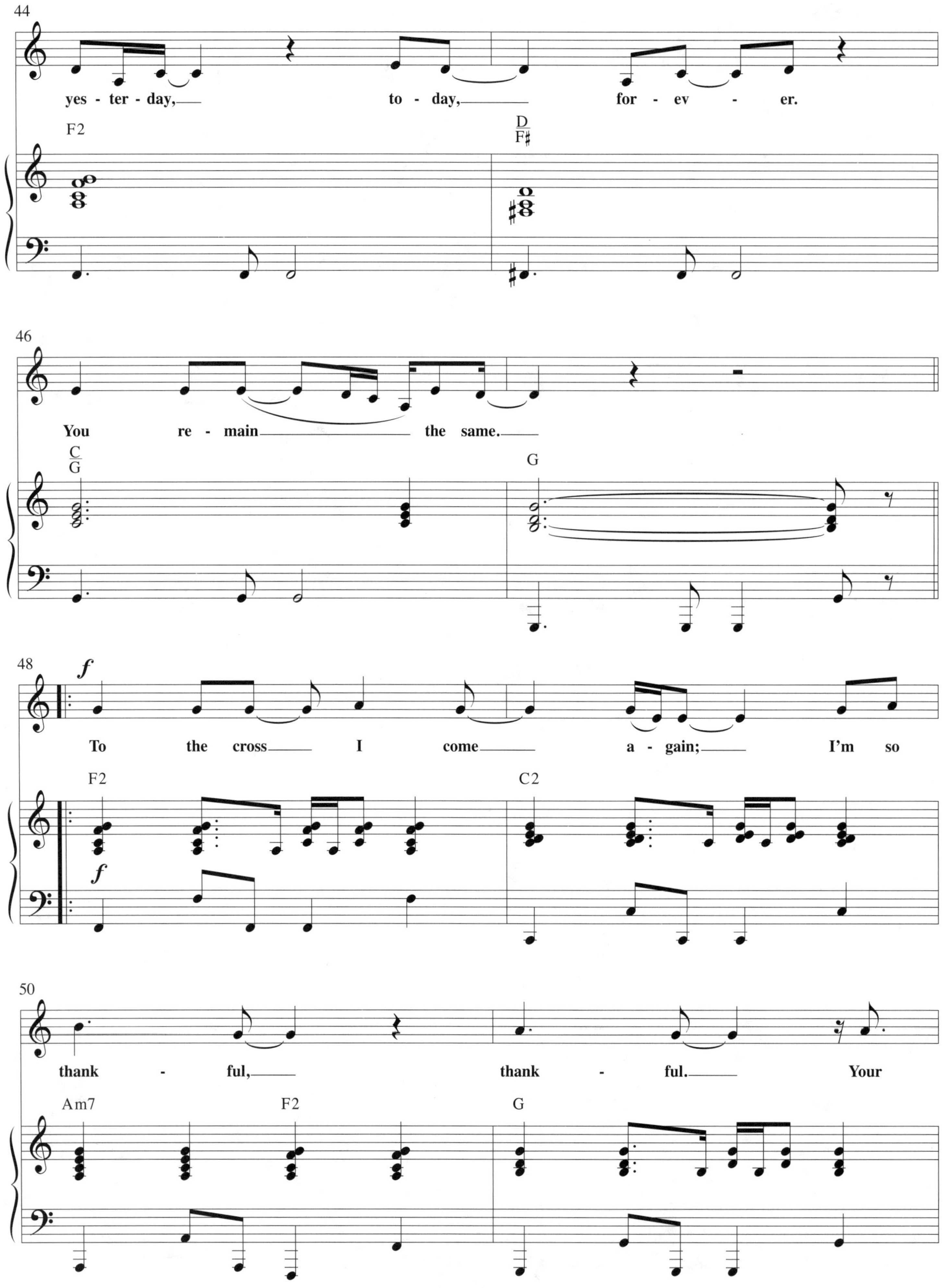
44
yes - ter - day, to - day, for - ev - er.
F2
D/F♯
46
You re - main the same.
C/G
G
48
f
To the cross I come a - gain; I'm so
F2
C2
f
50
thank - ful, thank - ful. Your
Am7
F2
G

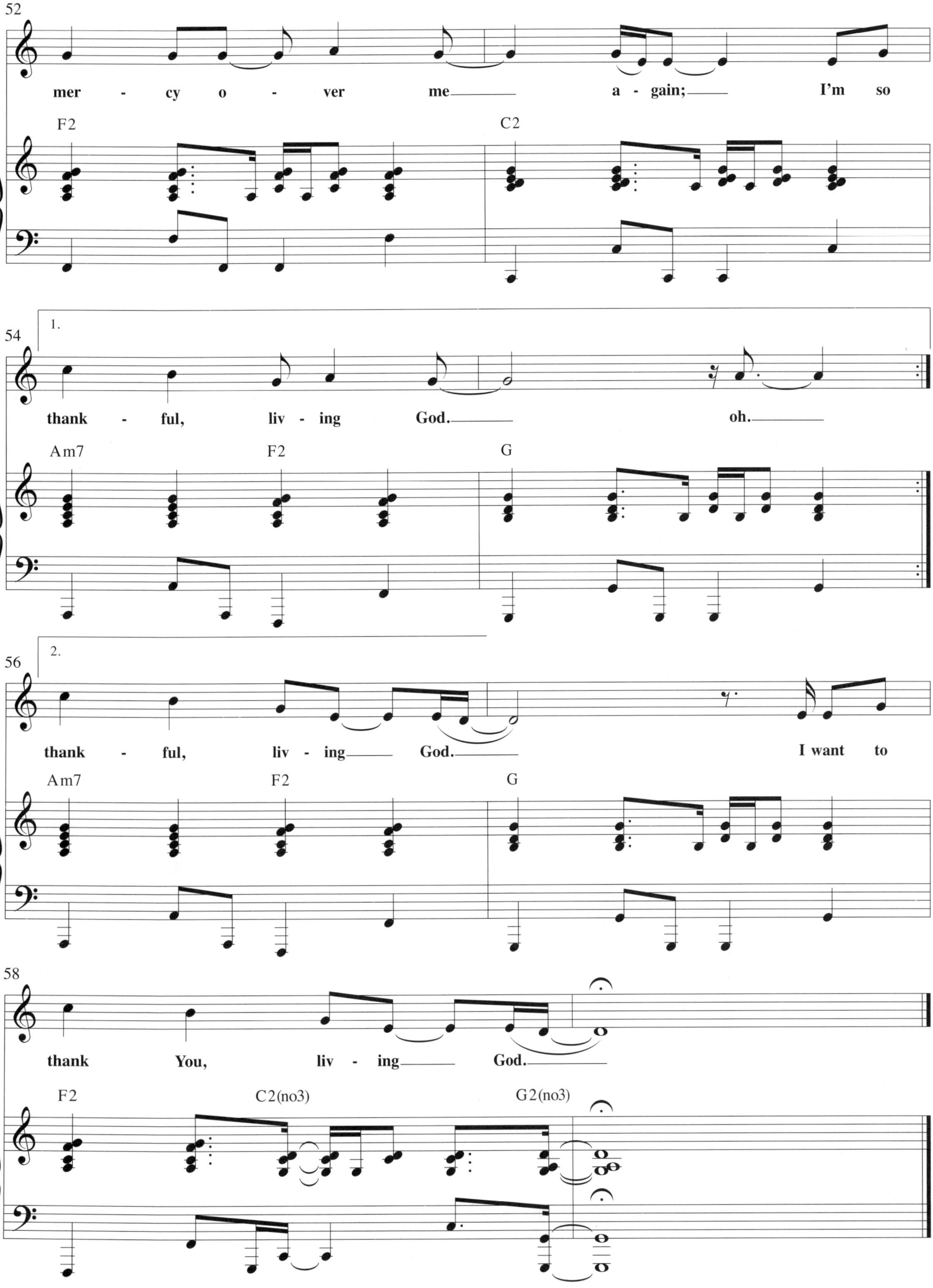
52
mer - cy o - ver me
a - gain;
I'm so
F2
C2
54
1.
thank - ful, liv - ing God.
oh.
Am7
F2
G
56
2.
thank - ful, liv - ing God.
I want to
Am7
F2
G
58
thank You, liv - ing God.
F2
C2(no3)
G2(no3)